Meatballs

"Good basic recipe and easy to make."

Serves 25

1 pound ground beef
1 cup bread crumbs
½ cup milk
1 teaspoon salt
Pepper to taste

Sauce
½ cup water
½ cup catsup
1½ tablespoons Worcestershire sauce
¼ cup vinegar
1 teaspoon sugar
½ cup green pepper, chopped
½ cup onion, chopped

Heat oven to 375 degrees. Blend first 5 ingredients and make into meatballs. Mix remaining ingredients and pour over meatballs. (You do not brown the meatballs first.) Bake at 375 degrees about 45 minutes.

Viola B. Jones

▲ To decrease fat content: Substitute ground round for ground beef.

Sm

"Great

Serves 50

2 pounds ground chuck
¼ cup chopped onion
1 teaspoon salt
¼ teaspoon pepper
¼ teaspoon garlic salt
½ cup cracker crumbs
1 egg
¼ cup milk
2 tablespoons salad oil
1 1-pound, 2-ounce bottle smokey
    barbecue sauce
1 cup cold water

Mix beef, onion, salt, pepper, garlic salt, cracker crumbs, egg and milk. Shape into meatballs. Brown on all sides in hot salad oil. In large pan mix together barbecue sauce and water. Place browned meatballs in sauce and simmer for 15 minutes. Serve in chafing dish. Yields approximately 100 meatballs.

Diane Radford

▲ To decrease fat content: 1) substitute ground round for ground chuck, 2) use skim milk, 3) use lowfat barbecue sauce, 4) use egg substitute for egg.

Mystery Hot Dip

"Your guests will not know exactly what this is. Keep 'em guessing."

Serves 20

1 1-pound box pasteurized process cheese
  spread
1 7-ounce can tuna, drained and flaked
1 cup mayonnaise
1 small jar stuffed olives
Salt and red pepper to taste

Heat all in double broiler. Transfer to chafing dish. Serve with thin wheat crackers or Melba rounds.

Nell Catherwood

Hot Crab Dip

"Mix ahead of time and pop in oven just before your guests are to arrive."

Serves 20

8 ounces cream cheese
1 tablespoon milk
1 pound crab meat
2 tablespoons onion, finely chopped (or
  dried onion)
1 teaspoon lemon juice
½ teaspoon cream style horseradish
¼ teaspoon salt
Dash of pepper

Combine all ingredients and bake at 350 degrees for 15 minutes or until bubbly. Keep warm in chafing dish and serve with toasted chunks of French bread, black rye bread or Quick Bread Wafers*.
*(Note index - under bread)

Joyce Moorman

▲ To decrease fat content: use lowfat cream cheese and skim milk.

Artichoke Hors d'Oeuvres

"Serve hot, with Melba rounds."

Serves 20

1 can artichokes, drained and cut into
  small pieces
1 cup sour cream
½ cup mayonnaise
1 cup Mozzarella cheese, cut into cubes
Garlic powder, as desired
Melba rounds

Mix all ingredients except Melba rounds. Bake in serving dish in microwave 3 minutes. Stir and turn; heat 1 minute more.

Jean M. Clay

▲ To decrease fat content: 1) substitute low fat yogurt or mock sour cream, 2) substitute no-fat mayo for mayonnaise.

Mexican Cornbread

"Add more beef and serve as a main dish."

Serves 8-20

1 cup yellow cornmeal
2 eggs, well beaten
1 cup sweet milk
½ teaspoon baking soda
¾ teaspoon salt
1 (#303) can cream style yellow corn
½ cup bacon drippings
½ pound ground beef
1 large onion, finely chopped
½ pound sharp cheese, grated
1 to 4 jalapeño peppers, chopped

Mix the cornmeal, eggs, milk, soda, salt, corn
and bacon drippings to make a batter. Set
aside.

Sauté the ground beef and put on a paper
towel to drain grease. Prepare the onion,
cheese and jalapeño peppers and place in
separate mounds, ready to be used.

Grease a large black iron skillet. Heat; sprinkle
a very thin layer of meal in the skillet and let
brown slightly. Pour ½ the batter into the
skillet, then sprinkle the meat over batter; next
make a layer of the onions, then the layer of
peppers, and finally the layer of cheese. Pour
the remaining batter on top. Bake at 350
degrees for 20-50 minutes depending upon the
baking container. Serve hot.

Beverly Hudson

▲ To decrease fat content: 1) use egg substitute, 2) use skim milk, 3) try bouillon for
bacon drippings, 4) substitute ground round
for hamburger, 5) use lowfat shredded cheese.

Cheese Ball

"Standard holiday fare."

Serves 25

½ pound American cheese, grated
4 ounces Bleu cheese, crumbled
¼ pound sharp Cheddar cheese, grated
8 ounces cream cheese
½ cup mayonnaise
1 small onion, chopped
1 tablespoon garlic salt
1 tablespoon prepared mustard
1 teaspoon red pepper
Pecans, crushed

Mix all ingredients except pecans. Form into 2
balls and roll them in pecan meal. Refrigerate
several hours (at least) before serving.

Pat Moss

Holiday Cheese Ball

"Can't go wrong when you serve this at a party."

Serves 25

2 8-ounce packages cream cheese
1 8-ounce can crushed pineapple, well
  drained
1 cup pecans, chopped
¼ cup green pepper, diced
2 tablespoons onion, chopped
1 tablespoon seasoning salt

Add all ingredients to softened cream cheese.
Shape into ball. Roll in parsley flakes or
chopped nuts. Can be frozen. Makes two balls.

Eleanora Clary and Tracy Magin

▲ To decrease fat content, use lowfat cream
cheese.

Cheese Crisps

"Good for eating and giving."

Serves 20

2 sticks margarine
½ pound sharp cheese, grated
2 cups flour
¼ teaspoon red pepper
2 cups crispy rice cereal

Soften margarine and grated cheese to room temperature. Cream thoroughly and add flour and pepper. With your hands, mix in crispy rice cereal. Pinch off small balls of dough (about size of a pecan), roll into round balls and flatten out in your hands. Place on a cookie sheet and bake in a 350 degree oven for about 15 to 20 minutes. These have to be done by hand to prevent crushing the rice cereal. Dip your fingers in flour if dough is sticky.

Edith Buford

▲ To decrease fat content, substitute lowfat margarine and lowfat shredded cheese.

Cheese Straws

"A party is incomplete without Emily's cheese straws."

Serves 35

1 pound sharp Cheddar cheese, grated
2 sticks margarine
2¼ cups flour
1 teaspoon salt
¼ to ½ teaspoon red pepper

Grate the cheese and mix with margarine, seasonings and most of flour right in food processor. May need to mix the last of the flour with your hands. Or you can use an electric mixer for mixing until the last of the flour makes it difficult. When mixed put through cheese press and bake at 350 degrees about 10 minutes.

Emily Harrison

▲ To decrease fat content, substitute lowfat margarine and lowfat shredded cheese.

*The **May-Turnbull House** was the site of many meetings held by the town leaders to discuss the future of the youth of Harmony Grove.*

Cheese Puffs

"These appetizers 'fly off' the tray."

Serves 10

2 3-ounce packages cream cheese
2 sticks margarine
8 ounces grated sharp Cheddar cheese
5 egg whites
1 loaf Italian/French or any coarse bread

Heat cream cheese, margarine and Cheddar cheese in heavy saucepan very slowly and blend. Beat the egg whites until stiff and fold into cheese mixture. Cut crust off bread and cut into cubes. Coat the bread with the cheese mixture. Place on greased cookie sheet and bake at 400 degrees for 5-7 minutes. (Can be put on a cookie sheet, uncooked, placed in freezer until frozen, stored in plastic bags until ready to use.)

Belle Blount

▲ To decrease fat content, use lowfat cream cheese, fat-free margarine and lowfat shredded cheese.

Brie Hors D'Oeuvres

"Serve with crackers and Granny Smith apples."

Serves 8-12

¼ cup brown sugar
2 tablespoons whiskey
Chopped nuts

Microwave above ingredients until melted (on high for 1 minute).

Spread on wedge of Brie and put in micro-wave for 1 minute or until melted.

Ellen McCracken

Pineapple-Chutney Dip

"Delicious with Melba rounds."

Serves 20

1 fresh pineapple shell with pretty top
8 ounces cream cheese
¼ cup chutney
¼ teaspoon dry mustard
1 teaspoon curry powder

Cut top from pineapple and remove fruit from shell. This is to be used for the serving "bowl." Put aside. Soften cream cheese; stir in other ingredients. Put in pineapple shell to serve and garnish plate with the pineapple top.

Maureen J. Harris

▲ To decrease fat content use lowfat cream cheese.

Toni's Spiced Pineapple

"Disappears quickly."

Serves 10-12

2 cans pineapple chunks
1¼ cups sugar
1 stick cinnamon
¾ cup vinegar
1 cup pineapple juice
6 to 8 cloves

Drain pineapple, reserving juice. Combine the sugar, cinnamon, vinegar, pineapple juice and cloves in a saucepan. Bring to a boil and let boil 5 minutes. Then add pineapple. Let season for at least 24 hours in refrigerator. Will keep several weeks. Drain with slotted spoon to serve. Have toothpicks handy.

Lacey Virginia Harrison

Dip for Vegetables

"Rabbit food."

Serves 25

8 ounces sour cream
1 cup mayonnaise
2 teaspoons curry powder
2 teaspoons lemon juice
1 teaspoon minced onion
1 teaspoon Worcestershire sauce
½ cup chili sauce
3 dashes red pepper
Salt - several sprinkles

Blend all together and chill. Serve with raw vegetables.

Nell Lashley Catherwood

▲ To decrease fat content, use lowfat yogurt or mock sour cream, and use non-fat mayo.

Fruit Ball

"A wonderful snack for children or use for a party."

Serves 15-20

1 4-ounce package cream cheese
⅔ cup crushed pineapple (drain well)
6 ounces coconut
½ cup sour cream
4 ounces chopped cherries
2 cups chopped pecans (1 cup in fruit ball, 1 cup for rolling)

Mix together and roll in the remaining cup of chopped pecans. Serve with vanilla wafers.

Kaye Samford

▲ To decrease fat content, use lowfat cream cheese and lowfat yogurt or mock sour cream.

Cucumber Sandwiches

"A must for a southern garden party."

Serves 25

2 cucumbers, peeled and chopped
1 small white onion, grated (less if desired)
½ cup slivered almonds, toasted and finely chopped
Salt and pepper to taste
Mayonnaise to bind
Bread with crust removed

Drain chopped cucumbers well. Mix with remaining ingredients and drain again. Spread at last minute and cut into finger sandwiches. A bit of parsley adds a pretty color.

Joyce Moorman

▲ To decrease fat content, use non-fat mayo.

Zesty Spinach Dip

"Serve in a hollowed out round of bread for something different."

About 5 cups - serves 25

2 cups mayonnaise
2 cups sour cream
1 10-ounce package frozen, chopped spinach, cooked and drained
4 teaspoons dill weed
1 1-ounce package regular ranch salad dressing mix
½ cup onion, minced
Garlic salt, to taste

In a bowl, combine all ingredients, mixing well. Cover and chill 12 hours. Spoon into a serving bowl and serve with cut up vegetables, crackers or chips.

Eleanora Clary

▲ To decrease fat content, use non-fat mayo and lowfat yogurt or mock sour cream.

Ham Spread

"Use on crackers as an appetizer or on bread for sandwiches."

Serves 6-20

1 cup chopped or ground ham
⅓ cup chopped celery
1 tablespoon chopped onion
1 grated carrot
¼ cup mayonnaise or salad dressing

Mix all ingredients well.

Pat Perkinson

▲ To decrease fat content, use lowfat/turkey ham and use non-fat mayo or salad dressing.

Marinated Mushrooms

"Always gets rave reviews."

Serves 30

2 pounds mushrooms
1 cup vinegar
½ cup oil
1 clove garlic, minced (or 1 teaspoon garlic powder)
1½ teaspoons salt
½ teaspoon black pepper
2 teaspoons chopped chives
1 bay leaf
½ teaspoon thyme
½ teaspoon oregano
3 tablespoons fresh chopped parsley
1 onion, sliced in rings
1 teaspoon dry mustard
1 tablespoon Worcestershire sauce
¼ teaspoon basil
½ teaspoon paprika

Clean mushrooms. Mix all remaining ingredients and pour over the mushrooms. Marinate for at least 24 hours prior to serving.

Julia Jones

Taco Dip

"Great for an informal party or after a football game."

Serves 25

1 large can refried beans
1 package taco seasoning mix
1 8-ounce package cream cheese
1 avocado
1 8-ounce container sour cream
4½ ounces chopped ripe olives
1 tomato, diced
4½ ounces chopped green chilies (less if desirable)
8 ounces grated Cheddar cheese

Mix together refried beans and taco seasoning and spread on the bottom of a 9 x 13-inch platter. Mix the mashed avocado and cream cheese until smooth. Spread on first layer leaving a ½-inch rim. Spread sour cream on top of second layer, leaving a ½-inch rim. Put olives, green chilies and tomato on top of sour cream and sprinkle cheese over the entire dish. Serve with nacho chips.

Kim Lucy

▲ To decrease fat content, use lowfat cream cheese, lowfat yogurt or mock sour cream, and use lowfat shredded cheese.

Salmon Ball

"Company is a'coming!"

Serves 25

1 large can salmon, drained
2 8-ounce packages cream cheese, softened
1 tablespoon horseradish
1 tablespoon onion, minced
1 tablespoon lemon juice

Blend salmon and cream cheese together. Add seasonings and mix well. Form into a ball and roll in chopped nuts. Serve with crackers.

Lorraine Freeman

▲ To decrease fat content, use lowfat cream cheese.

Sausage Balls

"So easy to make. Makes a wonderful hostess gift."

Serves 50

1 pound mild sausage
4 cups dry biscuit mix
½ pound sharp cheese, grated

Work uncooked sausage into biscuit mix. Add grated cheese and mix well. Roll into balls. Bake on ungreased cookie sheets at 350 degrees for 15 to 20 minutes. Makes 100 balls. Freezes well.

Virginia Vaughan

▲ To decrease fat content, use turkey-sausage and lowfat shredded cheese.

Shrimp Spread

"Serve at your fanciest party. Do not use frozen or fresh shrimp!"

Serves 25

4 small cans shrimp
3 3-ounce packages cream cheese
2 tablespoons onion, grated
1 8 ounce (small) jar mayonnaise
1 teaspoon Worcestershire sauce
½ cup catsup
Juice of 1 lemon
1 cup celery, cut finely

Drain shrimp and mash. Work cream cheese till soft and smooth and blend with mayonnaise. Mix all ingredients together. Refrigerate in covered bowl or jar. DO NOT FREEZE. Will keep several days in refrigerator. Serve with crackers or as elegant spread for sandwiches.

June Thomas

▲ To decrease fat content use lowfat cream cheese and non-fat mayo.

Mimosas

"Great start for a bridal luncheon."

Champagne, chilled
Orange juice
Strawberries

Combine equal parts of champagne and orange juice in a champagne glass. Add strawberry. Easy for a party.

Allene Barkley

Champagne Punch

"Delicious for a bride's party."

Yields 30-35 cups

6 bottles champagne
2 bottles sautérne
1 pint brandy
6 oranges
3 lemons
1 cup sugar (or to taste)
Fresh mint sprigs
Ice ring

Into a chilled bowl, pour 3 bottles champagne and 2 bottles sautérne, all well chilled. Add 6 oranges and 3 lemons, sliced but not peeled. Add sugar, stir well to dissolve. Add brandy. Just before serving, add ice ring and 3 more bottles of champagne. Serve in punch cups or champagne glasses.

June Thomas

Sara's Champagne Punch

"A wonderful light punch for an afternoon gathering."

Serves 30

4 6-ounce cans lemonade concentrate
4 lemonade cans of water
2 quarts dry champagne
2 quarts club soda

Thaw lemonade concentrate. Pour concentrate and water into punch bowl. Add the club soda and champagne and mix. Add an ice ring with frozen fruit to keep cool and look pretty.

Sara Bishop

Bride's Punch

"A pretty and non-alcoholic way to celebrate a wedding."

Serves 25

1 quart vanilla ice cream
1 quart lime sherbet
1 46-ounce can unsweetened pineapple juice
1 28-ounce bottle ginger ale

Chop ice cream and sherbet into pieces. Add juice and ginger ale.
To serve 40 to 50 people, double the recipe and add 3 bottles of ginger ale.

Lorraine Freeman

▲ To decrease fat content, use ice milk or fat-free vanilla ice cream.

"Mock" Champagne Punch

"Refreshing without the dizzy head."

Serves 25

2 bottles sparkling white grape juice
2 bottles ginger ale
1 32-ounce bottle white grape juice
1 6-ounce can frozen lemonade (thawed and undiluted)

Mix all ingredients in a punch bowl and add ice ring to keep cool.

Evelyn Carpenter

Banana Crush

"So easy to make ahead and freeze. Put together at the last minute for serving."

Serves 25

4 cups sugar
6 cups water
2½ cups orange juice
½ cup lemon juice
4 cups pineapple juice
5 bananas, mashed
1 64-ounce bottle or lemon-lime carbonated beverage

Combine sugar and water in a medium saucepan, cook over medium heat until sugar dissolves, stirring constantly. Add juices and bananas, mixing well. Pour into a plastic container and freeze. To serve, thaw slightly. Place in punch bowl and stir with a fork to break into chunks. Add carbonated beverage.

Edith Marcuson

Lazy Day Lemonade

"Old fashioned lemonade."

Serves 6 glasses

1¼ cups sugar
½ cup boiling water
1½ cups fresh lemon juice
4½ cups cold water
Lemon slices for garnish

Combine sugar and boiling water, stirring until sugar dissolves. Add lemon juice and cold water; mix well. Chill and serve over ice. Garnish with lemon slices.

Alice Wood

Hot Spiced Percolator Punch

"This spicy aroma will fill your home and will greet your guests as they arrive."

Yield: 20 cups

9 cups unsweetened pineapple juice
9 cups cranberry juice cocktail
4½ cups water
1 cup brown sugar
4½ teaspoons whole cloves
4 cinnamon sticks broken in pieces
¼ teaspoon salt

Combine pineapple juice, cranberry juice and brown sugar. Place in a 30-cup automatic coffee maker and add water. Combine spices and put in basket of coffee maker. Percolate and serve hot.

Allene Barkley

Irish Coffee

"Quick and Easy."

Serves 8

6 to 8 cups coffee
6 to 8 ounces bourbon
½ pint heavy cream, whipped and
**   sweetened**

This beverage recipe should be made at the table with your guests. Put coffee in a silver pot. Pour bourbon in a decanter. Put whipped cream in a silver serving bowl. Pour coffee into cups about two-thirds full (no more). Add 1 ounce bourbon and top with a couple dollops of whipped cream. Cup should be completely full. Serve as it is made. Do not stir.

Lacey Virginia Harrison

▲ To decrease fat content, substitute low fat whipped topping for sweetened heavy cream.

Coffee Punch

"Brunswick Garden Club favorite."

Serves 28 cups

1 gallon strong coffee (16 cups)
2 quarts vanilla ice cream
1 quart whipping cream
5 tablespoons sugar
2 teaspoons vanilla extract

Brew the coffee, cool and chill in the refrigerator (May be brewed the day before). Whip the cream. Add sugar and vanilla and continue whipping until soft peaks form. Place the ice cream in the bowl and pour chilled coffee over it. Chop up ice cream into small lumps. Stir in whipped cream. Stir until thickened and fairly smooth. (Some small lumps are "ok".)

Brunswick Garden Club

▲ To decrease fat content, use ice milk or fat-free ice cream substitute, and replace whipping cream and sugar with non-fat whipped topping.

Russian Tea

"A generous dash of rum in each cup improves the recipe."

1 teaspoon whole cloves
1 1-inch stick cinnamon
3 quarts water
2½ tablespoons black tea
Juice of 3 oranges
Juice of 1½ lemons
1 cup sugar

Tie spices in bag and bring to boiling in water. Add tea tied in bag loosely. Steep 5 minutes. Remove bags. Heat fruit juices and sugar. Add to tea. Can be made ahead of time - best when reheated, but be careful not to boil tea.

Helen Dortch

Old Virginia Wassail

"Garnish with orange slices."

Serves 20

2 quarts sweet apple cider
2 cups orange juice
1 cup lemon juice
Juice from 2 #2 cans pineapple
1 stick whole cinnamon
1 teaspoon whole cloves
Sugar or honey to taste

Combine ingredients and bring to a simmer.
Strain and serve hot.

Gay Neale

Easy Russian Tea

"Always in cupboard, ready for a cold wintry day."

1 1-pound, 2-ounce jar of Tang
1 cup sugar
⅔ cup instant tea
1 teaspoon ground cinnamon
½ teaspoon ground cloves
1 large envelope of lemonade mix

Mix all ingredients well. Use 1-2 tablespoons
mix for each cup of boiling water.

Irene Kirchman

Hot Mocha Coffee Drink Mix

"For a warm-up on a cold day."

2 cups sugar
2 cups instant nonfat dry milk
2 cups non-dairy creamer
1 cup cocoa
½ cup instant coffee

Combine ingredients and mix well. Use 2
tablespoons mix in 1 cup boiling water. Top
with a marshmallow or whipped cream.

Irene Kirchman

Mulled Cider

"Health conscious - leave out butter."

Serves 20

1 gallon apple cider
½ cup sugar
⅓ stick butter
6 sticks cinnamon
8 whole cloves
Nutmeg to taste

Bring to boiling point. Add rum or vodka if
desired.

Nita Lane Fleshood

Bloody Mary

"Serve in a glass with a stalk of celery."

Serves 6

1 cup gin or vodka
1 quart tomato juice
2 tablespoons clam juice
1 tablespoon Worcestershire sauce
½ teaspoon celery salt
⅛ teaspoon ground black pepper
1 tablespoon lemon juice

Mix all ingredients and shake well. Pour into
glasses and garnish with celery stalks.

Beth Parker

Peach Daiquiris

"Cool drink on a hot day."

Serves 2

2 fresh peaches, peeled and sliced
2 teaspoons sugar
1 small can frozen lemonade
1 can of rum
2 cups crushed ice

Combine all ingredients in a blender and
blend until smooth.

Betty Lowe

Grandpapa's Eggnog

1 dozen eggs, separated
18 tablespoons sugar for yolks
6 tablespoons sugar for whites
About 1 pint apple brandy "cut" with some
rum
Whipping cream, whipped
Nutmeg

Put yolks in bowl large enough for good beating and stirring. Put whites in large flat platter for whipping by hand. (An electric beater and a bowl would probably make just as good eggnog, but Grandpapa wouldn't agree.) Begin by stirring the yolks well with a big spoon, adding the 18 tablespoons of sugar a few tablespoons at a time. Then add brandy very slowly with plenty of stirring as this "cooks" the yolks. The whites are to be beaten to peaks and the 6 tablespoons sugar well mixed in. Fold whites slowly into the yolks and brandy mixture. When mixed it should be thick and smooth. Cover and refrigerate. When ready to serve, stir and spoon into mugs, garnishing with whipping cream partially folded into the brew; sprinkle with nutmeg if desired.

Grandpapa's rule was to add 2 level tablespoons sugar per egg with ¾ of this going to yolks and ¼ to whites. And "the rule is a pint of brandy to a dozen eggs, which is rather a strong rule."

Jenny Showalter

Grape Wine

Wash grapes and squeeze by hand and put in a stone jar if available (plastic or glass jar may be substituted.) Add to grapes 1 cup of water and 1 cup of sugar per gallon. Cover jar with cloth or Reynolds Wrap. Let stand for about 3 to 4 days depending on how warm weather is. The warmer the weather the faster the grapes will ferment. Stir daily with wooden spoon.

After the 3 to 4 days, squeeze the hulls from juice by hand and remove, then add to pulp and juice, 2 pounds of sugar per gallon. Each day as pulp works to the top skim it off with a spoon, do this for several days until most of the pulp has worked to the top and been removed. Then strain juice through either cheesecloth or kitchen screen wire strainer and put in gallon glass jugs and put air lock valves on jugs or tie a rubber balloon over top of jug. The balloon permits gasses to escape which blows the balloon up. When the balloon goes down the juice has begun to slow down fermenting. After the sediments have settled to the bottom of jar (3 to 4 weeks) use a plastic siphon tube and siphon off wine leaving sediments in bottom. Put wine back in jugs and let it settle again a few more weeks and repeat siphoning process.

Wine should not be sealed up tight in jars until 10 to 12 weeks from starting time. Wine will be ready to use after aging, 6 months to several years.

W.R. Wright

"Most people who have grown up in rural areas have sooner or later performed the chore of bringing in wood. Wagons, sleds and wheelbarrows helped make the job easier."

"My father, brother and I cut our family's firewood. Dead or diseased trees as well as trees intruding on cultivated areas provided most of our wood. Using a saw hooked up to our tractor, we cut the firewood into suitable lengths for the wood heater and the cookstove in the kitchen."

Eldridge Bagley

"WOOD WAGON"
Appears through the courtesy of the painting's owners, Ralph A. and Nancy H. Amos.

Gazpacho

"Chunky or smooth, this is summer fresh."

Serves 8

2 cloves garlic, crushed
2 pounds medium size tomatoes (6 or 7), peeled and chopped
1 medium cucumber, peeled and diced
1 large green pepper, remove seeds and chop
2 slices white bread (1 cup), trim off crusts and crumble
¼ cup red wine vinegar
2 cups tomato or cocktail vegetable juice
1 cup water (or ½ cup for chunky version)
¼ cup olive oil
½ teaspoon salt
¼ teaspoon fresh ground pepper
Optional garnishes: ½ cup chopped green pepper, ½ cup chopped green onions, ½ cup packaged garlic croutons, cucumber slices

To make smooth gazpacho: combine garlic, tomatoes, cucumber, green pepper, bread and vinegar in blender; mix until smooth. Press mixture through sieve, discarding solids. Add juice, water, oil, salt and pepper to the mix. Chill well. Serve in bowls, garnish with green pepper, green onions, or croutons if desired.

To make chunky gazpacho: blend tomato chunks, garlic, salt, pepper, oil and vinegar in blender at moderate speed. Empty contents of blender into large container; pour in juice and ½ cup water, stir. Then stir in 1 cup diced cucumber, green pepper and sliced green onions. Serve chilled in bowls using garnishes if desired.

Frances Hampton

Chilled Cucumber Soup

"Cool and refreshing."

Serves 2 to 3

1 tablespoon reduced-calorie margarine
1 medium cucumber, peeled, seeded, and chopped
2 tablespoons sliced green onions
2 teaspoons cornstarch
1¼ cups skim milk, divided
1 teaspoon chicken-flavored bouillon granules
¼ teaspoon dried whole dillweed
½ cup plain lowfat yogurt
Thin cucumber slices (optional)
Fresh parsley sprigs (optional)

Melt margarine in a small saucepan; add cucumber and onions, and sauté until vegetables are tender.

Combine cornstarch and ¼ cup milk, stirring until blended; add cornstarch mixture, remaining 1 cup milk, bouillon granules, and dillweed to saucepan. Cook, stirring constantly, over medium heat until thickened. Pour mixture into container of an electric blender; process until smooth. Let cool slightly.

Stir yogurt into cucumber mixture; cover and chill 2 hours. Garnish with cucumber slices and parsley, if desired.

Cherrill Robertson

Chilled Mushroom Soup

"Great for a summer luncheon."

Serves 4

1 pound fresh sliced mushrooms
4 tablespoons butter
4 cups water
½ cup chopped celery
½ cup chopped onion
2 tablespoons flour
2 cups milk or half and half
1¼ teaspoons salt
⅛ teaspoon paprika
⅛ teaspoon dill weed
4 tablespoons sherry (optional)

Sauté mushrooms in 2 tablespoons of the butter. Add the water, celery and onions. Simmer until tender, about 20 minutes. Drain, reserving liquid. There should be at least 3 cups of liquid; if not, add water until you have 3.

Puree the onion, celery and mushrooms and put back in liquid.

In saucepan on medium heat, stir 2 tablespoons flour in melted butter. Gradually add the milk or half and half, whisking or stirring continually until thickened. Do not boil. Reduce heat and stir in the mushroom and vegetable stock.

Add salt, paprika, dill weed and sherry (optional). Stir well, chill in covered bowl. Serve cold with dash of paprika and fresh cut dill weed for garnish, if desired.

Gay Neale

Hint - Every time you make a mushroom dish, save stems and pieces in a bag in the freezer. When you get a pound or more, you can use them for this soup.
▲ To decrease fat content, use no-fat margarine and skim milk.

Mock Vichyssoise

"Delicious and refreshing chilled soup."

Serves 8

2 14-ounce cans chicken broth
2 10¾-ounce cans cream of potato soup
2 8-ounce cartons sour cream
2 teaspoons onion, finely minced
Chives, for garnish

Combine all ingredients in blender. Chill for several hours. Garnish generously.

Jean Clay

▲ To decrease fat content, use lowfat chicken broth or bouillon, lowfat cream of potato soup, and lowfat yogurt or mock sour cream in place of the commercial sour cream.

French Onion Soup

"Quick and classic. If you want cheese slightly brown, stick under broiler for a couple of minutes."

Serves 6

6 large onions
4 cans consommé
¾ stick butter
1 cup champagne (optional)
French bread
Parmesan cheese
Mozzarella cheese

Slice onions thinly. In large pot melt butter and add onions. Cooking slowly, let onions brown, but do not burn. Add consommé and champagne. Simmer for 30 minutes. Use small crocks, ladle soup into each one and top with a slice of French bread sprinkled with grated Mozzarella and Parmesan cheese. Bake in 350 degree oven until hot and bubbly.

Carolyn Kirchman

Broccoli and Crab Soup

"This is so good, no one will believe it's quick and easy."

Serves 3 to 4

**1 8-ounce package frozen Alaska King
    Crab, thawed, or 1 7½-ounce can Alaska
    King Crab**
**1 10-ounce package frozen, chopped
    broccoli, completely thawed**
3 tablespoons butter
½ cup onion, chopped
2 tablespoons flour
2 cups milk
2 cups half and half
2 chicken bouillon cubes
½ teaspoon salt
½ teaspoon black pepper
**½ teaspoon cayenne (for milder use ¼
    teaspoon or less)**
¼ teaspoon thyme

In a skillet, melt butter and sauté onion. Blend in flour until thoroughly mixed and gradually add milk and half and half. Stir constantly and cook until thickened and smooth. Add bouillon cubes and stir until dissolved. Season to taste. Add crab and broccoli and heat through.

Kay Outten

▲ To decrease fat content, use no-fat margarine, skim milk and lowfat evaporated milk.

Scallop Stew

"You can vary portions of ingredients to suit your taste. If you substitute half and half for milk it will be much richer."

Serves 3 to 4

3 to 4 tablespoons butter
1 large onion, chopped
3 to 4 white potatoes, diced

**¾ to 1 pound scallops (if using sea
    scallops, quarter before using)**
1 cup vacuum packed yellow corn, drained
Approximately 3 cups milk
Freshly ground pepper to taste

Melt butter in saucepan. Add onions and potatoes. Sauté until tender, covering pan if necessary to help cook potatoes. Add scallops to pan and cook covered on low for 5 to 10 minutes or until scallops are opaque. Uncover and add corn, milk, and lots of freshly ground pepper to taste. Heat over medium until stew is piping hot, but do not let boil.

Virginia Caldwell Brown

▲ To lower fat content, use non-fat margarine and skim/lowfat milk.

Southside Peanut Soup

"If extra seasoning is needed, add a chicken bouillon cube."

Serves 4

2 tablespoons butter
1 tablespoon celery leaves, chopped
1 tablespoon onion, minced
1 tablespoon chopped parsley
3 cups chicken stock
½ cup crunchy peanut butter

Sauté in butter until done, but not brown, celery leaves, onion and parsley. Add to this chicken broth (canned chicken broth or cream of chicken soup, diluted, may be substituted). Add peanut butter and simmer 30 minutes.

Mary Sheppard Flinn

▲ To decrease fat content, use no-fat margarine, lowfat chicken stock or bouillon and lowfat peanut butter.

Bea's Bean Soup

"Good served with apple salad and sweet muffins."

Serves 6

1 pound white beans
1 cup ham scraps (lean and fat)
1 slice white meat (fatback)
2 small carrots
1 large onion
3 stalks celery
2 tablespoons tomato sauce
Crushed red pepper
Salt
Freshly ground black pepper

Soak beans overnight in a generous amount of cold water. When ready to cook, put ham scraps, white meat and beans on to cook in large pot in cold water, well covered, and boil for at least 1 hour and 15 minutes. Sauté chopped carrots, onion and celery in butter and add to soup along with tomato sauce, salt and pepper. Boil another 30 minutes or longer. Add more water if needed.

Virginia Harris

▲ To decrease fat content, use lean ham scraps only, omit the white meat.

Sausage Soup

"You could also call this 'chili soup'."

Serves 6

1 pound pork sausage
2 15-ounce cans kidney beans
1 large can tomatoes
1 quart water
1 large onion
1 bay leaf
1½ teaspoons salt
½ teaspoon garlic salt
½ teaspoon thyme

⅛ teaspoon pepper
2 cups potatoes, diced
½ green pepper, chopped

Brown sausage in skillet and pour off fat. In a large kettle combine all other ingredients. Add sausage and simmer covered for 1 hour. Remove bay leaf before serving.

Pat Perkinson

▲ To lower fat content, use lowfat turkey sausage.

Sherwood Manor Soup

"You may add tomatoes or water to get the desired thickness."

Serves 12

1 whole chicken or 3 to 4 pounds chicken
   leg quarters
1 to 2 cups chopped celery
7 to 8 diced potatoes
3 chopped medium onions
1 chopped leek
1 32-ounce package frozen mixed
   vegetables
1 10-ounce package green peas
3 quarts tomatoes
2 packages vegetable soup recipe mix
Salt, pepper, little bit of sugar and hot
   sauce to taste

Cook chicken in water (enough to cover) until tender. Cool and debone chicken, return chicken to broth along with remaining ingredients and seasoning to taste, including sugar. Cook until vegetables are done, about 1 hour to allow for flavors to come together.

Pat Temple

▲ Using skinless chicken will lower the fat.

Mushroom and Potato Soup

"Very mushroom rich, an elegant potato soup."

Serves 4 to 8

2 tablespoons butter
½ small green pepper (optional)
1 small onion, diced
1 stalk celery, chopped
1 8-ounce package sliced fresh mushrooms
2 cups peeled and diced potatoes
2 cups chicken broth
½ teaspoon thyme
2 to 3 teaspoons fresh parsley
    or 1 teaspoon parsley flakes
2 cups milk
½ teaspoon salt
3 tablespoons flour

Sauté the onion, celery, green pepper and mushrooms in butter, then set aside. Cook potatoes in chicken broth with parsley and thyme seasonings. When potatoes are tender, add sautéed mushrooms, onions, green pepper and celery. To thicken, combine flour with ¼ cup of the milk, shaking vigorously in a small jar or whisking vigorously in a bowl until smooth. Add thickener to simmering mushroom and potatoes, stirring constantly. Gradually add remaining milk, stirring constantly. Season to taste with salt and fresh ground pepper. Serve piping hot.

Linda McPeters

▲ To decrease fat content, use lowfat chicken broth and skim/lowfat milk.

Vegetable Bean Soup

"Don't be put off by the long list of ingredients. They all go in pot at same time (except rice)."

Serves 10 to 12

¼ pound salt pork, finely diced or leftover
    ham, cubed
2 quarts hot water
½ cup tomato or cocktail vegetable juice
1 can pinto beans
1 can bean with bacon soup
6 beef bouillon cubes
1 cup diced carrots
1 cup chopped celery
1 cup shredded cabbage
1 cup chopped green onion
½ package frozen chopped spinach
1 teaspoon basil
1 teaspoon monosodium glutamate
½ teaspoon salt
½ teaspoon pepper
¾ cup uncooked rice
Parmesan cheese

If using salt pork, brown cubes using a large pot, then add all ingredients except rice and cheese. Bring to boil, cover and simmer 1 hour. Add rice and simmer an additional 30 minutes. Sprinkle with Parmesan cheese before serving, if desired.

Weezie Rawlings

▲ To decrease fat content, use lowfat turkey ham and lowfat bean with bacon soup.

Brunswick Stew

"Cooked on stove but just as good, maybe better than stew cooked outside in the big black pot."

Serves 12 to 16

2½ to 3 pounds chicken
2 pieces celery
1 small onion
2 quarts tomatoes (4 - 29 oz cans)
1 quart green butter beans (drain if canned) (4 - 15 oz) & 2-16 oz frozen
1 quart whole kernel corn (drain if canned) (2 - 29 oz) & 2-16 oz frozen
3 medium white potatoes
1 cup onion, chopped
5 tablespoons sugar
Salt, red and black pepper

Place chicken, celery and small onion in large kettle. Add about a quart of water. Simmer until meat is tender or begins to loosen from bones. Lift chicken from broth; cool; discard celery. Remove meat from bones and cut into small pieces.

Add tomatoes, chopped onions, whole potatoes to chicken broth and continue cooking over medium heat. Remove potatoes when tender, mash and return to stew.

Add cut-up chicken, butter beans, corn and sugar. Salt and pepper to taste.

Bring to a boil while stirring; cover, lower heat and simmer slowly - stirring occasionally to prevent sticking 3 to 5 hours or until tomatoes have cooked to pieces.

Makes about 6 quarts. Freezes well.

Van Doyle

▲ To decrease fat content, use skinless meat.

Girl Scout Stew

"Quick and easy."

Serves 4

1 pound ground beef
2 tablespoons butter
1 can vegetable soup
½ cup water
Salt and pepper

Brown ground beef in butter in a large skillet; add soup and water. Season with salt and pepper. Cover; cook slowly for 15 minutes. Serve with thick slices of garlic toast.

Evelyn Carpenter

*When court is in session at the **Brunswick County Courthouse**, the broad street in front of it is clogged with traffic.*

Tennessee Brunswick Stew

"As the name says, this is the way it's made in Tennessee. The bread makes the difference."

Serves 6

1 stewing chicken, squirrel or rabbit
4 potatoes, diced
1 pint butter beans
1 or 2 diced onions
½ pint okra
1 pint tomatoes
½ pint corn
1 tablespoon butter
1 cup biscuit or bread crumbs
Salt to taste
Black pepper, use a lot

Combine all ingredients in a large pot except the biscuit or bread crumbs. Cover well with water, bring to a boil. Simmer until done, stirring occasionally and picking out bones. Cook at least 2 hours. The longer the better. Keep adding water as it cooks down. Add butter and bread crumbs to thicken.

Louise Weeks

▲ To decrease fat content, use skinless meat.

Freeman F. Browder's Brunswick Stew

"Real honest-to-goodness cooked outdoors over an open fire, black pot stew."

Serves 50 to 60

18 squirrels*
2 pounds white meat (fatback)
6 quarts tomatoes
4 quarts butter beans
4 quarts corn
3 pounds onions

Scrub pot well. Bring the pot to a good heat and put in the diced fat meat. Cook until all of the grease has been extracted from meat. Pour in 3 gallons of very hot water. Bring the water to a boil. Put in the squirrels and cook until the meat leaves the bones. Pick out as many bones as possible. Drop in the onions and tomatoes. Cook until the tomatoes fall apart. Put in the butter beans and cook until they test done. Put in the corn and that will be done in a very short time. Set the pot off the fire and the stew is ready. Makes 5 gallons of stew.
Note: Stir all of the time.
*Chicken, lamb or kid may be substituted for squirrel.

Gay Neale

▲ To decrease fat content, omit the white meat.

Little League Beef Stew

"So nice to come home to."

Serves 6

1½ pounds beef
4 potatoes
4 carrots
1 onion (or more)
1 can cream of celery soup
½ cup red wine
Salt and pepper to taste

Cut beef, potatoes, carrots and onion into pieces. Mix all ingredients in a large casserole. Cover and cook 4 hours at 300 degrees.

Barbara Roehrich

Oven Beef Stew

"Don't let it get dry while cooking, you may have to add liquid."

Serves 4

1½ pounds chuck steak or stew beef, cut
  into cubes
1 or 2 onions, chopped
3 carrots, cut up
Green pepper, if desired
2 or 3 stalks celery, cut up
1 3-ounce can mushrooms, undrained
⅓ cup red wine or water
Salt
Pepper
Bay leaf

Sauté vegetables in a little oil. Remove vegetables from pan and then add a little more oil, flour meat, put in pan and brown on all sides. After meat has browned, remove from pan and drain off excess fat.

Stir in mushrooms undrained and wine or water. Add seasonings. Bring this to a boil to loosen brown bits from pan. Remove from heat and combine meat, vegetables and mushroom mixture. Put in casserole and cover tightly (can use aluminum foil if you don't have a casserole with top). Bake in 350 degree oven from 1¼ to 1½ hours, or until meat is tender.

Serve with noodles or rice.

Jean Cyrus

Chili

"Top with grated Cheddar cheese if desired."

Serves 4 to 6

2 pounds lean ground beef
2 large onions, chopped
1 small green pepper, chopped
2 1-pound cans whole tomatoes
  (do not drain)
2 large garlic cloves, crushed and minced
2 rounded tablespoons chili powder
  (I always add more)
2 rounded teaspoons oregano leaves
  (use less or more to taste)
2 teaspoons salt
1 1-pound can kidney beans, drained

Brown meat in oil; add onions and green pepper stirring along with meat till they are sautéed. Add the tomatoes with their juice, chopping whole tomatoes up as you stir them in. Add all other ingredients except kidney beans and bring to boil. Stir well, reduce heat, cover; simmer for about 1 hour. Stir occasionally, chopping tomatoes more if necessary. Add beans and simmer uncovered for at least 20 more minutes. Taste and add extra chili powder, if desired, and dash of red and/or black pepper. Serve hot in bowls; garnish with grated Cheddar cheese, if desired, saltines or cornbread on the side.

Jenny Showalter

Beef Stew Bourbonnais

"Especially good reheated the next day."

Serves 6

1½ pounds beef chuck, cut into 1-inch
    cubes
1 tablespoon shortening
1 clove garlic, minced
1 medium onion, chopped
½ teaspoon salt
½ teaspoon pepper
1 can condensed tomato soup
¾ cup red wine
¼ cup water
¼ teaspoon basil
¼ teaspoon thyme
½ cup tomato catsup
3 medium carrots, cut into ½-inch
    diagonal pieces
1½ cups celery, diced into 1-inch diagonal
    pieces
4 medium potatoes, pared and quartered

In large skillet or Dutch oven lightly brown
meat in shortening. Add garlic and onion;
sauté until transparent. Sprinkle with salt and
pepper. Stir in soup, wine, water. Cover and
simmer 30 minutes. Add herbs and catsup.
Arrange vegetables on top of meat and gravy;
cover; simmer 1½ hours or until meat and
vegetables are tender. Add more water if
necessary and cook very slowly. Freezes well.

Connie Peebles

Hamburger Stew

*"You can add whatever vegetables you happen to
have or have a taste for at the moment."*

Serves 6 to 8

1½ pounds hamburger
1 10-ounce bag frozen mixed vegetables
2 cans stewed tomatoes
1 12-ounce can cocktail vegetable juice

Any fresh vegetable you desire,
    suggestions are: carrots, celery, onion,
    zucchini, potatoes, etc.
Season to taste

Brown hamburger and drain off grease.
Combine all ingredients together in large pot.
You may need to add water or more stewed
tomatoes in order to cover all well with liquid,
it will depend on how much fresh vegetables
you use. Let cook at least 2 hours. Salt and
pepper to taste.

Gray Rawlings

Rusty Buck Stew

*"Use any vegetables you have. I have also used
turnips and butter beans."*

Serves 12

Loin of venison, cut into ¾-inch slices
Seasoned meat tenderizer
1 tablespoon salad oil
½ to 1 cup water
2 quarts tomato juice
6 to 7 potatoes, cubed
6 to 8 carrots
1½ pints frozen corn, cooked
1 pint frozen green beans
Season to taste with:
1 to 2 teaspoons salt
½ teaspoon onion salt
Dash of marjoram, basil, chili powder and
    oregano

Season venison with tenderizer and brown in
oil in pressure cooker. Add ½ to 1 cup water
and cook under 15 pounds pressure for 30
minutes.

Heat tomato juice in Dutch oven. Add all
vegetables. Shred the cooked meat and add to
juice and vegetables. Add desired seasonings
and simmer 1 to 2 hours.

Maureen Harris

"Spending hours in the garden picking vegetables, in between other farm chores, was tiring and usually a hot job. So when it came time to shell peas, snap beans, or shuck garden corn we tried to find a way to make those jobs more enjoyable. What better way than with cool shade, an icy drink and a radio?"

Eldridge Bagley

"THE SHELLING TABLE"
Appears through the courtesy of the painting's owners, Russell and Barbara Mait.

Congealed Asparagus Salad

"A creative way to get your family to eat asparagus."

Serves 8 to 12

¾ cup sugar
1 cup water
½ cup vinegar
2 envelopes unflavored gelatin
   (soaked in ½ cup cold water)
½ teaspoon salt
½ cup pecans, chopped
1 cup celery
2 pimentos, chopped
2 teaspoons onion, grated
Juice of ½ lemon
1 small can asparagus tips, drained

Mix and boil sugar, water, salt and vinegar.
Add soaked gelatin to hot mixture. Cool well.
Add other ingredients and pour into mold.

Harriette Newsom

Congealed Cauliflower Salad

"A good way to use left-over party vegetable tray hors d'oeuvres."

Serves 8

1 package lime gelatin
1 cup hot water
1 cup cold water
2 or 3 teaspoons grated onion
1¼ cups small pieces raw cauliflower
¼ cup diced pimentos
2 tablespoons vinegar
1 teaspoon salt
Dash of pepper

Dissolve gelatin in hot water. Add cold water
and chill until it thickens. Prepare remaining
ingredients and let stand to blend. When
gelatin is slightly thick, fold in seasoned
vegetables. Chill in molds until firm.

Elizabeth Watkins

Beet Aspic Salad

"A colorful addition to any meal."

Serves 8

2 packages lemon gelatin
1 cup boiling water
¾ cup beet juice
1 tablespoon horseradish
2 tablespoons chopped onion
5 tablespoons vinegar
1 cup chopped celery
1 cup chopped cooked beets
Dash of red pepper

Dissolve the gelatin in boiling water. When the
gelatin begins to congeal add the remaining
ingredients.

Mary Jane Powell

Broccoli Salad

"If you haven't tried broccoli this way - try it, you'll like it."

Serves 8

1 bunch fresh broccoli
1 medium sweet onion
1 cup sharp cheese
¼ to ½ pound bacon

Dressing
½ cup mayonnaise-type salad dressing
1½ teaspoons vinegar
¼ cup sugar

Use only flowerets of broccoli and cut into
pieces. Cut onion in half and slice thin. Grate
cheese. Fry bacon and crumble. Toss broccoli,
onion and cheese. Pour dressing over salad
and toss again. Put crumbled bacon on top.

Louise Frazier

▲ To decrease fat content, use lowfat/no-fat
salad dressing.

Broccoli Delight Salad

"For a crisper taste - add bacon last. Sunflower seeds are optional."

Serves 6 to 8

1 large bunch fresh broccoli
1 cup raisins
¼ cup onion, diced (red onion preferred)
7 to 10 strips bacon, fried and crumbled
1 cup sunflower seeds

Dressing
3 to 4 tablespoons sugar
½ cup mayonnaise
1 tablespoon vinegar or lemon juice

Put washed, well-drained broccoli which has been cut in small pieces in a large bowl; add raisins, onion, bacon and sunflower seeds. Mix together dressing ingredients; pour over salad and toss. Refrigerate several hours before serving.

Maureen J. Harris

▲ To decrease fat content, use lowfat/no-fat mayonnaise and omit the bacon or use bacon bits.

Cucumber Salad

"Can be served on tomato wedges."

Serves 10 to 12

1 large box lime gelatin
2 teaspoons salt
2 cups boiling water
2 tablespoons vinegar
2 teaspoons grated onion
⅛ teaspoon black pepper
2 cups sour cream
½ cup mayonnaise
2 cups grated cucumber, peeled
1 tablespoon unflavored gelatin

Combine unflavored gelatin (soften in a little cold water) with lime gelatin and salt in a large bowl. Add the boiling water. Stir until dissolved. Add vinegar, grated onion, and pepper. Chill in refrigerator until it looks the consistency of an egg white. Now fold in sour cream, mayonnaise and cucumber.

Lucy Wiley

▲ To decrease fat content, use lowfat/no-fat mayonnaise and replace sour cream with lowfat yogurt or mock sour cream.

Carrot And Coleslaw Salad

"Serve in lettuce cups."

Serves 6 to 8

1 3-ounce package lemon-flavored gelatin
1 cup hot water
½ cup cold water
2 tablespoons vinegar
½ cup mayonnaise or salad dressing
¼ teaspoon salt
¼ teaspoon pepper
1 cup shredded carrots
1 cup shredded cabbage
1 green pepper, finely chopped
½ onion, finely chopped
Lettuce cups

Dissolve gelatin in hot water. Add cold water, vinegar, mayonnaise, salt and pepper. Stir until well blended. Chill until partially set.

Beat chilled mixture and add carrots, cabbage, green pepper, and onion. Chill until firm.

Edie Bell

▲ To decrease fat content, use lowfat/no-fat mayonnaise or salad dressing.

Marinated Broccoli Salad

"When the occasion calls for you to bring a 'covered dish', how much simpler could this be?"

Serves 8 to 12

1 bunch fresh broccoli
1 cup celery, diced
1 jar artichoke hearts, drained
1 small jar pimentos, drained
1 small can sliced ripe olives
1 cup fresh mushrooms
1 cup Italian Dressing

Separate broccoli into bite-size pieces. Add rest of the ingredients (remember to drain pimento and artichoke hearts). Marinate with dressing for 24 hours before serving.

Ann P. Lewis

▲ To decrease fat content, use lowfat or no-fat Italian dressing.

Pea Salad

"How easy can serving vegetables be?"

Serves 6 to 8

1 pound frozen green peas (thawed but not cooked)
½ cup onion, chopped
1 cup celery, chopped
½ cup bacon bits
½ cup sour cream
½ cup Spanish peanuts

Combine all ingredients except peanuts in bowl. Let set several hours. About ½ hour before serving, add the Spanish peanuts. Mix well.

Ann P. Lewis

▲ To reduce fat, replace sour cream with lowfat yogurt or mock sour cream.

Layered Cole Slaw

"Will keep several days in the refrigerator."

Serves 10

1 large cabbage
1 large onion
1 green pepper
1 cup sugar
¾ cup oil
1 cup vinegar
1 teaspoon dry mustard
1 teaspoon celery seed
1 tablespoon salt

Shred in order listed. Do not stir. Pour sugar over vegetables, do not stir. Combine remainder of ingredients and bring to boiling point and pour over shredded vegetables while hot. Do not stir. Refrigerate overnight.

Polly Harris

Dilled Tomatoes And/Or Cucumbers

"Don't let a single fresh garden tomato or cucumber go to waste!"

Serves 6 to 8

3 large tomatoes
⅓ cup vegetable oil
3 tablespoons vinegar
½ teaspoon dry dill weed
¼ teaspoon sugar
½ teaspoon salt
⅛ teaspoon pepper

Place sliced tomatoes in a shallow container. Combine remaining ingredients in a small jar. Cover tightly and shake vigorously. Pour over tomatoes. Chill at least 6 hours but best to chill overnight. Drain and serve on lettuce bed. Can also use cucumbers.

Cherril Robertson

Danish Potato Salad

"Nice for a summer supper."

Serves 8

4 cups white potatoes, diced and cooked
2 beaten eggs
¼ cup vinegar
¼ cup water
¼ cup sugar
2 hard-boiled eggs
1 cup mayonnaise
Pickle relish or ⅓ cup cucumber, diced
small
Salt and pepper to taste

Bring water, sugar and vinegar to a boil, then
add 2 beaten eggs, beat constantly until
thickens. Remove from heat and cool. Add
mayonnaise and relish or cucumber. Mash 2
boiled eggs and add to potatoes. Pour mixture
over potatoes. Season with salt and pepper.

Minnie Welton

▲ To decrease fat content, use lowfat or no-
fat mayonnaise.

Tomorrow Salad

"Suggested options are sliced water chestnuts or
sliced olives in addition to or in place of listed
ingredients."

Serves 8

1 head iceberg lettuce, cut up in small
pieces
4 to 6 celery ribs, diced
1 green pepper, diced
2 bunches green onions, diced
1 cucumber, peeled and sliced
1 10-ounce package frozen peas, cooked
and drained
1½ cups sour cream
1½ cups mayonnaise

Parmesan cheese
Bacon bits (optional)

Using a 9 x 13-inch casserole dish, layer in
order of first 6 ingredients. Do not mix.
Combine sour cream and mayonnaise and
spread over top of entire dish. Top generously
with Parmesan cheese and bacon. Refrigerate
for 24 hours (or at least overnight) before
slicing to serve. May be garnished with sliced
hard-boiled eggs before serving.

Kay Outten

▲ To decrease fat content, use lowfat or no-
fat mayonnaise and replace sour cream with
lowfat yogurt or mock sour cream.

*The bell in the tall, white steeple of the **First Presbyte-***
***rian Church** at the edge of downtown Harmony*
Grove has been calling the town's faithful to worship
since the early 1800's.

Vegetable Salad

"Great for summer cookouts."

Serves 10 to 14

1 15½-ounce can tiny peas, drained
1 15½-ounce can white corn, drained
1 cup onion, diced
1 cup green pepper, diced
1 cup celery, chopped
1 small jar pimento
1 cup Cheddar cheese, cubed (optional)

Dressing
½ cup sugar
½ cup vinegar
½ tablespoon pepper
1 tablespoon salt
¼ cup oil

Mix all dressing ingredients together and bring to a boil. Pour over vegetables. Refrigerate for several hours.

Marion Barkley

▲ To reduce fat content, use lowfat Cheddar cheese or omit.

Garbeano Salad

"Packed full of nutritional foods."

Serves 8

1 15½-ounce can kidney beans, drained
1 15½-ounce can garbanzo beans, drained
1 9-ounce package frozen cut green beans, cooked and drained
½ cup julienned carrots, 1½-inches
½ cup sliced celery
½ cup sliced onion
½ cup julienned green peppers, 1½-inches
2 tablespoons chopped parsley
2 tablespoons chopped pimento

1 package Italian with cheese salad dressing mix
2 tablespoons water
¼ cup red wine vinegar
⅔ cup salad oil
1 clove garlic, crushed
½ teaspoon seasoned salt
½ teaspoon seasoned pepper

Combine beans, carrots, celery, onion, green pepper, parsley and pimento. Combine Italian salad dressing mix and water in a jar, shake well, add vinegar; shake again. Add oil, garlic, salt and pepper, combine thoroughly. Pour over bean mixture; toss. Chill several hours before serving.

Justine Jones

Rice-Spinach Salad

"Suggested way to use left-over rice."

Serves 4 to 6

1 cup rice, uncooked
½ cup Italian dressing
1 tablespoon soy sauce
½ teaspoon sugar
2 cups fresh spinach cut in thin strips
½ cup celery
½ cup green onions with tops
⅓ cup crumbled crisp bacon

Cook rice, transfer to large bowl, cool slightly. Combine dressing, soy sauce and sugar. Stir into warm rice, cover and chill. Add remaining ingredients just before serving.

Anne Walker

▲ To decrease fat content, use lowfat/no-fat Italian dressing.

3 Bean Salad

"If vegetables want to float, place a plate on top to keep them down or press down with a spoon periodically while chilling."

Serves 10 to 14

1 1-pound can green beans
1 1-pound can wax beans
1 1-pound can kidney beans
¾ cup sugar
⅔ cup vinegar
½ cup cooking oil
½ to 1 teaspoon salt
¼ to ½ teaspoon pepper
½ cup or more thinly sliced onion
½ cup green pepper and/or celery, chopped (I use both)

Drain and rinse beans in cold water. Mix sugar, vinegar, oil salt and pepper. Put layer of beans mixed together, then onion, pepper, celery; repeat layers, topping with a few onion and pepper rings to look pretty. Pour dressing over all. Try to use a casserole dish the right size so that all the vegetables get well covered with the dressing. Cover dish and refrigerate overnight.

Virginia Allen

Normany Sauce

"Half and Half or coffee cream may be substituted."

Serves 3 to 4

¼ cup whipping cream
½ cup peanut oil
2 tablespoons vinegar
Salt and pepper to taste

Blend well and serve on Bibb or Boston lettuce.

Susan Slayton

Spinach Salad Dressing

"Try on other greens also."

Yields approximately 2 cups

1 cup oil
¼ cup vinegar
½ cup sugar
⅓ cup catsup
1 tablespoon minced onion
1 tablespoon Worcestershire sauce
1 teaspoon salt

Mix oil and vinegar with electric mixer, then add other ingredients. Chill.

Cherril Robertson

White House Dressing

"There's nothing like a freshly made dressing for a green salad."

Yields 2 to 3 cups

1 cup mayonnaise
2 tablespoons sour cream
2 tablespoons tarragon vinegar
2 tablespoons minced chives
6 fillet anchovies (drain)
1 clove of garlic
Salt and pepper
1 tablespoon lemon juice

Mix all ingredients in blender. Chill.

"Sookie" Peebles

▲ To decrease fat content, use lowfat/no-fat mayonnaise and replace sour cream with lowfat yogurt or mock sour cream.

Bleu Cheese Dressing

"Great on any green salad."

Yields 2 to 3 cups

½ pound Bleu cheese
1 cup sour cream
1 cup mayonnaise
2 teaspoons onion, finely grated
Dash of red pepper

Blend mayonnaise and sour cream. Add grated onion and crumbled Bleu cheese. Mix. Add dash of red pepper. Place in covered jar. Refrigerate.

June Thomas

▲ To decrease fat content, use lowfat/no-fat mayonnaise and replace sour cream with lowfat yogurt or mock sour cream.

French Dressing

"The blender is the best way to mix this dressing."

Yields 5 to 6 cups

1 cup sugar
1 cup vinegar
1 egg
1 bottle chili sauce
1 cup vegetable oil
½ teaspoon salt
½ (1-ounce) wedge Bleu cheese, crumbled
2 cloves garlic
2 medium onions
Dash of Worcestershire sauce

Mix in blender or electric mixer. Cover well and store in refrigerator.

Alta Brown

Clear Garlic Dressing

"Improves with age."

Yields 2 cups

1⅓ cups olive oil
½ cup vinegar
1 teaspoon sugar
1½ teaspoons salt
½ teaspoon dry mustard
4 garlic cloves, sliced

Combine in bottle or jar. Cover and shake with vigor.

Rebecca Peebles

*The mouth-watering aroma that escapes the front door of the **Green Front Grocery** means that Christmas is not far away.*

"Several apple trees on our farm provided us with fall fruit. My mother used the apples for making pies, applesauce, and Waldorf salads. The extra apples were stored for later use and lasted well into the winter."

Eldridge Bagley

"WINESAPS"
Appears through the courtesy of the painting's owners, Eldridge and Beth Bagley.

Blueberry Salad

"Your guests will think you picked them yourself."

Serves 8

2 3-ounce packages blackberry gelatin
2 cups boiling water
1 15-ounce can blueberries, drained
1 8½-ounce can crushed pineapple
1 8-ounce package cream cheese
½ cup sugar
½ pint sour cream
½ teaspoon vanilla
½ cup chopped pecans

Dissolve gelatin in boiling water. Drain blueberries and add enough water to make 1 cup of liquid and add to gelatin. Stir in blueberries and pineapple. Pour into a 1-quart flat pan and put in refrigerator until firm. Combine cream cheese, sugar, sour cream and vanilla and spread evenly over congealed salad. Sprinkle with chopped pecans.

Justine Jones

▲ To lower fat content, use lowfat cream cheese and replace sour cream with lowfat yogurt or mock sour cream.

Banana Split Salad

"Serve on a bed of lettuce."

Serves 10 to 12

1 12-ounce carton prepared whipped topping
1 14-ounce can sweetened condensed milk
1 can cherry pie filling
1 8-ounce can crushed pineapple, drained
4 medium bananas, cubed
½ cup nuts, chopped

Blend whipped topping and milk together. Add remaining ingredients and mix well. Pour into a 3-quart bowl and chill for several hours.

Dora T. Poythress

Congealed Cranberry Salad

"Great to serve with a chicken casserole."

Serves 10 to 12

1 3-ounce package cherry or raspberry gelatin
1 cup boiling water
1 package unflavored gelatin
¼ cup cold water
1 16-ounce can whole cranberry sauce
1¼ cups crushed pineapple, drained
½ cup nuts, chopped
(May add 1 peeled orange cut into small pieces)

Dissolve cherry gelatin in hot water and dissolve plain gelatin in cold water. Add plain gelatin to cherry mix. Add cranberry sauce and mix thoroughly. Add crushed pineapple, nuts (and orange). Chill in a flat bottom baking dish until set.

Margaret Andrews

Jellied Waldorf Salad

"Great to serve with ham."

Serves 6

1 3-ounce package raspberry gelatin
1 cup boiling water
¾ cup cold water
1 tablespoon lemon juice
½ cup apples, diced
½ cup celery, sliced
2 tablespoons raisins
2 tablespoons walnuts, chopped

Dissolve gelatin in boiling water; add cold water. Chill until thick. Pour lemon juice over apples, stir into gelatin along with celery, raisins and nuts. Pour into molds and refrigerate.

Rubye Moseley

Cranberry Sour Cream Salad

"Great holiday salad - pretty and delicious."

Serves 8 to 12

1 3-ounce package cherry gelatin
1 cup hot water
1 11-ounce can whole cranberry sauce
½ cup celery, diced
¼ cup nuts, chopped (pecans and walnuts)
1 cup commercial sour cream

Dissolve gelatin in hot water; let chill until slightly thickened. Break up cranberry sauce and stir into gelatin. Add chopped celery and nuts. Pour half of mixture into mold. Spread evenly with sour cream. Pour remaining cranberry sauce mixture on top and chill. Makes 1 quart.

Lorraine Freeman and Gwen Allen

▲ To decrease fat content, substitute lowfat yogurt or mock sour cream for commercial sour cream.

Christmas Gelatin Salad

"So pretty on the table Christmas Day."

Serves 8 to 10

1 3-ounce package strawberry flavored
  gelatin
1 3-ounce package raspberry flavored
  gelatin
3 cups boiling water
1 cup pineapple juice
1 pound cranberries, ground
1 small apple, grated
1 15¼-ounce can crushed pineapple,
  drained
1 cup sugar
1 cup nuts, chopped

Dissolve gelatin in boiling water; add pineapple juice. Cool. Combine remaining ingredients. Add to gelatin mixture. Pour into a 13 x 9 x 2-inch pan; chill until firm. Cut into squares to serve.

Ruth Finch

Sunshine Delight Salad

"Think tropical."

Serves 8 to 10

1 6-ounce package orange flavored gelatin
2 cups boiling water
1 11-ounce can mandarin oranges, drained
  and chopped
1 8¾-ounce can fruit cocktail, drained
½ cup pecans, chopped
1 medium banana, sliced
1 3-ounce package cream cheese, softened
¼ cup commercial sour cream
Lettuce leaves

Dissolve gelatin in boiling water; add oranges, fruit cocktail, pecans and bananas, stirring gently. Pour half of gelatin mixture into a lightly oiled, 9-inch square dish. Chill until firm. Combine cream cheese and sour cream in a small mixing bowl; beat at medium speed with electric mixer until smooth. Spread evenly over gelatin layer; chill slightly. Pour remaining half of gelatin mixture on top; chill until firm. Cut into squares and serve on lettuce leaves.

Essie R. Wesson

▲ Substitute lowfat yogurt or mock sour cream for commercial sour cream.

Cherry Salad

"Serve on George Washington's birthday."

Serves 8 to 12

1 can cherry pie filling
2 cups boiling water
½ cup sugar (optional)
1 large package cherry gelatin
1 medium can crushed pineapple, drained

Dissolve gelatin in boiling water and add remaining ingredients. Place in mold to congeal.

Sour Cream Dressing
1 cup sour cream
1 to 2 tablespoons sugar
2 tablespoons white vinegar
½ teaspoon salt

Stir together sour cream and vinegar; add sugar and salt to taste.

Myrtha Reese

▲ To lower fat content, substitute lowfat yogurt or mock sour cream for sour cream in dressing.

Orange Salad

"A pretty orange frosted salad."

Serves 16

2 3-ounce (or 1 6-ounce) packages orange
   gelatin
1 cup boiling water
2 11-ounce cans mandarin orange
   sections, undrained
1 8¼-ounce can crushed pineapple
2 cups miniature marshmallows
½ teaspoon vinegar
Dash of salt

Topping
½ cup salad dressing or mayonnaise
1 cup prepared whipped topping
Grated cheese

Pour boiling water over gelatin and marshmallows. Add remaining ingredients. Place in refrigerator. After it has hardened, spread on topping.

Make topping by mixing salad dressing or mayonnaise with prepared whipped topping and spread. Grate cheese and sprinkle on top.

Van Doyle

▲ Substitute no fat salad dressing or mayo and lowfat whipped topping to decrease fat content.

Congealed Grapefruit Salad

"Very pretty to serve - resembles melon."

Serves 8 to 12

1 package lime gelatin
1½ cups juice or water (hot)
Dash of red pepper
1 teaspoon vinegar
1 small can crushed pineapple
Fruit from 2 or 3 grapefruits
1 package plain gelatin (for extra
   firmness)

Save juice from the fruits for use with gelatin. Save the grapefruit halves. Combine the other ingredients with fruit and gelatin. Cool. Pour into grapefruit halves to congeal. When ready to serve, cut in half again and place the quarter wedge on lettuce. Use mayonnaise, if desired.

Frances Walton

Ruby Red Salad

"When the color red is called for - this is your salad."

Serves 12

1 16-ounce can beets, sliced and drained
1 15½-ounce can pineapple chunks,
drained
1¼ cups juice of pineapple and beets
A little salt
¼ cup lemon juice
2 3-ounce boxes red gelatin (cherry,
strawberry or raspberry)
½ cup nuts, chopped

Heat juice in pan and add gelatin, mixing well.
Add other ingredients and let set until congealed.

Dorothy J. Jones

Strawberry Pretzel Salad

"Use as a salad or a dessert."

Serves 8

First Layer
2 cups pretzels, crushed
¾ cup butter, melted
3 teaspoons sugar (optional)

Mix and press into a 1½-quart rectangular
baking dish. Bake at 450 degrees for 8 minutes. Cool.

Second Layer
1 8-ounce package cream cheese, softened
1 cup sugar
1 4½-ounce (small) container prepared
whipped topping

Beat sugar into softened cream cheese and stir
in whipped topping. Spread over cooled
pretzel crust and chill until set.

Third Layer
1 large package strawberry gelatin
2 cups boiling water
2 10-ounce containers frozen strawberries

Mix gelatin and water; add frozen strawberries.
Let stand 10 minutes. Pour over chilled cream
cheese. Chill.

Christie Hales

▲ To lower fat content, use no-fat margarine,
lowfat cream cheese and lowfat whipped
topping.

Strawberry Frozen Salad

"Strawberries are good at anytime of the year."

Serves 8 to 12

8 ounces cream cheese
1½ to 2 cups sugar
1 10-ounce package frozen, sliced
strawberries
1 20-ounce can crushed pineapple,
drained
1 cup miniature marshmallows
3 to 4 bananas
1 9-ounce carton prepared whipped
topping
½ to 1 cup nuts, chopped

Cream sugar and softened cream cheese
together; add strawberries (thawed), pineapple, bananas, and nuts. Fold in whipped
topping and marshmallows and freeze. Thaw
½ hour before serving. May be served as a
dessert.

Peggy Martin

▲ To lower fat content, use lowfat cream
cheese and lowfat whipped topping.

Strawberry Salad

"You'll love that wild strawberry taste."

Serves 8

1 3-ounce package wild strawberry gelatin
1 16-ounce can crushed pineapple
  (do not drain)
1 9-ounce carton whipped topping
1 12-ounce carton cottage cheese

Put gelatin and pineapple in pan. Heat until gelatin is dissolved. Chill until it begins to thicken. Add cottage cheese and whipped topping. Refrigerate until it is congealed.

Doris Hill

▲ To lower fat content, use lowfat whipped topping and lowfat cottage cheese.

Pineapple-Cheese Mousse

"Marvelous molded salad."

Serves 9

1 3-ounce package lemon gelatin
1 3-ounce package cream cheese
1 tablespoon mayonnaise
½ cup chopped pecans
1 small jar pimento, chopped (use little
  less than the whole jar)
1 medium can crushed pineapple

Drain pineapple. Use juice and water to make 2 cups of liquid. Heat to boiling. Add to gelatin. Set aside to partially gel. Add remaining ingredients to gelatin. Put in a large mold or 8 x 8-inch casserole dish.

Jean Clay

▲ To lower fat, use lowfat cream cheese and non-fat mayo.

Frosted Salad

"Too good to be called a salad."

Serves 10 to 12

1 3-ounce box orange gelatin
1 3-ounce box lemon gelatin
1 lemon
1 No. 2 can crushed pineapple
  (reserve 1 cup juice)
2 bananas, diced
1 cup miniature marshmallows

Frosting
2 tablespoons flour
½ cup sugar
1 egg, slightly beaten
1 cup pineapple juice
1 tablespoon margarine
1 small carton prepared whipped topping

Dissolve orange and lemon gelatin in 2 cups hot water. Add 1½ cups cold water and juice of lemon. Chill until slightly thick, then add pineapple, bananas and marshmallows. Chill.

To make frosting, mix first 5 ingredients and cook until thick. Cool, then add whipped topping and spread over salad.

Viola Jones

▲ To lower fat content, use lowfat whipped topping.

Frosted Lime Salad

"A really pretty salad to serve."

Serves 8

1 small package lime gelatin
1 cup boiling water
1 No. 2 can crushed pineapple
1 cup small curd cottage cheese
½ cup finely chopped celery
½ cup chopped English walnuts or pecans

Dissolve gelatin in boiling water. Add drained pineapple. When it begins to thicken add celery, nuts and cottage cheese. Pour into a 12 x 8 x 2-inch pan and refrigerate until firm. Spread with following topping.

Topping
1 3-ounce package cream cheese
1 tablespoon mayonnaise
2 teaspoons of lemon juice

Blend the above ingredients and spread as a frosting. Decorate with chopped maraschino cherries and chopped nuts.

Jean Dennis

▲ To decrease fat, use lowfat cottage cheese, lowfat cream cheese and non-fat mayo.

Heavenly Pink Salad

"Pretty to serve for a young lady's birthday meal."

Serves 8 to 10

1 8-ounce package cream cheese, softened
1 6-ounce bottle maraschino cherries (red), cut in half, reserve juice
1 20-ounce can crushed pineapple, drained
2 bananas, sliced
2 cups miniature marshmallows
1 8-ounce carton whipped topping

Slowly cream together the cream cheese and the juice from the cherries. Add cherries, pineapple, bananas, and marshmallows. Mix well. Fold the whipped topping into the mixture. Chill and serve.

Hilda Caldwell

▲ Lowfat cream cheese and lowfat whipped topping may be substituted to lower the fat content.

Cherry Frozen Salad

"If doing cupcake style, divide nuts by putting 2½ nuts in each cupcake liner before filling."

Serves 8 to 12

1 can cherry pie filling
1 can condensed milk
1 20-ounce can crushed pineapple, undrained
1½ bananas
1 tablespoon lemon juice
½ cup nuts
Muffin pans

Mix all ingredients together. This can be frozen in large dish and cut into squares or put in foil-lined cupcake cups. After the salad is frozen it will keep well in freezer bags.

Frances D. Wright

▲ Substitute lowfat condensed milk to lower fat content.

Frozen Fruit Salad

"So easy to make."

Serves 12

1 8-ounce carton sour cream
1 9-ounce carton prepared whipped
  topping
½ cup or less sugar
2 tablespoons lemon juice
1 teaspoon vanilla
2 medium bananas, diced
1 cup fruit cocktail, drained
1 cup crushed pineapple, drained
1 cup strawberries, drained (if frozen)
½ cup pecans, chopped

Blend together first 5 ingredients. Fold in fruits and nuts. Freeze several hours. Serve in blocks on lettuce. Will keep well in freezer.

Hilda Anderson

▲ To lower fat content, use lowfat yogurt or mock sour cream and a lowfat whipped topping.

Frozen Fruit/Cherry Salad

"Another good frozen salad."

Serves 8

1 teaspoon plain gelatin
3 tablespoons pineapple juice
12 marshmallows
2 tablespoons lemon juice
1 tablespoon maraschino cherry juice
½ cup chopped maraschino cherries
½ cup mashed bananas
⅓ cup mayonnaise
1 9-ounce can crushed pineapple, drained
1 cup heavy cream, whipped

Soften gelatin in pineapple juice. Melt marshmallows over hot water; add lemon juice,

cherry juice and blend. Chill until it thickens. Add other ingredients. Fold in whipped cream and freeze.

Betty Clausen

▲ Using lowfat mayo or nonfat mayo and substituting lowfat whipped topping for the heavy cream will lower the fat content.

Apricot Delight

"A wonderful 'anytime' salad."

Serves 8 to 12

1 6-ounce package apricot gelatin
2 cups boiling water
2 cups ice water
1 cup crushed pineapple (reserve juice)
2 bananas
1 cup miniature marshmallows
½ cup pecans

Mix gelatin and water and chill until it thickens. Add remaining ingredients and chill until set. Top with the following topping.

Topping
½ cup pineapple juice
¼ cup sugar
2 tablespoons flour
1 egg, beaten
2 tablespoons margarine
1 3-ounce package cream cheese, softened
1 package whipped topping, whipped

Combine first 5 ingredients in saucepan and cook until thick. Cool. Mix with cream cheese and whipped topping. Spread over gelatin and refrigerate.

Justine Jones

▲ To lower fat, use an egg substitute, no-fat margarine, lowfat cream cheese and lowfat whipped topping.

Frozen Apricot Fruit Salad

"May be decorated on top with slices of maraschino cherries before freezing."

Serves 12 to 14

1 1-pound can pitted apricots, crushed
1 1-pound can crushed pineapple
4 tablespoons powdered sugar
1 can sweetened condensed milk
1 egg
2 tablespoons white vinegar
1 large package cream cheese
½ pint whipping cream

Sprinkle powdered sugar over apricots and pineapple, let stand. Beat well milk, egg and vinegar and add cream cheese and beat again. Beat whipping cream, add all ingredients together and pour into freezer trays to freeze.

Mary Ann Keith

▲ To lower fat content, use lowfat whipped topping.

Williamsburg Frozen Fruit Salad

"A Christmas time favorite."

Serves 8 to 9

2 cups fruit cocktail
1 cup mandarin orange sections
1 3-ounce package lemon gelatin
2 tablespoons lemon juice
½ cup mayonnaise
½ teaspoon salt
1 cup miniature marshmallows
½ cup whipping cream
Lettuce

Lightly oil 8 molds or an 8-inch square pan. Drain the fruit cocktail and orange sections, reserving 1 cup of fruit juice. Heat the fruit juice, add the gelatin, and stir until dissolved. Add the lemon juice and chill until partially set. Fold in the fruit cocktail, orange sections, mayonnaise, salt, and marshmallows. Whip the cream and fold it in. Turn into the prepared molds or pan and freeze until firm. Serve on lettuce.

Joyce Moorman

▲ Use lowfat or nonfat mayo and lowfat whipped topping to lower fat content.

The Harmony Grove Train Station *is one of the busiest spots in town.*

Pickled Peach Salad Mold

"May also be put in a 9 x 13-inch pan in case you prefer not to use a mold."

Serves 12

1 2½-pound jar pickled/spiced peaches
1 cup peach syrup from jar of peaches
¼ teaspoon salt
1 cup water
1 teaspoon whole cloves
2 3-ounce boxes orange-pineapple gelatin
2 cups orange juice

Drain peaches, reserving the 1 cup juice. Chop peaches and set aside. Simmer for 10 minutes the following: peach juice, salt, water and cloves; pour hot liquid over the gelatin. Remove the cloves and add orange juice. Chill until slightly thickened. Add chopped peaches and pour into mold. Refrigerate until congealed.

Mabel Brewer

Poppy Seed Dressing

"Especially good over apples."

Serves 20

1½ cups sugar
2 teaspoons dried mustard
2 teaspoons salt
⅔ cup vinegar
3 tablespoons onion juice
2 cups salad oil
3½ tablespoons poppy seed

Mix sugar, mustard seed, salt and vinegar. Add onion juice. Slowly add oil, beating until thick. Add poppy seed and beat.

This dressing is good over all types of canned fruit - the greater the variety, the better. Makes a large quantity. Keeps weeks when stored in refrigerator. Beat each time served.

Jane Sebrell

Fruit Salad

"Serve on a bed of lettuce."

Serves 10 to 12

1 small can fruit cocktail
1 small can crushed pineapple
1 can coconut
1 jar maraschino cherries
Grapes, seeded and sliced
1 can mandarin orange slices
Bananas
1 bag miniature marshmallows
Walnuts or other nuts
1 8-ounce carton sour cream

Drain and mix all fruits together. Add nuts and marshmallows. Add sour cream, mix and chill. All juice may be mixed together for a fruit juice drink.

Nancy Clary

▲ Replace sour cream with lowfat yogurt or mock sour cream to decrease fat.

Pistachio Salad

"Pretty green color, nice at Easter."

Serves 8 to 10

1 large can crushed pineapple with juice
1 box pistachio instant pudding mix
1 large container whipped topping
1 cup miniature marshmallows
½ cup chopped nuts

Mix all ingredients and let stand for 2 hours prior to serving.

Alice Wood

▲ Using lowfat whipped topping will lower fat content.

"Making the rounds on the farm might include a walk to the mailbox, a pause to gather spring flowers, and a stop by the chicken house. The rising temperature and humidity would encourage the shedding of a shirt and cap. In this painting, the fruits of these activities have been placed inside a barn door, perhaps while the owner of the shirt and cap is working at other tasks."

Eldridge Bagley

"JONQUILS"
Appears through the courtesy of the painting's owners, Dolores and Stanley Feldman.

Egg, Sausage And Bacon Casserole

"Get ready for the crowd ahead of time."

Serves 16

1 pound bacon
1 pound sausage
2 dozen eggs
1 pound Cheddar cheese
1 can cream of mushroom soup
  (do not dilute)

Scramble eggs to soft doneness, do not use any milk. Brown sausage and bacon, crumble.

In large flat casserole, place half of crumbled sausage and bacon. Add eggs, all. Cover egg layer with remaining sausage and bacon. Pour soup over all. Cover with grated cheese. Make the day before and store in refrigerator. Remove from refrigerator and let sit awhile before baking. Cook at 325 degrees for 20 minutes.

Rose Jones

▲ To lower the fat content, you may substitute turkey bacon or turkey sausage for the sausage and bacon, and use an egg substitute, lowfat cheese and lowfat soup.

Sausage Casserole

"Serve with fruit in season."

Serves 6

1 pound hot sausage
8 eggs
2 cups milk
Cubed bread crumbs
8 ounces Cheddar cheese

Cover bottom of 9 x 13-inch baking dish with cubed bread. Brown sausage in frying pan and pour off grease. Put sausage on top of bread. Mix egg and milk and pour over sausage. Top with Cheddar cheese.

Bake at 350 degrees for approximately 45 minutes, or until well done.

Virginia Hill

▲ To decrease fat, use turkey sausage, an egg substitute and lowfat cheese.

Baked Cheese And Eggs

"This is a good meat substitute."

Serves 4

5 slices bread (stale bread is best)
3 eggs
½ teaspoon Worcestershire sauce
½ teaspoon brown sugar
¼ teaspoon salt
½ pound sharp Wisconsin cheese, grated
1¾ cups milk, scalded
½ teaspoon dry mustard
Dash of red pepper

Trim some of crust from bread, and butter on both sides (use melted butter and pastry brush). Then cut bread into ½-inch squares. Grease baking dish; put in layer of bread, then thick layers of cheese (2 layers of each). Beat eggs; add dry ingredients, then milk. Mix well. Pour this mixture over cheese and bread. Make day before in the A.M. (for evening meal) and put in refrigerator. Set out to get room temperature before baking. Bake in pan of water at 300 degrees for 1 hour. Serve hot.

Virginia Bragg

▲ To decrease fat, use an egg substitute, lowfat cheese, and lowfat/skim milk.

Hearty Company Breakfast Soufflé

"May garnish with wedges of assorted melons and clusters of grapes."

Serves 8

16 slices coarse grained white bread, crusts removed
8 thin slices American cheese
8 thin slices fully cooked or Danish ham
8 thin slices Swiss cheese
6 eggs, slightly beaten
½ to ¾ teaspoon dry mustard
3 cups milk
½ cup butter or margarine, melted
1 cup crushed corn flakes

Grease a 13 x 9 x 2-inch baking dish. Arrange 8 slices of bread over bottom of dish. Top each bread slice with 1 slice of American cheese, 1 slice of ham and 1 slice of Swiss cheese. Cover each "sandwich" with a slice of bread. In a large bowl, combine eggs and mustard, mixing well. Blend in milk; pour over sandwiches. Cover and refrigerate 12 hours. Remove cover; evenly pour melted butter over casserole and sprinkle with corn flake crumbs. Bake in a moderate oven (350 degrees) for 55 to 60 minutes or until casserole is puffed and lightly browned. Cut into 8 squares and serve at once. May substitute crab meat or shrimp for ham, if desired.

Jean Clay

▲ To lower fat, use lowfat cheese, lowfat ham, skim/lowfat milk, lowfat margarine and an egg substitute.

Cheese Omelet

"Simple and light."

Serves 2

4 eggs, separated
½ teaspoon salt
2 tablespoons butter
¼ teaspoon baking powder
4 teaspoons milk
Dash of pepper
1 cup cheese, grated

Beat egg yolks with milk, salt and pepper. Beat whites, with baking powder added, until stiff. Fold whites into yolks. Pour into a large frying pan in which the butter has been melted. Sprinkle the cheese over this and cook slowly. Fold over and cook until firm.

Emily Harrison

▲ To decrease fat content, use lowfat cheese.

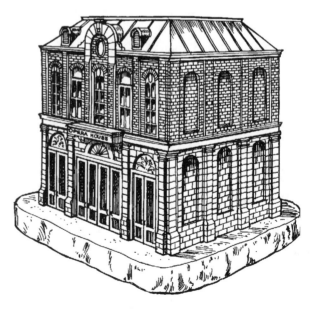

Few performers of the stage pass through the region without drawing an enthusiastic audience at the **Tidewater Opera House**.

Quiche Lorraine

"Can use bacon instead of sausage."

Serves 4 to 6

1 9-inch pie shell
⅓ pound sausage
1 spring onion, sliced
2 slices Swiss cheese
2 eggs
¾ cup coffee cream (or half and half)
Pinch salt
1 tablespoon butter

In frying pan, scramble sausage, pour off grease, then sauté onion lightly. Place cooked sausage and onions in bottom of pie shell. Cut cheese into matchstick strips and arrange over sausage and onions. Beat eggs. Add cream and salt to eggs, stir and then pour into pie shell. Dot top with bits of butter. Bake at 375 degrees for 30 minutes or until filling puffs high and golden.

Byrd Perkinson

▲ To lower the fat, use turkey sausage or turkey bacon, lowfat cheese, and an egg substitute.

Frozen Cheese Soufflé

"Freezing ahead lets you control more accurately when to bake to be able to serve a beautiful soufflé."

Serves 6 to 8

3 tablespoons margarine
¼ cup flour
½ teaspoon salt
1 cup milk
1½ cups grated sharp cheese
4 eggs
¼ teaspoon cream of tartar

Make a cream sauce of the first 4 ingredients. Add grated cheese; stir until cheese has melted and sauce is smooth. Add yolks of eggs, stirring each in well. Let cool.

Beat whites of eggs until slightly stiff; add cream of tartar and continue beating until stiff, but not dry. Fold cheese mixture into egg whites. Blend well but gently. Pour into ungreased 1½-quart baking dish and freeze at once, covered tightly with plastic wrap.

To bake - Place frozen soufflé in cold oven. Set oven temperature at 300 degrees and bake 1 hour and 25 to 30 minutes without opening oven. Serve at once.

Cam Rawlings

▲ To lower fat, use lowfat/skim milk and lowfat cheese.

Creamed Chipped Beef

"Very rich, wonderful brunch dish."

Serves 6

½ an 8-ounce carton whipped cream cheese
2 tablespoons milk
1 3-ounce package thinly sliced beef
½ cup (2 ounces) shredded Swiss cheese
2 hard-cooked eggs, chopped
1 hard-cooked egg, sliced
3 English muffins
Chopped parsley

Combine cream cheese and milk, stirring until smooth. Add beef, Swiss cheese, and 2 chopped eggs to cream cheese. Spread this mixture on 6 English muffin halves. Serve cold or broil 2 to 3 minutes. Garnish each half with egg slice and parsley.

Pat Perkinson

▲ To lower fat, use lowfat cream cheese and lowfat Swiss cheese.

Cheese And Sausage French Toast

"Serve garnished with kiwi fruit, strawberries."

Serves 4 to 8

1 8-ounce package sausage patties
**1 8-ounce loaf Italian bread (about 16
    inches long)**
¼ pound sliced Muenster cheese
4 large eggs
1 cup milk
1 tablespoon sugar
Salad oil
Warm maple syrup

Cook sausage patties. Cut bread into 8 diagonal slices ½-inch wide. Cut each slice almost all the way through, cutting from top crust toward bottom. This will form a pocket for stuffing.

Place cheese and sausage in pocket, cutting cheese and sausage to fit. Press together.

In a 13 x 9-inch baking dish, beat eggs, milk and sugar with fork until blended. Place filled bread slices in egg mixture, turning to coat both sides, and making sure all egg mixture is absorbed.

In large skillet over medium heat, in 1 tablespoon hot salad oil, cook stuffed sandwiches about 10 minutes, until golden brown on both sides, carefully turning sandwiches once and adding 1 more tablespoon oil after turning. Serve with maple syrup.

Kay Outten

▲ To lower fat, use lowfat (turkey) sausage, lowfat cheese, lowfat/skim milk and an egg substitute.

Cheese And Ham Turnovers

"A great use for leftover ham."

Serves 5

**1½ teaspoons butter or margarine,
    softened**
1 teaspoon dried onion flakes
¾ cup diced cooked ham (about 4 ounces)
**½ cup (2 ounces) shredded Cheddar
    cheese**
1 6-ounce can refrigerated biscuits
1 tablespoon milk

Combine first 4 ingredients in a small bowl; set aside.

Separate biscuits and place on an ungreased baking sheet. Press or roll each biscuit into a 5-inch circle. Spoon about ½ cup ham mixture onto half of each biscuit. Brush edges of biscuits with water; fold dough over filling, pressing edges with a fork to seal.

Make a 1-inch crescent-shaped slit on top of each turnover. Brush with milk, and bake at 375 degrees for 15 minutes or until golden brown.

Kay Outten

▲ To lower fat content, use lowfat ham and lowfat cheese.

Three Cheese Noodle Casserole

"Elegant cheese dish."

Serves 8 to 10

1 pound medium egg noodles (about 8
   cups)
4 to 6 quarts boiling water
½ cup butter or margarine
2 cloves garlic, crushed
¼ cup flour
½ teaspoon dry mustard
¼ teaspoon black pepper
½ teaspoon Worcestershire sauce
1 quart (4 cups) milk
2 cups (8 ounces) grated natural Swiss
   cheese
1 cup (4 ounces) grated sharp Cheddar
   cheese
½ cup grated Romano or Parmesan cheese
½ cup fine dry bread crumbs
2 tablespoons butter or margarine, melted

Cook noodles in water, adding salt. When
tender drain, rinse off with cold water and set
aside.

In Dutch oven melt ½ cup of butter. Add garlic
and sauté. Stir in flour, salt, pepper and
Worcestershire sauce. Gradually add milk,
stirring constantly. Allow to thicken, continuing to stir. Add all cheeses, stir over low heat
until cheeses are melted.

Add noodles to cheese sauce, tossing well. Put
all into buttered baking dish. Top with bread
crumbs and melted butter mixture. Bake at 350
degrees for 30 to 40 minutes.

Carolyn Lee

▲ To decrease fat content, use lowfat margarine, lowfat/skim milk and lowfat cheese.

Baked Cheese Grits Casserole

"Perfect accompaniment with ham."

Serves 8

1 cup quick grits
1 teaspoon salt
4 eggs, beaten
1 stick butter
3½ cups water
1 cup milk
½ pound New York State cheese, grated

Bring water to a boil; add salt, slowly stir in
grits, cooking 5 to 10 minutes till thick.
Remove from heat. Stir in butter, cheese, milk,
eggs. Pour into a large casserole dish. Bake for
1 hour at 300 degrees or till firm in center.

Lucy Heartwell

▲ To lower fat, use an egg substitute, lowfat
margarine, lowfat/skim milk and lowfat
cheese.

Garlic Cheese Grits

"The garlic flavor adds a lot to these grits."

Serves 8

2 cups cooked grits
1 6-ounce roll garlic cheese
1 stick butter
3 eggs, lightly beaten
1 cup milk
Salt to taste
½ cup grated cheese

Melt butter and garlic cheese. Add to other
ingredients. Top with grated cheese. Bake at
350 degrees for 1 hour. Let sit for 15 minutes
before serving.

Rosalie Lafoon

▲ To lower fat, use lowfat margarine,
lowfat/skim milk, lowfat cheese and an egg
substitute.

Garden Macaroni Salad

"Fresh and flavorful."

Serves 8

1 8-ounce package elbow macaroni
1 cup cucumber, diced
1 cup celery, sliced
¼ cup green pepper, chopped
¼ cup radishes, sliced
2 teaspoons green onion, chopped
2 medium tomatoes, diced
¾ cup mayonnaise
1 teaspoon salt
¼ teaspoon dried whole basil

Cook macaroni according to package directions, omitting salt; drain well. Combine macaroni and next 6 ingredients, tossing well. Stir together mayonnaise, salt, and basil; toss with macaroni mixture. Cover and chill at least 3 hours.

Bettie N. Vaughan

▲ You can also use lowfat mayonnaise to further lower fat content.

Sea Shell Supper Salad

"A meal in itself."

Serves 4

5 ounces sea shell macaroni, cooked and drained
1½ cups diced cooked meat or poultry
3 tablespoons pickle relish
½ cup diced celery
½ teaspoon salt
½ cup mayonnaise
½ small onion, minced
¼ cup green pepper strips
¼ teaspoon pepper
¼ cup sour cream

Combine cooked macaroni with remaining ingredients and toss lightly. Chill an hour or more. Spoon onto salad green.

Milly Johnson

▲ To lower fat, use lowfat mayo and lowfat yogurt or mock sour cream.

Tomato Cream With Penne Pasta

"Serve in warm shallow soup bowls."

Serves 6

¼ cup extra-virgin olive oil
4 plump fresh garlic cloves, minced
¼ teaspoon red pepper flakes
Salt
1 28-ounce can crushed tomatoes
1 pound penne pasta (or something similar)
2 tablespoons vodka
1 cup heavy cream
¼ cup flat leaf parsley, snipped with scissors

In a very large skillet, combine oil, garlic, pepper and a dash of salt. Stirring, cook until garlic is golden. Add crushed tomatoes and simmer until sauce begins to thicken (10 or 15 minutes). Taste for seasoning, add as desired.

Cook pasta according to directions on package. Cook until tender but firm. Drain in colander. Add to skillet with tomatoes. Toss together. Add vodka, toss again. Add cream, toss again. Cover and cook for 3 minutes. Add parsley and toss again.

▲ To lower fat content, use skim evaporated milk instead of heavy cream.

Tomato Pasta Toss

"Light, delicious and all you need for a meal along with hot bread."

Serves 4 to 6

3 to 4 tablespoons olive oil
3 to 6 cloves garlic, sliced
4 to 6 tomatoes, cut up
1 cup cubed Mozzarella cheese
Fresh basil (may substitute green onion or other fresh green)
1 pound penne (or any short tubed pasta), cooked

Sauté garlic in oil. Place in bowl and let cool. Add cut up tomatoes, cheese and basil (or green of your choice). Add pasta last!

Kelly Stokes

▲ Lowfat cheese may be substituted to lower fat content.

Pasta With Basil And Sweet Pepper

"Tasty and good for you, lowfat."

Serves 4 to 6

3 tablespoons olive oil
1 medium red or yellow pepper, finely chopped
1 large garlic clove, minced or pressed
⅓ cup water
1 chicken bouillon cube
2 tablespoons chopped fresh basil or 1 teaspoon basil
1 teaspoon red wine vinegar
7 ounces pasta, cooked and drained

In skillet, heat oil over medium heat. Add garlic and pepper; sauté 3 minutes. Add water, bouillon cube and basil and bring to boil. Reduce heat; simmer 4 minutes. Remove from heat, stir in vinegar. Toss with pasta.

Linda Anderson

Chili With Macaroni

"Recipe can be doubled for a big crowd."

Serves 8

1 pound ground beef
1 onion, cut up small
2 cans tomatoes (3½ cups)
½ teaspoon chili powder
2 teaspoons salt
½ teaspoon pepper
1 large can pork and beans (3½ cups)
1 can kidney beans
2 cups cooked elbow macaroni

Brown ground beef and onion in small amount of oil. Add tomatoes, chili powder, salt and pepper. Simmer. Add cooked macaroni to the meat mixture, pork and beans and kidney beans. Bring to a boil and serve.

Justine Jones

▲ Use ground round to lower fat.

Beef And Macaroni Cassoulet

"Marvelous stew, fruit salad accompanies it nicely."

Serves 6 to 8

1 pound stew beef, cut into cubes
1 tablespoon oil
1 envelope onion gravy mix
1 1-pound can tomatoes
1 package Italian style green beans, frozen
1 cup shell macaroni, cooked

Brown cubed stew beef in oil. Stir in onion gravy mix and tomatoes. Cover and simmer for 1 hour, until beef is tender. Add green beans and cooked macaroni. Cook 10 to 15 more minutes.

Mildred Johnston

Messetti

"All you need is a tossed salad to have a great supper."

Serves 6

1 6-ounce package egg noodles, cooked
2 pounds hamburger
1 large onion, chopped
1 large green pepper, chopped
1 package Mozzarella cheese
1 can cream of mushroom soup
1 can tomato soup
½ cup water
¼ teaspoon chili powder

Brown together the hamburger, onion and pepper; drain off grease. Mix together the soups, water and chili powder and heat thoroughly. In baking dish alternate layers of cooked egg noodles, meat mixture, soup mixture and cheese. Bake at 350 degrees for approximately 30 minutes.

Jackie Browder

▲ To lower fat content, use ground round, lowfat cheese, and lowfat soup.

Pasta Fagioli

"Very filling, very good, and very lowfat."

Serves 6 to 8

1 cup (½ pound) dried white beans
5 cups water
1 teaspoon salt
¼ cup olive oil
1 medium onion, finely chopped
2 cloves garlic, finely chopped
2 stalks of celery, finely chopped
1 1-pound can tomatoes
½ teaspoon leaf rosemary, crumbled
½ teaspoon freshly ground black pepper

1½ cups small elbow or seashell macaroni
¼ cup chopped fresh parsley
Parmesan cheese

Soak beans in water overnight at room temperature.

Place beans and water in kettle and bring to a boil. Simmer 1 hour and add salt.

Meanwhile, sauté the onions, garlic and celery in the oil until tender.

Add sautéed vegetables to bean mixture along with tomatoes, rosemary and pepper. Bring to a boil, add pasta and cook 8 minutes or until al dente. Add parsley. Serve with Parmesan cheese.

Melissa Anderson

Shrimp With Fettucini

"Simple and really pleasing."

Serves 2 to 3

2 tablespoons each olive oil and butter
1 clove garlic, chopped
½ pound raw shrimp, cleaned
¼ cup lemon juice
Salt and pepper to taste
Parmesan cheese
Fettucini
2 teaspoons each of several fresh chopped
   herbs such as basil, parsley, chives, dill,
   watercress, green onion (dried herbs
   will do if fresh unavailable)

Sauté shrimp in oil and butter with garlic until pink. Add herbs and lemon juice to pan. Toss gently with pasta cooked according to directions. Served with grated Parmesan.

John Walker

▲ Using ½ tablespoon each olive oil and butter will lower fat content.

All Day Spaghetti Sauce

"Long and slow cooking is the secret."

Serves 4 to 6

2 pounds hamburger
2 onions
2 peppers
6 stalks celery
2 6-ounce cans tomato paste
1 large can tomatoes
1 teaspoon basil leaves
½ teaspoon parsley flakes
Dash garlic salt

Brown hamburger and onion in skillet, then drain off excess fat. Combine remaining ingredients and cook slowly all day.

Wendy S. Smith

Italian Spaghetti Sauce

"Very thick, meaty sauce."

Serves 4 to 6

1½ pounds hamburger
1 medium onion, chopped
2 stalks celery, chopped
1 green pepper, chopped
1 can tomato soup
1 6-ounce can tomato paste
½ soup can water
½ tablespoon Worcestershire sauce
2 dashes hot pepper sauce
2 bay leaves
1 teaspoon oregano
1 teaspoon thyme
½ teaspoon garlic salt
½ teaspoon chili powder

Crumble and brown hamburger, add chopped onion, celery and green pepper. Sauté with hamburger until onion is tender. Add soup, tomato paste, water and remaining ingredients.

Simmer covered on low heat for at least 1 hour. This makes a very thick sauce. As it cooks you may need to add small amounts of water. Remove bay leaves before serving.

Joyce Moorman

▲ Use ground round instead of hamburger to lower fat.

Shrimp And Feta With Pasta

"An exceptional way to serve shrimp."

Serves 4 to 5

3 tablespoons olive oil
(add more if needed)
1 teaspoon garlic, minced
1½ teaspoons oregano
1 pound large fresh shrimp, peeled, with
tails remaining, uncooked
⅛ teaspoon hot red pepper flakes
(optional)
1 box rigatoni (or other similar pasta),
cooked
½ pound Feta cheese
1 large jar chunky garden style tomato
sauce

Heat oil, oregano and garlic, and sauté shrimp until it is pink (about 1 minute). Drain oil. Add tomato sauce to shrimp and let simmer on low heat for about ½ hour. Place cooked rigatoni in greased baking dish, pour shrimp in sauce over rigatoni and crumble Feta cheese on top. Bake, uncovered, in a 350 degree oven for about 15 minutes, or until bubbly hot.

Carolyn Clay Oliver

Canoe Trip Lasagna

"This is the traditional finalé for the annual Memorial Day canoe trip."

Serves 100

6 pounds Mozzarella cheese
6 quarts Ricotta cheese
Parmesan cheese
8 boxes of lasagna noodles
1 large can of tomato juice
4 gallon cans of tomatoes, crushed or
    whole
4 8-ounce cans tomato paste
2 gallons water
10 onions, chopped fine
8 to 12 cloves of garlic, chopped
6 pounds ground beef
1 4-ounce jar Italian seasoning
4 tablespoons hot pepper sauce
2 tablespoons black pepper
2 tablespoons salt

Simmer in at least 2 large pots, the tomatoes, tomato paste and water. Meanwhile in a large skillet, adding oil as necessary, brown the onions and garlic. Divide and add proportionately to pots.

Continue with skillet and brown the hamburger, add this to pots, proportionately. Add the Italian seasoning, hot pepper sauce and black pepper to the tomato sauce, again dividing proportionately. Let simmer on low heat for 1 hour.

Boil lasagna noodles 1 package at a time, and drain in a colander when they are just cooked to flexibility.

In pans that are at least 3 inches deep and 12 x 18-inches, put a thin layer of oil or oil spray on the inside.

Put a ladle full of sauce on the bottom and spread it around. Start with a layer of noodles, laid to cover the bottom, then sauce, then grated Mozzarella sifted over all, blobs of Ricotta and a dusting of Parmesan. Lay another layer of noodles, and put sauce and cheeses. Continue until pan is almost full. For the top layer, pour in enough tomato juice to fill the air spaces in layers below, then liberally cover with sauce and Mozzarella.

This makes 6 large pans of lasagna. At this point you can hold them in a refrigerator for 2 days, or freeze.

Bake in 350 degree oven for an hour. Can be frozen after baking, too.

Gay Neale

▲ To lower fat content, use lowfat cheese, skim milk cottage cheese instead of Ricotta, and ground round.

Turkey Tetrazzini

"This is especially good when made the night before and refrigerated before baking."

Serves 4

1 fryer chicken or 2 cups leftover turkey
    chunks
8 ounces thin spaghetti
1 can cream of mushroom soup
1 3- to 4-ounce can mushrooms and juice
4 to 6 ounces Cheddar cheese, cut in
    chunks

Boil fryer till tender in salted water, then remove fryer from water and cook spaghetti in same broth. Cut or break meat into bite sized pieces, then mix all ingredients in a greased 10 x 12-inch casserole dish or pan. Bake at 350 degrees for 30 minutes.

Mrs. R. A. Saville

▲ To lower fat content, use lowfat soup and lowfat cheese.

Lasagna

"Classic dish, can't be beat."

Serves 8

1 pound ground beef
½ pound ground lean pork
1 28-ounce can whole tomatoes
1 12-ounce can tomato paste
2 teaspoons garlic salt
1½ teaspoons oregano
1 teaspoon basil leaves
2 cups cottage cheese
½ cup grated Parmesan cheese
3 4-ounce packages Mozzarella cheese, shredded
12 ounces lasagna noodles, cooked and well drained
½ cup grated Parmesan cheese
1 package pepperoni (optional)

In Dutch oven or large skillet, cook and stir meats till brown. Drain off fat. Add tomatoes; break up with fork. Stir in tomato paste, garlic salt, oregano, basil, pepperoni. Heat to boiling, stirring occasionally. Reduce heat; simmer, uncovered, 20 minutes or until mixture is consistency of spaghetti sauce. Preheat oven to 350 degrees. Stir together cottage cheese and ½ cup Parmesan cheese. Set aside 1 cup of meat sauce and ½ cup Mozzarella cheese. In an ungreased pan (13 x 9 x 2-inches), alternate layers of ⅓ each noodles, remaining meat sauce, remaining Mozzarella cheese and the cottage cheese mixture. Finish with reserved meat sauce on top, ½ cup Parmesan cheese, then reserved Mozzarella cheese. Bake uncovered 45 minutes. Let stand 15 minutes before cutting into 3-inch squares.

Ann Burke

▲ To lower fat content, use ground round, skim milk cottage cheese, lowfat cheese, and omit the pepperoni.

Linguine With Clams

"Delicious, low in calories and fat."

Serves 4

18 littleneck clams
2 tablespoons olive oil
2 large cloves of garlic, sliced
2 cups chopped, seeded tomatoes
1½ tablespoons fresh basil or 1 teaspoon dried
1½ tablespoons minced Italian parsley
1 teaspoon dried oregano
Salt to taste
Hot pepper flakes or fresh ground pepper to taste

Wash clams; then place them in a pot with ½ cup water and steam over medium high heat until clams begin to open. Remove clams from shells. Discard any that do not open. Save liquid. Coarsely chop clams and set aside.

In a wide skillet, heat olive oil and brown the garlic in it; do not allow garlic to burn. Remove browned garlic from oil, and discard. To the skillet add tomatoes, basil, parsley, oregano, salt and pepper.

Add the clams and the reserved liquid and continue to cook over moderate heat for 3 minutes.

In the meantime, cook the linguine for 6 minutes. Drain thoroughly. Add the linguine to the sauce in the skillet; turn up the heat and continue cooking, tossing constantly until the sauce saturates the pasta and the pasta is done.

Carolyn Kirchman

"Tobacco was the chief cash crop of our family, as it has been for many families in the south. Our entire family, which included my parents, my sister, my brother and myself, were all involved in the never-ending work that tobacco requires. Suckering and pulling leaves were part of the hardest work. Neighborhood young people helped us with the harvest. The best part of the day was when we took a break for lunch. My mother, in addition to stringing leaves all day, would prepare a delicious meal for all of us. 'In To Lunch' portrays a deserted tobacco bench and offers a look at some of the elements that were a part of this aspect of farm life."

Eldridge Bagley

"IN TO LUNCH"
Appears through the courtesy of the painting's owners, Garnet O. and Lucy A. Gillispie-Queen.

Chicken Salad

"Try adding apples or grapes for a variation."

Serves 8 to 10

4 cups cooked chicken breast, cubed
1½ cups celery, diced
1 cup slivered almonds, toasted
1 cup cooked dressing (recipe follows)
1 cup mayonnaise (more or less to taste)
Salt and pepper to taste

Combine mayonnaise with the cooked dressing recipe which follows. Combine all ingredients, mixing well. You may prefer to use less dressing.

Emily Harrison

▲ To decrease fat content, use lowfat/no-fat mayo.

Cooked Dressing For Chicken Salad

"Keeps indefinitely."

Makes 2 cups

4 egg yolks
1 heaping teaspoon dry mustard
⅓ cup sugar
1 light cup milk
1 teaspoon salt
⅛ teaspoon red pepper
¾ cup diluted vinegar
3 tablespoons butter

Add dry ingredients to yolks, then add vinegar and milk. Cook in double boiler until thick. Take off stove and add butter. Keep top on until cool. Store in refrigerator and use on chicken salad.

Allene Barkley and Emily Harrison

Fried Chicken

"Extraordinary, Sunday fried chicken."

Serves 4 to 6

1 frying chicken, cut up
1 chicken bouillon cube
1 cup evaporated milk
1 teaspoon salt
¼ teaspoon pepper
1 cup flour

Place cut up and rinsed chicken in cold salted water for 10 to 15 minutes. Drain thoroughly. Dissolve chicken bouillon cube in 1 tablespoon boiling water. Add to evaporated milk. Place chicken in milk mixture and let stand for 10 to 15 minutes. Mix salt, pepper and flour together. Dip milk-soaked chicken into flour mixture, lightly. Fry slowly in hot oil until golden brown, about 10 minutes on each side. Remove from oil and crisp in hot oven for a few minutes.

Nora Peterson

Company Chicken

"Always well received."

Serves 8

1 jar dried beef
8 pieces chicken breast, skinned and
**   boned**
8 strips bacon
1 small carton sour cream
1 can cream of mushroom soup

Line casserole with dried beef. Wrap each piece of chicken breast in a strip of bacon and place in dish. Mix sour cream and soup, pour over chicken. Bake at 300 degrees for 3 hours.

Sarah Bishop

▲ To decrease fat content, use lowfat soup and replace sour cream with lowfat yogurt or mock sour cream.

Fried Chicken On A Roll

"A really special sandwich."

Serves 6

6 boneless chicken breasts
6 slices country ham, cooked
Salt
Pepper
Paprika
Flour
1 teaspoon prepared mustard
¼ cup cooking oil
¼ cup butter, softened
6 seeded rolls
¼ teaspoon dill weed
1 tablespoon dried parsley
1 teaspoon lemon juice

Wash and bone (if not boneless already) chicken breasts; salt and pepper. Coat with flour mixed with paprika. Fry in hot oil and butter until tender, about 10 to 15 minutes. Drain on paper towel. Meanwhile, combine ¼ cup butter with dill weed, parsley, lemon juice and mustard. Split rolls and spread generously with herb butter. Place a piece of ham and a piece of chicken on each roll. Makes 6 rolls.

Justine Jones

▲ To decrease fat content, use lowfat ham and grill the chicken breast rather than coating it in flour and frying. Use lowfat margarine in spread.

Chicken Pie

"You can substitute stew beef for chicken and have a different dish."

Serves 4

1 whole chicken
Cream of chicken or cream of mushroom
  soup
Broth
1 stick margarine
½ teaspoon black pepper
1 cup self-rising flour
1 cup buttermilk
½ teaspoon salt

Cook chicken till tender. Reserve broth. Take chicken from bone; cut into small pieces.

Put 2 cups of chicken broth and 1 can of undiluted cream of mushroom soup or cream of chicken soup in saucepan and bring to a boil.

Mix 1 stick melted margarine, ½ teaspoon pepper, 1 cup flour, 1 cup buttermilk and ½ teaspoon salt. Mix thoroughly to form soft dough.

Put chicken in a 9 x 12 x 2-inch pan. Pour broth mixture over chicken. Then spoon dough mixture on top. Bake at 425 degrees for 30 minutes.

Shelia J. Walker

▲ To lower fat, use lowfat margarine, lowfat soup, and skim buttermilk.

Crunchy Chicken

"Fried chicken in the oven."

Serves 8

2 frying chickens, cut up
2 cups round buttery cracker crumbs
¾ cup Parmesan cheese
¼ cup fresh parsley, chopped
  (or 1 tablespoon dried parsley flakes)
1 clove garlic, pressed
2 teaspoons salt
½ teaspoon pepper
1 cup melted butter

Blend cracker crumbs, Parmesan cheese, parsley, garlic, salt and pepper. Dip chicken in melted butter, then in cracker mixture. Arrange in shallow pan. Pour remaining butter over chicken. Bake, uncovered, for 1 hour at 350 degrees. Do not turn chicken.

Diane Radford

▲ To lower fat, use lowfat margarine.

Honey Chicken

"Tangy and tasty, easy."

Serves 4 to 6

3 tablespoons corn oil
½ cup honey
⅓ cup prepared mustard
1 teaspoon curry powder
1 chicken, cut up and skinned
¼ cup sliced almonds

Preheat oven to 375 degrees. Mix corn oil with honey, mustard and curry powder to make sauce. Place chicken parts in single layer in baking dish prepared with non-stick vegetable cooking spray. Pour sauce over chicken. Spread sliced almonds on top of chicken. Cover and bake for 1 hour.

Peggy Vaughan

Relish Crust Chicken Pie

"M-m-m good."

Serves 4

2 cups cooked chicken, diced
1 cup English peas, cooked, drained
½ cup celery, finely chopped
2 cups hot chicken gravy
1 teaspoon salt
1 tablespoon parsley, chopped (optional)

Combine all ingredients; heat. Pour all into buttered 1½-quart casserole. Top with Relish Crust Biscuits (recipe follows). Bake at 425 degrees for 20 to 25 minutes.
Note: 2 cups medium white sauce or diluted cream of chicken soup may be substituted for gravy.

Relish Crust Biscuits

Yields 6 servings

2 cups biscuit mix
⅛ teaspoon paprika
1 tablespoon parsley, chopped
2 tablespoons carrots, shredded
1 tablespoon green pepper, chopped
⅔ cup milk

Mix ingredients. Roll out; cut into biscuits.

Justine Jones

▲ Substituting thickened chicken broth for the gravy and using lowfat/skim milk, will decrease the fat content.

Baked Chicken Salad

"A luncheon delight."

Serves 6

2 cups chicken, cooked and chopped
4 hard-boiled eggs
2 cups celery, diced
½ cup toasted almonds, chopped
½ teaspoon salt
2 tablespoons onion, grated
2 tablespoons lemon juice
1 cup mayonnaise
1 cup potato chips, crushed
½ cup cheese, grated

Combine chicken, eggs, celery, almonds, salt, onion and lemon juice in bowl; fold in mayonnaise. Turn into a greased casserole; top with potato chips and cheese. Bake at 450 degrees for about 12 minutes or until salad is bubbly and cheese is melted.

Ann P. Lewis

▲ To decrease fat content, use lowfat/no-fat mayonnaise, lowfat cheese, and replace potato chips with saltines or bread crumbs.

Hot Chicken Salad

"So good with a congealed fruit salad and rolls."

Serves 6

2 cups croutons, toasted
2 cups cooked chicken, diced
1½ cups celery, chopped
1½ cups sharp cheese, grated
¼ cup slivered almonds, toasted
2 tablespoons onion, minced
¾ cup mayonnaise
½ teaspoon salt
1 tablespoon lemon juice

Combine half the croutons with all the remaining ingredients. Turn into baking dish and cover with remaining croutons. Bake at 350 degrees for 35 minutes. May be prepared ahead, but if so, do not put in croutons until baking time.

Mildred Rawlings

▲ To decrease fat content, use lowfat cheese and lowfat/no-fat mayonnaise.

Chicken And Chow Mein Noodle Casserole

"Crunchy texture."

Serves 6 to 8

1 cup celery, chopped
1 can cream of celery soup
1 can cream of mushroom soup
1 6-ounce can evaporated milk
2 cups chicken breast, cooked and
    chopped
½ cup green pepper, chopped
1 teaspoon salt
1 can sliced mushrooms, drained
¼ cup pimento, chopped
½ cup slivered almonds, toasted
3 cups chow mein noodles

Cook celery in salted water till tender; drain. Combine all ingredients, stir and place in casserole. Bake at 350 degrees for 50 to 60 minutes.

Clyde Peebles

▲ To lower fat, use lowfat soups and lowfat evaporated milk.

Chicken Casserole Deluxe

"Get ready for company ahead of time."

Serves 8 to 10

4 cups cooked chicken
1 can cream of chicken soup
¾ cup mayonnaise
3 hard-boiled eggs, sliced
2 ounce jar sliced pimentos, drained
1 small can whole water chestnuts
**   (sliced for casserole)**
2 teaspoons lemon juice
¼ cup green pepper, chopped
2 cups celery, chopped
1 cup sharp cheese, grated
1½ cups potato chips, crushed
Red pepper to taste
1 teaspoon salt

Blend all ingredients except the cheese, potato chips and eggs. Add eggs to mixture and put in a buttered 13 x 9 x 2-inch casserole. Sprinkle cheese on top, then the crushed potato chips. Bake 20 to 25 minutes in a 400 degree oven. Prepare the casserole the night before, refrigerate and bake the next day before serving.

Pat Temple

▲ To lower fat, use lowfat soup, lowfat/no-fat mayonnaise, lowfat cheese, and saltines or bread crumbs instead of potato chips.

Lenten Luncheon Chicken Casserole

"St. Andrews traditionally serves this casserole at the community Lenten Luncheon."

Serves 10 to 12

2 frying chickens
1 can cream of chicken soup
1 can cream of celery soup
1 13-ounce can evaporated milk
1 stick margarine
1 medium onion, chopped
1 small package herb-seasoned stuffing
**   mix**
1 cup broth from cooked chicken

Boil chicken and take off bones. Put chicken chunks in bottom of a 9 x 13-inch pan or casserole dish. Mix soups and evaporated milk and pour over chicken. Sauté onion in margarine, add cup broth and stir. Add stuffing and stir till moistened. Pat this mixture over chicken. Cover with foil. Bake at 350 degrees for 1 hour. This reheats well and may be frozen.

Donna Fowler

▲ To decrease fat, use lowfat soup and nonfat evaporated milk.

*In the summer, usually the Sunday closest to the Fourth of July, **St. Andrews Church** holds its annual homecoming picnic.*

Chicken And Broccoli Casserole

"The sauce really enhances the broccoli."

Serves 2 to 3

**2 chicken breasts, cooked, skinned
and cut into bite-size pieces**
**1 package frozen broccoli, cooked and
drained**
Grated cheese and bread crumbs

Layer the chicken and broccoli in buttered
dish. Make the sauce below and pour over all.
Top with grated cheese and bread crumbs and
bake at 350 degrees for 25 to 30 minutes.

Sauce
1 can cream of chicken soup
½ cup mayonnaise or salad dressing
½ teaspoon lemon juice
¼ teaspoon curry powder
½ tablespoon butter, melted

Ella Connell and Emily Harrison

▲ To decrease fat content, use lowfat cheese,
lowfat soup, lowfat margarine, and lowfat/no-
fat mayonnaise or salad dressing.

Three Soup Casserole With Rice

"Really good."

Serves 6 to 8

1 can cream of mushroom soup
1 can cream of chicken soup
1 can cream of celery soup
1 soup can water
1 2½-pound fryer, cut up
1 cup uncooked rice
¼ pound margarine
Salt and pepper

Combine soups with water in saucepan; add
butter and bring to a boil. Remove from heat
and add rice. Sprinkle chicken with salt and
pepper and place in 2-quart casserole. Pour
sauce with rice over the chicken. Cover and
bake at 300 degrees for 2 hours, or until rice is
tender.

Evelyn Carpenter

▲ Using lowfat soups and lowfat margarine
will reduce the fat content.

Chinese Walnut Chicken

*"The walnuts and chestnuts are a wonderful
combination."*

Serves 4

1 small can walnuts
2 tablespoons vegetable oil
**2 whole chicken breasts, deboned and
diced**
4 teaspoons cornstarch
4 tablespoons soy sauce
1 large onion, chopped
4 stalks celery, chopped
1 can water chestnuts, sliced
1 can mushrooms, sliced
1 cup chicken broth

Brown walnuts in oil. Drain and salt lightly.
Combine 2 teaspoons of cornstarch with soy
sauce. Coat the diced chicken in the soy sauce
mixture. Brown chicken in skillet just used to
brown walnuts. Add more oil if necessary.
Cook for 5 minutes. Add cut up vegetables,
water chestnuts and mushrooms. Mix 2
teaspoons cornstarch with ¼ cup water, add
this and browned walnuts to skillet. Serve with
rice.

Mary Bellone

Chicken And Rice Casserole

"This is hard to beat."

Serves 4

½ cup uncooked rice, cooked
2 cups cooked chicken breast, chopped
2 tablespoons onion, finely chopped
1 4-ounce jar sliced pimento
1 medium jar sliced mushrooms
½ cup sour cream
¼ cup mayonnaise
1 can cream of celery soup

Combine all ingredients and bake at 350 degrees for 30 minutes. Makes 12 x 8-inch casserole. Freezes well.

Betty Woofter

▲ To reduce fat content, replace sour cream with lowfat yogurt or mock sour cream, and use lowfat/no-fat mayonnaise and lowfat soup.

Polynesian Chicken

"Quick to put together."

Serves 6

1 green pepper, cut in thin strips
1 cup celery, chopped
1 10½-ounce can cream of chicken soup
2 tablespoons soy sauce
1 can mushrooms, drained
1 can pineapple chunks, drained
2 cups cooked chicken
1 can water chestnuts, drained
¼ cup slivered almonds, toasted

In 2 tablespoons oil, cook celery and pepper till crisp tender. Stir in other ingredients except almonds. Cook, stirring constantly, till hot. Serve over hot cooked rice. Garnish with toasted almonds.

Karen Burchinal

▲ To decrease fat content, use lowfat soup.

Baked Chicken And Rice

"The rice is fluffy and flavorful."

Serves 6

1 fryer, cut up
1 teaspoon salt
1 teaspoon paprika
¼ teaspoon pepper
1 cup uncooked rice
½ cup onion, chopped
2 tablespoons butter
1 teaspoon celery salt
3 cups chicken broth or boiling water

Sprinkle chicken with paprika and salt and pepper. Brown rice and onions in butter. Spread rice mixture in a 13 x 9 x 2-inch buttered baking dish. Add broth and celery salt. Place chicken on top of rice mixture. Cover dish tightly with foil. Bake at 350 degrees for 1 hour. Remove cover and bake 15 minutes longer or until tender.

Marion Barkley

Onion-Smothered Chicken

"A side dish of mashed potatoes goes nicely with the gravy."

Serves 4

2 tablespoons shortening
1 envelope onion soup mix
1 2½- to 3-pound broiler-fryer, cut up
2 cups water
2 tablespoons flour

In large skillet, heat shortening; brown chicken well. Add onion Soup mix and 2 cups of water. Simmer, covered, 45 minutes or until tender. Remove chicken to serving platter. Blend flour with ¼ cup water. Stir into broth in skillet and cook, while stirring, until thickened; spoon over chicken.

Mary Ann Keith

Slim Chicken Parmigiana

"You can use veal instead of chicken."

Serves 6

1½ pounds deboned chicken breast
¼ cup seasoned bread crumbs
1 tablespoon oil
2 8-ounce cans tomato sauce
2 teaspoons oregano, crumbled
1 teaspoon garlic salt
½ teaspoon salt
⅛ teaspoon pepper
3 ounces part-skim Mozzarella cheese

Dip chicken in bread crumbs. Tap off excess. Heat oil in a nonstick frying pan. Brown chicken, turning once. Place chicken in a shallow baking dish; spoon the tomato sauce over chicken; sprinkle with oregano, garlic salt, salt and pepper. Top with Mozzarella cheese. Bake in a moderate oven (350 degrees) for 20 minutes or until cheese is melted and bubbly.

Anne Butler

Chicken Piccata

"Very versatile. Serve with rice or pasta."

Serves 4

1 pound boneless chicken thigh/breast
**   fillets**
½ cup all-purpose flour
Salt and pepper to taste
1 egg beaten with 1 tablespoon water
¼ cup butter or margarine
1 tablespoon lemon peel, grated
2 tablespoons lemon juice
3 cloves garlic, minced
½ cup freshly chopped parsley
⅔ cup dry white wine
⅔ cup chicken broth
1 lemon, thinly sliced for garnish

Place each fillet between 2 sheets plastic wrap and pound with meat mallet or rolling pin. Combine flour, salt and pepper in shallow dish. Dip each piece in beaten egg, drain, then dredge in flour (for less crusty result, omit egg and just lightly flour).

Melt butter in large skillet. Add chicken pieces and sauté 2 minutes on each side until golden brown. Remove chicken from pan and set aside. Add lemon peel, lemon juice, garlic (may use garlic salt), parsley (may use dried if fresh not available), wine and broth to skillet. Bring to a boil, scraping up browned particles in bottom of pan. Return chicken to skillet, lower heat and simmer 15 minutes, turning occasionally.

Arrange chicken on warm serving platter. Bring sauce in skillet to a boil. Boil rapidly until reduced by half. Spoon sauce over chicken and garnish with lemon slices.

Kay Outten

*The steep pitch of the gables on the **Peebles House** make it one of the easiest to find in Harmony Grove.*

Chicken Cacciatore

"You can serve over pasta of your choice or use 'flaky rice' directions below."

Serves 4

¾ cup fresh mushrooms, sliced
½ of 8-ounce can (about ½ cup) tomatoes, cut up
½ cup green pepper, chopped
5 tablespoons dry red wine
½ teaspoon dried oregano
½ teaspoon salt and dash pepper
¼ cup onion, chopped
1 clove garlic, minced
2 whole chicken breasts (8 ounces each), skinned and halved
Paprika
2 tablespoons dry red wine
2 teaspoons cornstarch
Parsley

In medium skillet, combine first 8 ingredients and place chicken breasts on top. Sprinkle lightly with additional salt. Bring to boiling, then reduce heat, cover and simmer 25 minutes or till chicken is done. Remove chicken to warm casserole in oven; sprinkle with paprika. Combine cornstarch and 2 tablespoons wine and stir into skillet mixture. Cook and stir till thickened and bubbly. Cook a minute more, then spoon sauce over chicken. Garnish with parsley or may be held in warm oven, then garnished and served.

Flaky Rice

2 cups boiling water
3 bouillon cubes
1 cup converted rice

Add bouillon cubes and rice to boiling water. Simmer 25 minutes.

Doris Baker

Dirty Rice

"A meal in a skillet."

Serves 6 to 8

1 cup each green pepper, celery and onion, chopped
1 stick margarine
6 pieces boiled chicken, chopped (save broth)
1 small box regular rice

Cook rice according to directions on box using chicken broth in place of water. Meanwhile, sauté onions, celery, green pepper in butter until tender. Mix in chopped chicken and add all to rice when it's done. Add salt and pepper to taste. The more the better!

Peggy Vaughan

▲ To reduce fat content, use lowfat margarine.

Chicken Cordon Bleu

"Lots of extra calories, but worth it on occasion."

Serves 6

6 deboned chicken breasts
3 slices Smithfield ham (thin)
1 bag bread crumbs
1 stick melted butter
3 slices Swiss cheese
½ pint sour cream

Flatten chicken breasts. Put about ½ slice ham and ½ slice cheese in center. Wrap and secure with toothpicks. Dip in sour cream. Roll in bread crumbs. Place in greased baking dish. Pour melted butter over chicken. Bake 1 hour 15 minutes in 350 degree oven.

Kay Outten

▲ To decrease fat content, use lowfat margarine, lowfat cheese, and replace sour cream with lowfat yogurt or mock sour cream.

Chicken Chow Mein

"If you substitute non-stick vegetable spray for bacon drippings you have a lowfat dish."

Serves 4

½ cup onion, chopped
1 tablespoon bacon drippings
1 cup turkey or chicken, diced
¼ cup green pepper, diced
1 cup celery, diced
1 tablespoon cornstarch
¼ cup water
¾ cup hot water or stock
2 teaspoons brown sugar
1 can bean sprouts
Salt to taste
1 tablespoon soy sauce

Sauté onions in bacon drippings. Add meat, green pepper and celery to sautéed onions and simmer 10 minutes. Mix cornstarch in ¼ cup water, then add cornstarch mixture and remaining ingredients to meat mixture. Let come to boil, then serve over crisp noodles or rice.

Mary Willy Rawlings

Country Captain

"A meal for a crowd."

Serves 8 to 12

12 pieces chicken
½ stick butter
1 cup onion, chopped
½ cup green pepper, chopped
1 clove garlic, chopped fine
1 tablespoon curry powder
1 teaspoon thyme
2 cups canned tomatoes
½ cup raisins
½ cup toasted slivered almonds
Dash hot pepper sauce (optional)

Flour, salt and pepper the chicken pieces. Brown lightly in butter. Remove chicken. Brown onion, green pepper and garlic in same butter, also adding curry and thyme. Return chicken to pot. Add tomatoes. Cover and simmer until tender, about 40 minutes. Add raisins and almonds the last few minutes. Add salt and pepper to taste.

Dale Tynes

▲ To reduce fat content, use lowfat margarine.

Barbecued Chicken

"Use this sauce for outdoor grilling also."

Serves 6

1 chicken, cut up
1 medium onion, chopped
2 tablespoons oil
2 tablespoons vinegar
2 tablespoons brown sugar
¼ cup lemon juice
½ cup catsup
3 tablespoons Worcestershire sauce
½ tablespoon mustard
½ cup celery, chopped
1 cup water
Salt and pepper to taste

Sauté onion in oil. Add other ingredients except chicken and simmer 30 minutes. Brown chicken. Put in casserole dish. Pour sauce over the chicken and cook 1 hour in 325 degree oven.

Emily Harrison

Wild Duck In Bag

"A particularly good way to cook wild duck because it keeps it moist without having to baste."

Serves 2

1 tablespoon flour
½ cup orange juice
¼ cup dry white wine
1 wild duck
Butter or margarine, melted
Salt
½ apple

Preheat oven to 350 degrees. Shake 1 tablespoon flour in small size (10 x 16-inch) oven cooking bag and place in 2-inch deep roasting pan. Pour orange juice and wine into bag and stir until flour is well mixed with liquids. Brush duck with melted butter and sprinkle duck with salt all over, including within body cavity. Place apple within cavity and put duck in bag. Close bag with twist tie and make 6, ½-inch slits in top. Cook for 1½ hours.

Kay Outten

▲ To reduce fat content, use vegetable spray instead of melted butter to brush duck.

Oven Squirrel

"You can substitute just about any game, works well with rabbit and venison also."

Serves 6

3 squirrels, cut up and floured
Carrots
Salt
Thyme or bay leaf (optional)
½ cup peach wine
Potatoes
Onions
Pepper
2 cups water

Brown the squirrels in butter. Place in baking dish and add cubed potatoes, carrots and onions, salt and pepper and thyme. Add 2 cups of water to the pan squirrels were browned in. Add this liquid plus ½ cup peach wine to baking dish; cover. Bake at 325 degrees till tender, about 1½ hours.

Jem Jenkins

▲ To decrease fat content, drain and pat off excess butter before placing in baking dish.

Company Venison Steaks

"This is so elegant, great way to serve wild game to guests."

Serves 4

1 leg of venison, cut into 1-inch thick
   steaks
4 peppercorns
1 onion and 1 carrot, sliced
4 sprigs fresh parsley
1 bay leaf
½ cup white wine
5 tablespoons cooking oil
   (vegetable or olive)

Place steaks in large bowl, sprinkle with peppercorns, sliced onion and carrot. Add parsley, bay leaf, wine and oil. Marinate for 24 hours. Turn steaks 3 or 4 times.

To cook: Remove steaks from marinade and wipe dry with paper towels. Place 3 table-spoons oil in heavy frying pan and cook steaks in hot pan about 4 minutes on each side. Remove steaks and keep warm.

Sauce
2 tablespoons butter
1 small onion, finely cut
   (or 2 shallots, if available)
1 tablespoon flour
¼ cup white wine
Salt and pepper
1 cup sour cream

Remove excess fat from frying pan. In 2 tablespoons butter sauté onion lightly, then add 1 tablespoon flour, stirring well. Next add wine and salt and pepper to taste. Stir in sour cream, blending well (do not boil), pour sauce over steaks.

June Thomas

▲ To decrease fat, broil without oil in the last step and use lowfat yogurt or mock sour cream instead of sour cream in the sauce.

Venison Roast

"Versatile and good, venison is moist and tender."

Serves 6 to 8

Venison roast
2 cups buttermilk or sour cream
1 teaspoon celery salt
1 teaspoon garlic salt
2 teaspoons Worcestershire sauce
2 teaspoons soy sauce
Ground pepper
3 or 4 carrots, sliced
3 or 4 celery stalks, sliced
1 onion, sliced, if desired
1 cup red wine
Bacon

Combine the celery salt, garlic salt, Worcestershire sauce, soy sauce and pepper with the sour cream or buttermilk. Marinate the venison in this mixture for 24 hours. Remove from liquid and wipe some of the marinade off with a paper towel. Rub meat with celery salt, garlic salt and pepper. Wrap roast with bacon, completely covering. Shake 1 tablespoon flour in large browning bag. Add 1 cup red wine to floured brown-in-bag. Place bacon wrapped roast in bag and surround with sliced vegetables. Bake at 300 degrees for 15 minutes per pound. Do not overcook. This procedure can be varied by adding barbecue sauce or spices to the sour cream or buttermilk. Also add barbecue sauce to the wine. The roast should be turned every 30 minutes in the bag when using this method.

Joy Mullin

▲ To decrease fat, use skim buttermilk or mock sour cream.

Marinated Venison Tenderloin

"It always gets rave reviews."

Serves 6 to 8

7 pounds venison tenderloin
2 12-ounce beers
2 packages Adolph's meat tenderizer
 dissolved in 1 cup water
1 cup vegetable oil
1 cup vinegar
½ cup Worcestershire sauce
¼ cup A-1 sauce
2 teaspoons Texas Pete
2 teaspoons dry onion
2 teaspoons black pepper
1 teaspoon prepared mustard
1 teaspoon salt
1 stick butter

Heat the above ingredients to boiling point, pour onto a whole 7-pound venison tenderloin. Pour on 2 12-ounce beers. Marinate for 6 hours at room temperature, then marinate in the refrigerator overnight.

Next day, cook the whole roast over low temperature charcoal, using a rotisserie or covered on a grill and turning frequently. Baste every 15 minutes for about 2 hours. Can be cooked tightly wrapped in foil in a 350 degree oven for about 1 hour, done when pricks easily with fork. Either method results in a medium rare roast. You may want to save tenderest cuts of venison for outdoor cooking and cook tougher, smaller cuts in oven. Slice thinly and serve as main dish or may be served with assorted breads and Sweet and Sour Sauce (recipe follows) as an appetizer.

Sweet And Sour Sauce
½ cup vinegar
½ teaspoon pepper
½ teaspoon salt
2 teaspoons soy sauce
½ cup pineapple juice
½ cup brown sugar
4 tablespoons vegetable oil
2 tablespoons cornstarch
¼ cup beer

Combine vinegar, pepper, salt, soy sauce, pineapple juice, brown sugar, oil and heat. Add cornstarch and beer to the heated mixture.

Keith Washburn

"The title of this painting is really a play on words. There is more here than merely a tranquil farmhouse porch scene. Time spent in solitary reflection or relaxing with family and friends is being crowded out by busy lifestyles. Through windows of time, other influences have entered the picture. Porch talk seems to be in danger of becoming a lost art. How do we spend our 'prime time'?"

Eldridge Bagley

"PRIME TIME"
Appears through the courtesy of the painting's owners, Carolyn Gershfeld and Judy Schub.

Barbecued Beef

"This sauce works for chicken or pork also."

Serves 6

1½ pounds round steak

Sauce
1 clove garlic
¾ cup vinegar
1 tablespoon sugar
1 teaspoon paprika
2 tablespoons Worcestershire sauce
½ cup catsup
1 teaspoon salt
1 teaspoon mustard
⅛ teaspoon pepper

Cut steak into 1-inch pieces. Brown quickly in hot oil and put in casserole. Prepare sauce.

Mix all ingredients for the sauce and simmer 2 or 3 minutes. Pour over beef cubes and cover. Bake 1 hour at 350 degrees. Uncover and bake for 30 minutes longer.

Lucy Clary

Burgundy Beef

"Good served with toast points, mashed potatoes or rice."

Serves 2 to 3

1 pound steak or rump roast, cut in thin strips
1 4-ounce can mushroom pieces, drained
1 package brown gravy mix
3 tablespoons margarine or butter
¼ cup Burgundy

Brown strips of meat lightly in margarine. Remove meat from the pan and prepare gravy as directed on the package, in a saucepan with drippings from meat. Add mushrooms and cook slowly till gravy is thickened. Add meat to warm; add Burgundy and heat over slow heat several minutes. Do not boil.

Edie Bell

▲ To lower fat content, substitute lowfat mushroom soup mix for the mushroom pieces, brown gravy and margarine.

Beef Stroganoff

"Great way to use leftover roast beef. Very rich!"

Serves 3 to 4

1 to 1½ pounds sirloin or round steak, cut in 2½-inch strips or 2 to 2½ cups leftover roast beef cut into 2½-inch strips
½ cup flour
1 medium onion, diced
1 cup fresh mushrooms, sliced
2 to 3 tablespoons oil
1 cup water
1 bouillon cube
½ cup sour cream
½ teaspoon cooking sherry
½ teaspoon Worcestershire sauce
Salt and fresh ground pepper to taste

Sauté onion and mushrooms in oil and remove from skillet. Flour meat strips whether using leftover or fresh beef. Brown floured strips in skillet adding more oil if necessary. Add water and bouillon cube; if water does not cover meat, add more. Bring to a boil, return mushrooms and onions; reduce heat and cover, cook 1 to 1½ hours, until tender. Add water if necessary. Season to taste with sherry, Worcestershire, salt and ground pepper. Add sour cream, keeping warm but do not return to boil. Serve with rice, egg noodles or toast points.

Carolyn Lee

▲ To lower fat content, reduce amount of oil to 1 to 2 tablespoons and replace sour cream with lowfat yogurt or mock sour cream.

Easy Beef Stroganoff

"Rich, easy and delicious."

Serves 8

3 pounds stew beef (cut into bite-size pieces)
1 package dried onion soup mix
2 cans cream of mushroom soup
¾ cup sherry

Cook in a 250 degree oven, uncovered for about 3 hours. Serve over noodles or rice.

Van Doyle

▲ Using lowfat soup will reduce the fat content.

Easy Pepper Steak

"A tomato and green pepper dish."

Serves 3 to 4

Round steak
1 can tomatoes
1 onion
2 green peppers
1 tablespoon Worcestershire sauce

Slice steak into strips. Flour strips and brown well in oil. Drain and dry. Add juice from tomatoes and enough water to cover steak. Chop onion and sprinkle in pan of steak. Simmer 30 minutes. Add Worcestershire sauce and simmer 45 minutes. Cut green pepper into strips or rings and add to steak. Simmer 5 minutes. Add tomatoes and again simmer 5 to 10 minutes. May be served over cooked rice.

Barbara Wiley

Pepper Steak

"Remember, for crisper vegetables, wait until the last 5 or 10 minutes of the cooking time to return to skillet."

Serves 3 to 4

1 pound boneless round steak
2 tablespoons butter or margarine
1 medium green pepper, cut into strips
1 large onion
½ cup celery, chopped
¼ cup soy sauce
1 4-ounce can sliced mushrooms, drained
Pepper to taste
3 tablespoons water
1 tablespoon water and 1 tablespoon cornstarch
Cooked rice

Trim excess fat from steak, partially freeze steak and slice across the grain into 2 x ½-inch strips.

Melt butter in large skillet. Sauté green pepper, onion and celery in butter. Remove vegetables, reserving drippings in skillet.

Brown steak in reserved drippings. Return vegetables to skillet. Add mushrooms, soy sauce, pepper and 3 tablespoons water; cover and simmer 30 minutes or until meat is tender. Remove meat and vegetables, reserving drippings in skillet.

Combine cornstarch and 1 tablespoon water, stirring until cornstarch is dissolved. Add cornstarch mixture to liquid in skillet, cook, stirring constantly until smooth and thickened. Return meat and vegetables to skillet. Serve over rice.

Cherrill Robertson

▲ To reduce fat content use lowfat margarine.

Mary Lough's Meat Loaf

"Our family's favorite meat loaf."

Serves 6

2½ pounds hamburger
2½ cups bread crumbs
1 cup cheese, grated or cubed
Salt and pepper to taste
½ green pepper, chopped
1 small onion, diced
2 eggs
1 cup catsup

Combine all ingredients and form 2 loaves.
Top with extra catsup, if desired. Bake at 350
degrees for 1 hour and 15 minutes.

Joyce Moorman

▲ To decrease fat content, use lean hamburger or ground round, lowfat cheese and an
egg substitute.

Meat Loaf with Tomato Sauce

"Consider baking in small individual loaves."

Serves 6

1½ pounds ground beef
2 eggs, unbeaten
¼ cup chopped onion
½ cup chopped green pepper
¼ teaspoon pepper
¾ cup 1 minute quick oats (uncooked)
½ cup chopped celery
2 teaspoons salt
1 can tomato sauce
Beef broth
2 bacon strips

Combine all ingredients thoroughly. Add
enough beef broth to make good and soft.
Shape into loaf and put in baking pan. Top
with strips of bacon and bake in moderate
oven 350 degrees for about 1 hour until done.

Let stand before slicing or bake in individual
loaves and serve with tomato sauce.

Tomato Sauce
1 can tomato soup
¼ cup chopped onion
1 tablespoon vinegar
¼ cup sweet pickle relish
1 tablespoon brown sugar
1 tablespoon Worcestershire sauce

Simmer until onions are cooked and flavors
blended (about 10 minutes). Makes 1½ cups
sauce. Serve over meat loaf.

Lorraine Freeman

▲ To lower fat, use lean ground beef or
ground round and an egg substitute.

Corned Beef in Foil

"Great for sandwiches."

Serves 8 to 10

3 to 4 pounds corned beef
¼ cup water
2 tablespoons pickling spice
1 small orange, sliced
1 onion, sliced
1 stalk celery with leaves
1 carrot, sliced

Soak beef in cold water to cover for ½ hour.
Place large sheet of heavy duty aluminum foil
in a shallow baking pan. Pat meat dry. Place in
center of foil. Pour ¼ cup water over. Sprinkle
with spices. Arrange orange and vegetables
over and around meat. Seal meat with tight
double fold. Seal ends the same way, turned
up so juices won't run out. Bake 4 hours at
300 degrees. If using a larger roast, cook
longer (5 pounds, 5 hours, etc.). Drain, cool,
slice paper thin - good for sandwiches.

Isabelle Orgain

Double Cheese Meat Roll

"Cheese truly makes this a very special ground beef dish."

Serves 6 to 8

1½ pounds lean ground beef
1 egg
¾ cup cracker or bread crumbs
½ cup onion, chopped
2 8-ounce cans tomato sauce with cheese
1 teaspoon salt
½ teaspoon oregano
⅛ teaspoon pepper
2 cups Mozzarella or Cheddar cheese, shredded

Combine beef, egg, crumbs, onion and half cup of sauce. Mix well. Roll out about 10 x 12-inches on waxed paper. Sprinkle with shredded cheese. Roll as for jellyroll. Press ends of roll to seal. Bake at 350 degrees for 1 hour, on a large baking pan like a broiler pan. Drain off grease. Pour remaining sauce over roll and bake 15 minutes more.

Alice Vaughan

▲ Using lowfat cheese may reduce the fat content.

Hamburger Corn-Pone Pie

"All you need is a salad. Supper is ready."

Serves 4 to 6

1 pound ground beef
½ cup onion, chopped
1 tablespoon shortening
1 can drained tomatoes
2 teaspoons chili powder
1 teaspoon Worcestershire sauce
1 cup kidney beans, drained
1 cup cornbread batter (½ package corn muffin mix)

Brown meat and chopped onion in melted shortening. Add tomatoes and seasonings, cover, and simmer over low heat for 15 minutes. Add kidney beans. Pour mixture into a greased 1- or 1½-quart casserole. Top with cornbread batter (prepared according to package directions, halved), spreading carefully with wet knife. Bake at 425 degrees for 20 minutes.

Connie Woodroof

▲ Using lean beef or ground round and browning the meat and onion in the hamburger drippings will reduce the fat content.

Shipwreck Casserole

"Great on Friday night when you're just out of ideas of what to serve the troops."

Serves 6 to 8

2 onions, thinly sliced
2 or 3 potatoes, sliced
⅓ cup raw rice
1 green pepper, sliced
1 or 2 ribs celery, sliced
1 can kidney beans
1 to 1½ pounds browned and crumbled ground beef
1 6-ounce can tomato sauce or tomato juice
Salt, pepper, garlic powder, and seasoning salt to taste

Layer the first 7 ingredients in a baking dish. Season to taste. Pour tomato sauce or tomato juice over all. Sauce makes very thick casserole, tomato juice is juicier. Cover and bake in a 325 degree oven for 1 hour or until the potatoes are done. Take cover off for 15 minutes for browning. Use a 9 x 12-inch casserole dish.

Annie Ruth Clarke

Swedish Meatballs

"Serve over rice, if desired. A family favorite."

Serves 6

1½ pounds lean ground beef or 1 pound lean ground beef and ½ pound ground pork
1 slice bread of any kind (torn into small pieces)
2 tablespoons chopped onion, optional
1¼ teaspoons salt
¼ teaspoon pepper
1 cup sour cream
2 cups water
2 beef bouillon cubes
2 tablespoons flour
1 tablespoon chives

Mix together the meat, bread pieces, onion, salt, pepper and ½ cup sour cream. Reserve remaining sour cream for gravy. Shape mixture into meatballs and place on a rack in a baking pan. Bake for 10 minutes in a 400 degree oven. Put baked meatballs in a large saucepan or large skillet with the water and bouillon cubes. Simmer, covered for 30 minutes on stove. Remove meatballs from liquid. Blend into the liquid the remaining sour cream, flour and chives. Blend until thickened, about 5 minutes. Return meatballs to gravy and heat uncovered until steaming. Do not boil.

Beth Parker

▲ To reduce fat content, replace sour cream with lowfat yogurt or mock sour cream.

Burger Bundles

"Fun and good."

Serves 4

1 pound ground chuck
⅓ cup evaporated milk
1 cup cornbread stuffing mix (stove top type)
1 cup cream of mushroom soup
1 teaspoon Worcestershire sauce
3 tablespoons catsup (optional)

Mix ground chuck with evaporated milk and form 4 large patties. Prepare stuffing as directed on package. Place 1 to 2 tablespoons stuffing on each patty and shape patty into meatball. Place in baking dish. Mix soup, Worcestershire sauce and catsup (if desired) and pour over meatballs. Bake for 45 minutes covered, then 15 minutes uncovered in a 325 degree oven.

Ann Daniel and Pearl Settle

▲ Using skim evaporated milk and lowfat soup will help reduce fat content.

The Mayor's House has been Mr. Morehouse's home since the day he was born. He is Harmony Grove's youngest and most active leader.

Cabbage Meatballs

"Serve with rice or potatoes."

Serves 6 to 8

1 medium cabbage
1¼ pounds ground beef
½ cup cooked rice
2 teaspoons salt
Pepper
1 small onion, chopped
1 egg
½ teaspoon poultry seasoning or thyme
2 8-ounce cans tomato sauce
1 tablespoon brown sugar
¼ cup water
1 tablespoon lemon juice or vinegar

Make 1½-inch meatballs with beef, rice, salt and pepper, onion, egg, and poultry seasoning. Brown without using oil. Combine tomato sauce, brown sugar, water, lemon juice and pour over meatballs. Cut cabbage into 2-inch wedges and put into sauce, cover and simmer, stirring occasionally. Add water if sauce becomes too thick. Cooking time is 30 to 45 minutes.

Jean Cyrus

▲ To decrease fat content, use lean beef or ground round and an egg substitute.

Zucchini Lasagna

"No pasta in this lasagna. Great way to use all that zucchini from the garden."

Serves 6

½ pound hamburger
⅓ cup onion, chopped
1 15-ounce can tomato sauce
½ teaspoon salt
½ teaspoon oregano
¼ teaspoon basil
⅛ teaspoon pepper
4 medium zucchini, sliced
1 cup cottage cheese
1 egg
2 tablespoons flour
¼ pound Mozzarella cheese, shredded

In a 10-inch skillet, over medium high heat, cook beef and onion until onion is tender (about 10 minutes), stirring occasionally. Drain. Add tomato sauce, salt, oregano, basil, pepper; heat to boiling. Reduce heat to low and simmer 5 minutes. Preheat oven to 375 degrees. Meanwhile, with a sharp knife slice zucchini lengthwise into ¼-inch thick slices. In a small bowl, combine cottage cheese with egg until well mixed.

In the bottom of a large baking dish, arrange half of zucchini in a layer and sprinkle with a tablespoon of flour. Top with cottage cheese mixture and half of meat mixture. Repeat with remaining zucchini and flour; sprinkle with Mozzarella cheese and remaining meat mixture. Bake 40 minutes. Let stand 10 minutes for easier cutting.

Tracy Magin

▲ To reduce fat content, use lowfat cottage cheese and lowfat cheese.

♟ Pizza

"Fun to make. Create your own masterpiece pizza."

Serves 4

Crust
1½ cups flour
1 package active dry yeast
½ cup tepid water
1 tablespoon oil
1 teaspoon salt

Mix ¾ cup of flour and yeast. Combine the water, oil and salt, add to flour mixture, beat well. Add remainder of flour to make a stiff dough. Knead smooth, place in greased bowl, turn over, cover and let rise until more than double, punch down. Let rest 10 minutes. Roll out or spread until about ¼-inch thick in shape desired. Form edge, prick crust. Bake in 450 degree oven for about 10 minutes. Bake on a cookie sheet or pizza stone. For crisper crust bake directly on oven rack.

Sauce
½ cup dry red wine
1 8-ounce can tomato sauce
2 teaspoons minced onion
½ teaspoon basil
½ teaspoon oregano
½ teaspoon Worcestershire sauce
Desired toppings - pepperoni, sausage, green pepper, mushroom, Mozzarella cheese, anchovies, olives, etc.

Combine all ingredients except toppings. Bring to a boil, reduce to 1 cup. Spread over baked crust. Add desired toppings. Bake 10 more minutes or until done at 450 degrees.

Marilyn Creamer

▲ Stick to lowfat cheese and vegetable toppings to keep this lowfat.

Barbecue Pork Roast

"Tender and delicious."

Serves 4 to 6

2 pounds roast
⅓ cup sliced onion
2 tablespoons barbecue sauce (Sauers)
1½ teaspoons salt
½ cup catsup
1 tablespoon mustard
¼ teaspoon red pepper
¾ cup water
½ cup vinegar

Cut roast in 8 pieces. Place in covered casserole. Combine ingredients in saucepan. Bring to a boil, then pour over meat. Cover and bake at 375 degrees for 1¼ hours. Uncover and bake ½ hour longer, turning twice during this period.

Ann Burke

♟ Chop Skillet Dinner

"A stove-top casserole."

Serves 4 to 6

4 to 6 pork chops
1 green pepper
2 teaspoons salt or salt substitute
1 cup onion, sliced
½ cup water
4 cups pared, sliced potatoes
1 cup celery, diced
½ teaspoon pepper
1 can tomato soup, condensed

Brown chops, remove from skillet and pour off grease. Arrange vegetables in layers in skillet. Top with pork chops. Pour soup mixed with ½ cup water over casserole. Cover and cook over low heat ½ to 1 hour.

Margie Jamison

Roast Pork à la Davis

"Great next day sandwiches."

Serves 6 to 8

4 pounds loin of pork (trim fat off)
2 cloves garlic
2 teaspoons salt
1 teaspoon sage
½ teaspoon pepper
½ teaspoon nutmeg
2 carrots
2 onions
1 cup water
¼ cup currant jelly
1 teaspoon dry mustard
Whole cloves

Mash garlic cloves with salt, sage, pepper and nutmeg. Using your fingers, rub all well into the meat. Slice onions and carrots and spread in shallow pan. Place meat, fat side up, on vegetables. Splash water over meat and cook in 325 degree oven uncovered, 1½ hours.

Remove meat from oven. Slash fat in criss-cross pattern. Combine jelly and dry mustard. Spread this mixture over meat, stud with whole cloves, roast 1 hour more.

Joyce Davis

Pork Chops with Dill-Cream Gravy

"Most elegant company pork chops. You can prepare ahead of time except for addition of sour cream."

Serves 6

½ cup green onion, thinly sliced
½ cup fresh mushrooms, sliced
6 pork chops (¾-inch thick), trim fat
1 teaspoon salt
¼ teaspoon pepper
½ cup Chablis or other dry white wine
1 teaspoon Worcestershire sauce
1 teaspoon dried whole dillweed

⅓ cup water
2 tablespoons all-purpose flour
1 8-ounce carton sour cream

Sauté onions and mushrooms in butter in a large skillet until tender. Remove from skillet; set aside.

Sprinkle pork chops with salt and pepper; place in large skillet and brown on both sides. Combine sautéed vegetables, wine, Worcestershire sauce, and dillweed; pour over chops. Cover, reduce heat, and simmer 40 minutes or until pork chops are tender. Remove chops from skilled and set aside.

Combine water and flour, stirring until smooth; add to pan drippings in skillet. Cook over low heat, stirring constantly, until thickened and bubbly. Stir in sour cream and cook until thoroughly heated. Serve over rice.

Kay Outten

▲ To decrease fat content replace sour cream with lowfat yogurt or mock sour cream.

Pork Chops and Apples

"This was my father's favorite."

Serves 4 to 6

6 pork chops
3 to 4 unpeeled apples, cored and sliced
¼ cup brown sugar
½ teaspoon cinnamon
2 tablespoons butter

Preheat oven to 350 degrees. Brown pork chops. Place apples in greased baking dish; sprinkle with sugar and cinnamon. Dot with butter. Place pork chops on top. Bake, covered, for 1½ hours.

Kay Outten

▲ To decrease fat content, use only 1 tablespoon butter, or omit the butter completely.

Pork Chops with Sour Cream Gravy

"Delicious."

Serves 4 to 6

4 to 6 chops, regular thickness
Flour, oil, salt
2 medium onions, thinly sliced
1 tablespoon paprika
½ to 1 cup sour cream
1 cup water with 1 chicken bouillon cube
  or 1 cup chicken stock

Sprinkle chops on both sides with salt and dredge in flour. Brown chops in electric skillet in vegetable oil till brown on each side (use as little oil as possible and don't brown more than 3 chops at a time). Remove chops and add onions, cooking in remaining oil till tender, about 2 minutes. Stir in flour left from dredging chops (use about 1 tablespoon). Gradually add water, then dissolving bouillon cube in it and adding paprika. Heat to boiling, then add chops. Turn skillet to low (250 degrees), cover, and cook 45 minutes, turning once if desired. Add more liquid (water or broth) if it cooks down too much. When chops stick tender (45 to 60 minutes), remove chops to a platter and whisk sour cream into gravy. Simmer till thick and smooth, and serve over chops and rice. If you wish, you may return chops to the skillet, cover, and hold in sour cream gravy at very low temperature for a while.

Jenny Showalter

▲ Replacing sour cream with lowfat yogurt or mock sour cream will decrease the fat content.

Pork Chop and Sweet Potato Casserole

"A good pork variation."

Serves 4 to 6

3 large sweet potatoes, cooked and sliced
  (may use canned)
6 thin slices unpeeled orange
6 pork chops
1 teaspoon salt
¼ teaspoon pepper
⅓ cup light brown sugar

Preheat oven to 350 degrees. Drain sweet potatoes and place in greased oblong baking dish; top with orange slices, then pork chops. Season with salt and pepper; sprinkle with brown sugar. Bake in covered casserole for 1 hour.

Justine Jones

Sausage and Wild Rice Casserole

"Everybody wants more!"

Serves 6

1 box Uncle Ben's Wild Rice and Long
  Grain Rice
1 pound hot sausage
1 can cream of mushroom soup
  (undiluted)
1 small can mushrooms

Cook rice as directed and set aside. Brown and crumble sausage, drain off fat. Mix together cooked rice, cooked sausage, soup and mushrooms. Put in 2-quart casserole and bake uncovered for 30 minutes.

Faye Rutherford

Teriyaki Pork Chops

"You don't have to use the orange liqueur - very good without it."

Serves 4

⅛ teaspoon each: garlic salt, ground
   ginger, pepper
4 pork loin chops, cut ½-inch thick
1 small red sweet pepper, cut into thin
   strips (¾ cup)
¾ cup coarsely shredded carrot
½ cup bias-sliced green onion
¼ cup orange juice
3 tablespoons teriyaki sauce
2 tablespoons orange liqueur (optional)
1 teaspoon cornstarch
¼ teaspoon bottled hot pepper sauce
Hot cooked rice

In a small bowl, combine garlic salt, ginger and pepper. Trim fat from pork chops; rub both sides of each chop with ginger mixture. Preheat a 10-inch heavy skillet over high heat until hot. Add chops; reduce heat to medium. Turning once, cook chops until no longer pink, about 8 to 10 minutes. Remove chops from skillet; keep warm.

Add red pepper, carrot and green onion to skillet. Stirring often, cook over medium heat until crisp-tender, about 2 to 3 minutes. In a small bowl stir together orange juice, teriyaki sauce, liqueur, cornstarch and hot pepper sauce; add to vegetables. Cook and stir until thickened and bubbly; cook and stir for 2 minutes longer.

Serve pork chops on rice. Spoon vegetables mixture atop.

Lois Wainwright

Pork Chop and Rice Casserole

"A busy day meal."

Serves 3 to 4

1⅓ cups uncooked minute rice
1 can cream of mushroom soup
¾ can water
3 to 4 pork chops

Combine uncooked rice with cream of mushroom soup. Add ¾ can of water and mix. Put mixture into 9 x 13-inch casserole dish. Brown pork chops on both sides. Put on top of rice mixture. Bake at 350 degrees for 1 hour.

Justine Jones

▲ To reduce fat content, use lowfat soup.

Beans and Franks in Pot

"This served with salad and bread is a meal."

Serves 6 to 8

1 can baked beans
1 can kidney beans, drained
1 can lima beans, drained
1 medium onion, sliced
½ green pepper, diced
½ cup catsup
½ cup molasses
2 tablespoons vinegar
Dash hot pepper sauce
2 teaspoons dry mustard
1 pound franks, cut in diagonal slices

Combine all ingredients. Place in a large casserole or bean pot. Bake at 350 degrees for 1 hour. Serve warm. May be cooked in slow cooker (crock pot) for 1 hour on high then on low until serving time. Browned hamburger may be substituted for franks.

Frances Wright

Bacon, Corn and Potato Casserole

"A 'poor man's dinner', hearty and delicious."

Serves 4 to 5

5 or 6 medium potatoes, peeled and sliced
2 medium onions, sliced
8 to 10 slices bacon
1 can cream corn
1 13-ounce can evaporated milk
Salt and pepper to taste
Parsley flakes

Preheat oven to 375 degrees. Grease a 13 x 9 x 2-inch baking dish. Cook half the bacon and set aside. Layer potatoes, onions, corn, cooked bacon, then potatoes, onions, corn and uncooked bacon. Season each layer of potatoes with salt and pepper. Gently pour entire can of evaporated milk over top, then sprinkle with parsley flakes. Bake at 375 degrees about 50 minutes, until top is nicely browned and potatoes test done.

Margaret Cooke

Crackling Bread

"This is a main course dish, good with a big salad."

Serves 4

½ pound bacon, save ¼ cup drippings
2 cups regular cornmeal
3 teaspoons baking powder
1 cup sifted flour
3 tablespoons sugar
1½ teaspoons salt
1 teaspoon baking soda
1 cup buttermilk
2 eggs

Cook bacon until very crisp in 10-inch iron skillet; drain and reserve drippings. Crumble bacon. Do not wash skillet! Set oven at 375 degrees. Combine flour, cornmeal, sugar, baking powder, salt and soda in a bowl. Beat eggs, stir buttermilk and ¼ cup drippings in with eggs. Add liquids to dry ingredients all at once. Add bacon and beat well with spoon. Pour into skillet and bake 20 to 25 minutes until golden brown.

Gay Neale

Vaughan's Country Cured Ham

"This method finishes the ham so nicely."

Serves 18 to 24

Scrub ham thoroughly and put in heavy pot with lid. Cover with water, add ½ cup brown sugar. Bake in oven at 500 degrees until it starts to boil, then turn back to 250 degrees and bake for 20 minutes per pound.

One hour before done, take ham out, skin, and then put back to finish cooking. Let it cool in water.

Christine Vaughan

Country Ham

"This really works but only with smaller hams."

Serves 18 to 24

Scrub ham thoroughly and soak it overnight in cold water; cut off hock if necessary. Preheat oven to 375 degrees. Place ham and 5 cups of water in roaster, cover and place in oven. Turn oven to 500 degrees for 10 minutes and then turn oven off for 3 hours. Turn oven on again to 500 degrees for 15 minutes; then turn off again and leave for 6 to 8 hours. **Do not open oven door until the 8 hours are up.** Roaster should be covered and the oven door closed the whole time ham is cooking. This method works for smaller hams - not over 14 pounds.

Maggie Epperson

Yakimestti

"This is very colorful and kids love it."

Serves 6

2 cups cooked rice
1 tablespoon vegetable oil
3 medium carrots, sliced thin
½ cup celery, sliced
½ medium onion, chopped
1 cup peas
2 cups cooked ham, diced
Soy sauce

Heat oil in frying pan on medium high. Add all vegetables and meat. Stir fry until still barely crunchy. Add salt and pepper to taste, and 1 tablespoon soy sauce. Mix well. Add rice and heat thoroughly. Top with strips of egg (directions follow), when ready to serve.

Egg Strips
1 egg, beaten well
1 teaspoon water
1 tablespoon sugar

Mix egg with sugar and water. Pour half of mixture into hot frying pan with oil and cook through, like an omelette. Remove and cook remaining egg mixture the same way. Cut the cooked egg into thin strips.

Mary Ellen Saville

▲ To decrease fat content, use lowfat ham.

Perle Mesta's Cranberry Lamb Chops

"Wonderful and different lamb dish."

Serves 4

4 lamb shoulder chops, cut ½-inch thick
2 tablespoons lard or drippings
¼ teaspoon ground cloves

¼ teaspoon cinnamon
1 16-ounce can whole cranberry sauce
1 tablespoon flour
1 teaspoon salt
⅛ teaspoon pepper
¼ cup water

Brown lamb chops in lard or drippings. Pour off drippings. Season with salt and pepper. Combine cloves, cinnamon, ¼ cup water and cranberry sauce. Pour over lamb chops, cover tightly and simmer 45 minutes or until meat is tender. Remove meat to warm platter. Combine ¼ cup water and flour and add to drippings in pan. Cook, stirring constantly until thickened. Serve over lamb chops.

Kay Outten

▲ To decrease fat content, use lowfat margarine.

Dinner Lamb Chops

"Delicious."

Serves 6

6 lamb chops
Salt and pepper
1 green pepper, cut in rings
1 large onion, sliced
1 lemon, sliced
2 cups tomato juice

Brown chops in hot fat, season with salt and pepper. Place in baking dish and top each with pepper ring, onion slice, lemon slice. Pour tomato juice over chops. Cover with lid or foil. Bake at 325 degrees for 1½ hours.

Carolyn Lee

Leg of Lamb

"Garnish with slices of fresh tomato."

Serves 8 to 10

1 leg of lamb
1 cup flour
1 teaspoon salt
1 teaspoon pepper
1 teaspoon ginger
2 tablespoons shortening
1 small onion, sliced
1 tablespoon Worcestershire sauce
2 tablespoons catsup
Pinch of sugar
1 pint boiling water

Wipe leg of lamb with damp cloth. Combine flour, salt, pepper and ginger. Dredge leg of lamb in flour mixture. Sauté onion in shortening. Remove onion. Add Worcestershire sauce, catsup, sugar and water. Place lamb in baking pan and pour sauce over all. Bake slowly in 300 degree oven, basting frequently, about 1 hour per pound.

Virginia Woodroof

▲ To reduce fat content, use lowfat margarine.

Leg of Lamb Roast

"Paste is very spicy, do not lick fingers."

Serves 8 to 10

1 leg of lamb
1 tablespoon margarine
2 tablespoons flour
2 tablespoons vinegar
1 teaspoon red pepper
1 teaspoon crushed rosemary
3 teaspoons salt
1 teaspoon fresh ground pepper

Make a paste of all ingredients except leg of lamb. Rub over meat. Bake on rack at 325 degrees until thermometer reaches 180 degrees. Add cup water when needed to make basting broth. Baste 2 or 3 times. Probably will need to cook about 1 hour to the pound.

Beth Parker

Croquettes - Ham, Veal, Salmon

"Good way to use leftover ham."

Serves 4 to 6

2 cups ground meat
1 cup thick white sauce
1 cup bread crumbs, finely crushed
1 egg, beaten

White Sauce
3 tablespoons butter or margarine
⅓ cup flour
1 cup milk

To make sauce: in a heavy saucepan, melt butter. Blend flour into melted butter, stirring constantly. Stir in slowly the milk, being sure to stir constantly. Continue to cook and stir. Using a wire whisk aids in stirring to a smooth consistency.

Combine meat and white sauce seasoned with salt and pepper. Spread on plate and allow to cool in refrigerator, then shape into pyramids, dip in beaten egg and then roll in cracker meal. Chill to set bread crumbs firmly. Fry in hot oil until golden brown.

This can be prepared ahead of time and stored in refrigerator for a few days or freezer for several months. Takes only a few minutes to fry, great for a quick meal. Can be served with a little medium white sauce and parsley.

Snooze Barkley

"When August is mentioned, a couple of things come to mind: crepe myrtle and watermelon. We often picked ripe melons from our patches and cooled them for hours in springs near our tobacco fields. On the stickiest summer days, cold melons and abundant shade brought welcome relief and refreshment."

Eldridge Bagley

"MELON AND SHADE"
Appears through the courtesy of the painting's owner, Julia J. Norrell.

Hot Shrimp Sandwiches

"Just the thing for brunch or a very special lunch."

Serves 6

1 pound shrimp, cooked
Juice of ½ lemon
2 tiny onions, finely chopped or onion salt
2 hard-boiled eggs, diced
Mayonnaise
Parmesan cheese
Mozzarella cheese
Sliced bread

Mix together lemon juice, onions and diced hard-boiled eggs. Spread mayonnaise on a slice of bread, then spread the egg mixture; next place the cooked shrimp evenly on top of the egg mixture. Sprinkle a little Parmesan cheese over this and finally top all with Mozzarella cheese. Broil until golden.

Anne Butler

▲ To decrease fat content, use lowfat/no-fat mayonnaise and lowfat cheese.

Easy Shrimp Aspic

"Wonderful tangy flavor."

Serves 6

2 cans shrimp
1 3-ounce package lemon gelatin
1 cup boiling water
1 8-ounce can tomato sauce
1½ tablespoons vinegar
1 teaspoon horseradish
1 teaspoon grated onion

Mix gelatin with boiling water. Add other ingredients and refrigerate until set.

Sally Palmer

Seafood Salad

"Serve on crisp lettuce, sprinkle with paprika."

Serves 4 to 6

1 5-ounce can lobster, drained, boned, cut into bite-sized pieces
1 5-ounce can shrimp, drained
1 6½-ounce can crab meat, drained, boned and flaked
1 cup celery, diced
1 tablespoon lemon juice
¼ teaspoon pepper
1 tablespoon onion, minced
1 teaspoon salt
¾ cup mayonnaise

Toss seafood with all other ingredients, adding mayonnaise last. Mix well and cover and chill thoroughly. Serve with additional mayonnaise if desired.

Ruby Simmons

▲ To decrease fat, use lowfat/no-fat mayonnaise.

*Nothing gave Harmony Grove folks as much pride and confidence as the completion of the **Merchants and Farmers Bank** in 1898.*

Shrimp Mousse

"Lovely, cool, shrimp dish."

Serves 6

1 can shrimp
1 small jar pimentos, minced
2 hard-boiled eggs, chopped
3 teaspoons onion juice
1 package gelatin
1 cup cold water
¾ cup mayonnaise
¾ cup celery, chopped
1 small bottle of olives, minced
3 teaspoons lemon juice

Mix gelatin in cold water and put in double boiler over medium heat to dissolve. Combine all ingredients with mayonnaise. Cut up shrimp and add to mixture. Pack into individual oiled molds and chill. Unmold to serve.

Jean Clay

▲ To lower fat, use lowfat/no-fat mayonnaise.

Broiled Crab Puffs

"Do not put crab meat on the muffin too thick or the outside will brown before the inside cooks."

Yields 48 pieces

1 pound crab meat, special or backfin
1 5-ounce jar Old English sharp cheese
4 tablespoons mayonnaise
⅛ teaspoon ground red pepper
4 tablespoons melted butter or margarine
2 teaspoons regular mustard
½ teaspoon garlic salt
10 saltine crackers, crushed
6 English muffins, split and quartered

Gently pick over crab meat to remove any shell. Heat cheese to soften by placing jar in hot water. Combine all ingredients except crab and muffins, mixing well. Gently add crab. Spoon mixture onto triangles of English muffins. Place on a cookie sheet and freeze for at least 30 minutes. When ready to serve, broil for a few minutes, crab will be bubbly and slightly golden brown.

Beth Bagley

After frozen firm, pieces may be placed in a zipper bag and stored for 3 to 4 weeks until ready to broil and serve.

⚑ Dora's James River Crabcakes

"Dora suggested Uneeda crackers. I have found that the lowfat saltines on the market now work very well."

1 pound crab meat
1 egg
1 medium tomato
¾ teaspoon Worcestershire sauce
Dash of hot pepper sauce
8 saltine crackers, crumbled
Salt and pepper to taste

Beat egg slightly. Grate fresh tomato into egg (grate skin and all). Add Worcestershire sauce (amount given is a guess as I just splash some in), hot sauce and salt and pepper. Mix lightly then add crab meat and cracker crumbs. Blend together lightly and shape into patties. Patties will be loosely held together, however, they will hold if they are shaped and refrigerated for several hours before browning. Brown in skillet with butter or margarine at a medium-high temperature until golden brown on both sides, turning only once.

Kelly Stokes

Granny's Crab Imperial

"Our favorite crab dish when we want to dress it up a little."

Serves 4

1 pound backfin crab meat
1 tablespoon Durkee's dressing
2 tablespoons mayonnaise
1 tablespoon Worcestershire sauce
1 cup coarse cracker crumbs
1 tablespoon paprika
⅛ pound melted butter

Blend together the first 4 ingredients lightly. Pile in shells or small ramekins. Pat crumbs on top. Sprinkle with paprika. Pour melted butter over tops. Put shells in a baking pan and add about ¼-inch water to the pan. Bake in a 350 to 400 degree oven for 12 to 15 minutes.

Virginia Outten

▲ To decrease fat, use lowfat margarine and lowfat/no-fat mayonnaise.

Fannie Woodson's Crab Meat Casserole

"A touch of lemon really enhances flavor."

Serves 4

1 pound crab meat (pick over for shells, if you prefer)
3 slices bread, toasted, divided (1½ for topping)
¼ cup margarine, melted
½ cup mayonnaise
½ cup milk
1 teaspoon Worcestershire sauce
1 teaspoon dry mustard
1 teaspoon prepared mustard
½ teaspoon hot pepper sauce

½ teaspoon horseradish
Dash garlic salt
Dash pepper and salt to taste (it needs several or more good pinches of salt)

Combine ½ cup mayonnaise and ½ cup milk. Mix this with all other ingredients using crumbs from 1½ slices of bread, reserving rest for top. Put in a casserole dish and top with crumbs from remaining 1½ slices toasted bread. Dot generously with extra margarine. Bake in a 325 to 350 degree oven till bubbly hot and lightly browned. Serve with lemon.

Jenny Showalter

▲ Using lowfat margarine, lowfat/no-fat mayonnaise and lowfat/skim milk will decrease fat content.

Crab Mousse

"Especially good!"

Serves 4

1 can cream of mushroom soup
1 envelope unflavored gelatin
3 tablespoons cold water
¾ cup mayonnaise
1 8-ounce package cream cheese, softened
6½ ounces crab meat
1 small onion, grated fine
1 cup celery, grated fine

Heat soup over low heat till warm. Remove from heat. Dissolve gelatin in cold water. Add to soup and stir well. Add remaining ingredients and mix well. Oil a 4-cup mold with vegetable oil. Pour mousse into mold and chill till firm. To unmold, set mold in hot tap water for several minutes. Serve with crackers.

Patricia Samford

▲ To decrease fat, use lowfat soup, lowfat cream cheese, and lowfat/no-fat mayonnaise.

Crab Casserole

"Another superb crab dish."

Serves 4

1 pound crab meat (backfin is best)
4 slices of bread soaked in ¾ cup milk
  (use 5 slices if bread is thin sliced)
4 hard-boiled eggs, chopped
¼ cup green pepper, finely chopped
Onion salt (5 good shakes)
2 stalks celery, finely cut
¾ cup mayonnaise

Mix all ingredients and place in buttered casserole dish. Dot with butter and bread crumbs. Cook at 325 degrees for 30 minutes.

Carolyn Sykes

▲ To lower fat, use lowfat/skim milk to soak bread, lowfat/no-fat mayonnaise, and non-stick spray instead of butter on casserole dish.

Crab Meat Casserole

"A family favorite."

Serves 4

2 tablespoons butter
1½ cups light cream
1 cup grated cheese (sharp)
1 to 2 tablespoons cooking sherry
2 tablespoons flour
Salt and pepper to taste
2 cups crab meat
Buttered bread crumbs

Make a cream sauce of butter, flour, cream, salt and pepper. When thickened add cheese, crab meat and sherry. Fill buttered baking dish. Top with buttered bread crumbs and brown in hot oven (450 degrees).

Eloise Lucy

▲ To decrease fat, use skim milk/lowfat milk or nonfat evaporated milk instead of light cream, lowfat cheese, and use nonstick spray in baking dish instead of butter.

Baked Seafood

"This will freeze well despite the mayonnaise."

Serves 6 to 8

1 cup shrimp, cleaned and cooked
  (may use canned)
1 cup crab meat (may use canned)
½ to ¾ cup green pepper, chopped
1 cup celery, thinly sliced
¼ cup onion, minced
1 cup mayonnaise
1 teaspoon Worcestershire sauce
½ teaspoon salt
¼ teaspoon black or white pepper
½ cup soft bread crumbs
1 teaspoon butter or margarine, melted

Heat oven to 350 degrees. Cut shrimp in half lengthwise and flake crab meat. Mix these 2 and combine with all the other ingredients except crumbs and butter. Spread in baking dish. Toss bread crumbs with melted butter and sprinkle on top. Bake 30 minutes till browned. Serve with parsley sprigs and lemon quarters.

Nell Catherwood

▲ To decrease fat content, use lowfat/no-fat mayonnaise.

Crab and Shrimp Casserole

"A really good combination."

Serves 4 to 5

½ **pound shrimp**
1 **cup chopped celery**
¼ **cup chopped green pepper**
1 **cup mayonnaise**
½ **pound crab meat**
½ **cup chopped onions**
1 **tablespoon Worcestershire sauce**
1½ **cups crushed potato chips (save some**
   to sprinkle on top)

Mix all ingredients together and bake in uncovered casserole dish in preheated oven at 375 degrees for 15 to 20 minutes.

Ruth Sanders

▲ To lower fat, use saltines or bread crumbs instead of potato chips and use lowfat/no-fat mayonnaise.

Shrimp Newburg In a Shell

"This sauce can be made ahead, then wait to add shrimp just before serving, being sure to heat thoroughly."

Serves 4

⅓ **cup butter**
2 **tablespoons flour**
2 **cups light cream (half and half), warmed**
4 **egg yolks, slightly beaten**
2 **cups shrimp, cooked**
¼ **cup sherry**
2 **teaspoons lemon juice**
Salt to taste
1 **tablespoon parsley flakes**
4 **patty shells**

Melt butter and blend in flour. Stir in warmed cream and cook slowly, stirring constantly until mixture thickens. Stir small amount of hot mixture into egg yolks and gradually return this to hot mixture. Add shrimp and heat through. Add sherry, lemon juice, salt and parsley. Pour into cooked patty shells, overflowing them slightly.

June Thomas

▲ To decrease fat, use lowfat margarine and replace cream with lowfat/skim milk or nonfat evaporated milk.

Shrimp Newburg

"May be served in a chafing dish and used as an appetizer."

Serves 4

1 **pound shrimp, cleaned**
3 **tablespoons butter**
1 **teaspoon lemon juice**
1 **teaspoon flour**
½ **cup cream**
2 **egg yolks, beaten**
2 **tablespoons sherry**
Salt and pepper

Cook shrimp in 2 tablespoons of butter and lemon juice for 3 minutes. Set aside. Melt 1 tablespoon butter and stir in flour. Add cream gradually. Cook until thick. Add egg yolks, shrimp and sherry. If too thick, thin with additional cream. Season to taste. Serve over toast.

Anne Butler

▲ To reduce fat content, use lowfat margarine and replace cream with lowfat/skim milk or nonfat evaporated milk.

Seafood Casserole

"May use less mayonnaise, if desired."

Serves 4

**3 packages small or 1 large package cream
cheese
1 cup celery, cut up in small pieces
1 can crab meat
1 cup mayonnaise (can use less)
1 can tomato soup
1 can shrimp, cut shrimp up**

Mix cream cheese together and add ingredients. Sprinkle buttered bread crumbs over top. Bake in moderate oven about 35 to 45 minutes.

Louise Phipps

▲ To decrease fat, use lowfat cream cheese and lowfat/no-fat mayonnaise.

Shrimp Creole

"Best to prepare early in the day and allow time for all to season well together."

Serves 12

**¼ cup flour
¼ cup bacon grease
2 cups onion, chopped
½ cup green onion, chopped
2 cloves garlic, minced
1 cup green pepper, chopped
1 cup celery (with leaves), chopped
1 teaspoon thyme
2 bay leaves
3 teaspoons salt
½ teaspoon pepper
6 ounces tomato paste
1 16-ounce can tomatoes
8 ounces tomato sauce
1 cup shrimp stock or 1 cup water
3 pounds raw shrimp, cleaned
1 teaspoon hot pepper sauce**

**½ cup parsley, chopped
1 tablespoon lemon juice
2 cups cooked rice**

In a 4-quart Dutch oven, make a dark brown roux of flour and bacon grease. Add onion, green onion, garlic, green pepper, celery, thyme, bay leaf, salt and pepper. Sauté, uncovered, over medium heat until onions are translucent and soft, about 30 minutes. Add tomato paste and sauté 3 minutes. Add tomatoes, tomato sauce and shrimp stock or water. Simmer very slowly, partially covered, for 1 hour, stirring occasionally. Add shrimp and cook until shrimp are just done (5 to 6 minutes). Add hot pepper sauce, parsley and lemon juice. Stir, cover, and remove from heat. Serve over rice.

Pat Perkinson

Shrimp Creole

"This doesn't take long to get together."

Serves 3 to 4

**½ pound shrimp, shelled and cleaned
2 onions, chopped
1 green pepper, chopped
3 to 4 stalks celery, chopped
3 tablespoons oil or bacon fat
1 tablespoon flour
1 15-ounce can tomatoes
½ teaspoon salt
¼ teaspoon garlic powder
Dash of hot pepper sauce, if desired**

Sauté onions, green pepper and celery in oil until tender. Stir in flour. Add tomatoes and seasonings, including salt and pepper to taste. Simmer for 20 minutes, uncovered, stirring occasionally. Stir in shrimp. Simmer covered for 10 to 15 minutes. Serve on rice.

Lucy Heartwell

▲ You may want to lower the amount of oil or bacon fat you use to reduce fat content.

Sandy's Seafood Kebobs

"This marinade is also good for marinating sirloin steak before grilling."

Serves 6

½ cup peanut or olive oil
¼ cup lemon juice
1 teaspoon salt
1 teaspoon butter or margarine
1 teaspoon thyme
1 teaspoon oregano
1 or 2 cloves of garlic
¼ cup parsley
2 pounds shrimp or scallops
2 onions
2 green peppers
½ pound mushrooms

Chop or slice garlic cloves and place in a bowl. Melt butter; combine oil, lemon juice, salt, butter and spices in the bowl with the garlic. Pour the marinade over the peeled, raw shrimp or raw scallops. Quarter the onions and cut the green pepper into 1½-inch squares. Add onion, mushroom and green pepper to the marinade and marinate in the refrigerator overnight. Thread seafood and vegetables onto skewers and cook on grill until shrimp are firm, approximately 5 to 8 minutes for large shrimp. You may prefer to place the seafood and vegetables on different skewers since the vegetables may require longer cooking time.

Patricia Samford

Deviled Clams

"Can be frozen and baked when needed."

Serves 4 to 6

¼ cup onions, diced
¼ cup celery, diced
¼ cup green pepper, diced
¼ teaspoon minced garlic
¼ teaspoon seafood seasoning
Dash of curry powder
2 dashes Worcestershire sauce
2 dashes soy sauce
2 7½-ounce cans minced clams
¼ cup cracker meal

Sauté onion, celery, green pepper and garlic. Add spices and sauces to sautéed vegetables. Add clams, including liquid. Bring to a boil and stir until tender. Mix in cracker meal until wet mixture is formed. Spoon into clean shells on baking dish. Sprinkle with paprika. Bake at 350 degrees for 20 minutes.

Cherrill Robertson

You can also mix all (except cornmeal) in blender. After mixing, heat to a boil and add cornmeal, then continue as above.

Oyster Soufflé

"May be served without lemon sauce, but the sauce adds an extra touch."

Serves 6

2 10-ounce cans fresh or frozen oysters
½ cup chopped onion
⅓ cup butter or margarine
½ cup flour
1½ teaspoons salt
½ teaspoon paprika
Dash of white pepper and nutmeg
1 cup milk
4 eggs, separated

Thaw oysters, drain and reserve ½ cup liquor. Coarsely chop oysters. Cook onion slowly in saucepan in butter or margarine until tender - do not brown. Stir in flour, salt, paprika, pepper and nutmeg. Add milk along with reserve oyster liquor; cook until thickened, stirring constantly. Fold in chopped oysters. Beat egg whites until they hold soft peaks. Carefully fold egg whites into oyster mixture. Pour into ungreased 2-quart soufflé dish or deep casserole. Bake in slow oven, 325 degrees for about 60 or 70 minutes or until soufflé is puffed, browned and set. Serve with lemon sauce.

Creamy Lemon Sauce
2 tablespoons butter or margarine
2 tablespoons flour
½ teaspoon salt
¼ teaspoon paprika
1¼ cups milk
½ cup salad dressing or mayonnaise
1 tablespoon lemon juice (or more)

Melt butter or margarine in saucepan. Stir in flour, salt and paprika. Add milk. Cook until thickened and smooth, stirring constantly. Blend in salad dressing or mayonnaise and lemon juice. Heat slowly, never allowing to boil. Serve with oyster soufflé.

Katherine Dugger

▲ To decrease fat content, use lowfat margarine, lowfat/skim milk, and lowfat/no-fat mayonnaise or salad dressing in sauce.

Oyster Casserole

"For a special occasion, Thanksgiving, Christmas morning, etc."

Serves 6

1 pint oysters
½ stick butter (or more if you like)
20 saltine crackers
¼ teaspoon salt
⅛ teaspoon pepper
1 pint milk

Heat milk with butter, salt and pepper. In 2-quart baking dish alternate layers of crushed crackers and oysters. Pour heated milk over oysters and crackers. Bake in 350 degree oven for 30 minutes.

Cherril Robertson

Salmon Patties with Sauce

"Sauce adds a special touch."

Serves 4

1 15½-ounce can salmon, undrained
½ cup finely chopped onions
1 egg
½ cup all purpose flour
1½ teaspoons baking powder
1½ cups vegetable oil
3 tablespoons butter
¼ cup all purpose flour
1½ cups milk
¼ teaspoon salt
⅛ teaspoon pepper
1 8-ounce can English peas, drained

Drain salmon, reserving 2 tablespoons of liquid. Set reserved aside. In mixing bowl, flake salmon, then add onion and egg. Stir in ½ cup flour. Add the baking powder to the reserved liquid, stirring well. Add baking powder mixture to the salmon, mix well. Shape salmon mixture into 4 patties and fry in hot oil (375 degrees in electric skillet) until golden brown, about 5 minutes. Drain, keep warm.

In a small heavy saucepan, melt butter over low heat, add gradually ¼ cup flour, stirring constantly. Gradually add milk, stirring constantly. Continuing to stir, allow to cook over medium heat until mixture is thick and bubbly. Stir in salt, pepper and drained peas. Serve sauce over patties.

Nita Lane Fleshood

▲ Rather than frying, omit oil, try broiled or baked, coating lightly with nonstick spray for browning/crisping to reduce fat content.

♦ Low Cholesterol Salmon Patties

"My family likes their patties with a dash of catsup."

Serves 4

1 1-pound can salmon
4 egg whites or egg substitute to equal
  2 eggs
⅔ cup oat bran cereal (Quaker is the best)
1 medium onion, finely minced
1 tablespoon finely chopped parsley
1 tablespoon fresh squeezed lemon juice

Mix all ingredients together and make 8 patties. Spray a nonstick pan with non-stick vegetable spray (I use ⅓ cup olive oil). Fry until crisp.

Linda Anderson

*The young and the old are treated at **Dr. John Gorham's Office**, located on the south side of town.*

"Gardeners will probably never become extinct. There is a particular thrill that comes from playing a small part in the mysterious process of plant growth. To observe the daily changes as dormant seeds are transformed into robust vines or sturdy stalks is to witness a miracle. Then there is the satisfaction of gathering the yield. This painting depicts a couple of favorites grown in most home gardens."

Eldridge Bagley

"GARDEN CELEBRITIES"
Appears through the courtesy of the painting's owner, Lee M. Hylton.

Asparagus-Egg Casserole

"Serve as a side dish or a main dish and add a fruit salad."

Serves 4-6

1 can asparagus
1 cup milk
½ cup sharp cheese
1 cup bread crumbs
2 hard-boiled eggs, chopped
Salt and pepper
1 tablespoon flour
1 tablespoon butter or margarine

Boil eggs for 10 minutes. Put one layer of asparagus in casserole, cover with chopped egg. Add another layer of asparagus and top with other egg. Make a cream sauce of the butter, flour and milk; add cheese, salt and pepper. Pour this into the casserole and top with buttered bread crumbs. Bake in a moderate oven until done (bubbles).

Mary Francis Taylor

▲ To lower fat, substitute skim/1% milk and use lowfat cheese.

Asparagus with Sour Cream

"Wonderful - fresh asparagus!"

Serves 8

3 pounds fresh asparagus
1½ cups chicken broth

Sauce
1 cup sour cream
2 eggs, lightly beaten
1 tablespoon lemon juice
1 tablespoon sweet vermouth
Salt and pepper to taste
5 strips bacon, cooked crisp and crumbled
2 hard-boiled eggs, chopped

Place asparagus in pot with chicken broth. Cover and cook until tender, drain and place in warm buttered dish.

Over low heat, blend sour cream, eggs, and lemon juice, stirring constantly. When warm, stir in vermouth, salt and pepper and pour over warm asparagus. Serve with crumbled, crisp bacon and chopped hard-boiled egg yolks.

Pat Perkinson

▲ To decrease fat, replace sour cream with lowfat yogurt or mock sour cream and use an egg substitute and bacon bits instead of bacon strips.

Asparagus Casserole

"A nice addition to any meal."

Serves 8

1 can asparagus tips
1 cup cheese, grated
3 eggs, slightly beaten
1 cup sweet milk
¼ cup butter
1 cup cracker crumbs
½ teaspoon salt
⅛ teaspoon pepper

Mix all ingredients except butter and ⅓ cup cracker crumbs. Pour into buttered casserole and place remaining cracker crumbs and butter on top. Bake in a 350 degree oven until done.

Lucille Clary

▲ To decrease fat content, use lowfat cheese, egg substitute, and skim/1% milk.

Broccoli Casserole

"In place of bread crumbs use prepared cornbread dressing crumbs."

Serves 10

2 boxes frozen broccoli spears
2 eggs, well beaten
1 can cream of mushroom or cream of celery soup
2 teaspoons onion, grated
½ (or 1) cup mayonnaise, according to taste
1 cup sharp cheese, grated
Salt and pepper to taste
Bread crumbs

Place cooked broccoli in casserole. Cover with sauce made with eggs, soup, onion, mayonnaise, cheese, salt and pepper. Top with bread crumbs and bake at 350 degrees until bubbly.

Katherine Dugger

▲ To decrease fat, use an egg substitute, lowfat soup, lowfat/no-fat mayonnaise, and lowfat cheese.

Broccoli-Cheese Casserole

"Change the flavor by using pepper, paprika and Beau Monde (to taste) instead of lemon juice."

Serves 8

2 boxes frozen, chopped broccoli
1 package (⅓ of 3-tube box) round buttery crackers, crushed
1 8-ounce package pasteurized process cheese spread, cubed
1 stick margarine, melted
3 tablespoons lemon juice

Cook broccoli as directed on box; drain and place in a greased casserole. Mix cheese, ½ of

margarine, and the lemon juice and pour over broccoli. Combine remaining margarine and cracker crumbs and put on top. Bake at 350 degrees for about 20 to 25 minutes, until bubbly.

Van Doyle

▲ To decrease fat, use lowfat cheese and lower the amount of margarine or use lowfat margarine instead.

Broccoli-Cheese Pie

"Serve with a green salad or fruit."

Serves 6

1 bunch broccoli
2 to 3 eggs
1 cup low-fat cottage cheese
1 cup mild Mexican flavored pasteurized soft cheese
¼ cup chopped green onion
Dash nutmeg
1 pie shell, unbaked
Mustard, your preference
Parmesan cheese or bread crumbs
Pepper

Steam or microwave broccoli until just tender and combine with eggs, cheeses, onion and nutmeg in blender. Blend until just mixed.

Brush pie shell with mustard (if desired) and fill with blended mixture. Top with Parmesan and/or bread crumbs, pepper. Bake at 350 degrees for 35 to 45 minutes until brown and set.

Kay Outten

Cauliflower Casserole

"A sneaky way to serve cauliflower."

Serves 6

1 medium cauliflower
1 cup (4 ounces) Cheddar cheese,
 shredded
½ cup corn flake crumbs
⅓ cup green pepper, minced
¼ cup onion, finely chopped
1 8-ounce carton sour cream
½ cup Parmesan cheese, grated
Paprika

Cook cauliflower in boiling water until crisp
and tender. Drain. Combine cauliflower and
next 4 ingredients. Spoon mixture into a lightly
greased 2-quart casserole. Spread top with
sour cream; sprinkle with Parmesan cheese
and paprika. Bake at 350 degrees for 35
minutes.

Kathleen Newsom

▲ To decrease fat content, use lowfat cheese
and replace sour cream with lowfat yogurt or
mock sour cream.

Copper Pennies

"Keeps well in the refrigerator for several days."

Serves 12-14

2 pounds carrots, thinly sliced
1 small green pepper, chopped
1 medium onion, chopped
1 10¾-ounce can tomato soup
½ cup cooking oil
1 cup sugar
¾ cup vinegar
1 teaspoon prepared mustard
1 teaspoon Worcestershire sauce
Salt and pepper to taste

Cook carrots in small amount of salted water
for about 7 minutes. Cool and drain. Place a
layer of carrots, green pepper, and onion in a
1½-quart casserole. Combine tomato soup, oil,
sugar, vinegar, mustard, Worcestershire sauce,
salt and pepper; beat till well blended. Pour
over vegetables and cover with plastic wrap.
Refrigerate several hours to blend flavors. Bake
at 375 degrees until bubbly.

Evelyn Carpenter

Harvard Beets

"An easy way to fancy up canned beets."

Serves 3-4

1 pound can beets
2 tablespoons sugar
1 tablespoon cornstarch
¼ teaspoon salt
¼ cup vinegar
2 tablespoons butter

Drain can of beets, reserving ⅓ cup of liquid.
In saucepan, combine sugar, cornstarch and
salt. Stir in reserved liquid, vinegar and butter.
Cook and stir until mixture thickens and
bubbles. Add beets, heat thoroughly.

Evelyn Carpenter

▲ To decrease fat, lower the amount of
butter, or use lowfat margarine.

Scalloped Corn

"Use in place of scalloped potatoes."

Serves 8

1 stick margarine, melted
1 can creamed corn
1 cup sour cream
1 small box cornbread mix
1 can whole kernel corn, drained
2 eggs, beaten
Shredded cheese (optional)

Drain corn. Mix all ingredients except cheese. Bake at 350 degrees for about 65 minutes. Place shredded cheese on top and return to oven for 5 minutes.

Anne Walker

▲ To decrease fat content, use lowfat margarine, an egg substitute, lowfat cheese and replace sour cream with lowfat yogurt or mock sour cream.

Tangier Island Corn Pudding

"If you haven't been to Tangier Island, you must go just for the corn pudding."

Serves 8

1 16-ounce can creamed corn
1 6-ounce can evaporated milk
2 eggs, well beaten
¾ cup sugar
3 tablespoons flour
½ teaspoon vanilla
¼ cup margarine

Stir all ingredients together until well mixed. Pour in baking dish or pan. Bake at 350 degrees about 20 or 30 minutes.

Geraldine P. Lewis

▲ Using lowfat evaporated milk and an egg substitute will decrease the fat content.

Van's Corn Pudding

"Use fresh corn or drained canned corn."

Serves 4-6

2 cups corn
1 cup milk
2 tablespoons flour
½ teaspoon salt
2 eggs
5 tablespoons sugar
1½ tablespoons butter
Dash of pepper

Melt butter in 1-quart baking dish. Combine dry ingredients, add eggs, beat well. Add milk and then corn. Pour into baking dish. Bake about 30 minutes (at 400 degrees for 10 minutes and then reduce to 350 degrees).

Van Doyle

▲ To decrease fat content, use lowfat/skim milk and an egg substitute.

Squaw Hash

"This is an Indian recipe from the mid-West. They used wild mushrooms, but we don't advise that!"

Serves 4

½ pound bacon, cut in ¼-inch cubes
1 medium green pepper
½ pound fresh mushrooms
2 cups fresh corn, cooked

Fry bacon until crisp. Remove bacon from the drippings. Cut the green pepper into small pieces and put into bacon fat. Prepare the mushrooms by removing top skin and cutting in quarters. Fry mushrooms and pepper until done, then add the fresh sweet corn. Fry until golden brown. Return bacon back to the dish prior to serving.

Peg Walthall

Cabbage Casserole

"May be reheated for second day serving."

Serves 6

1 medium onion, chopped
2 tablespoons margarine or butter
1 pound ground beef
1 teaspoon salt
Dash of pepper
1 medium cabbage
2 cups American cheese, grated
1½ cups sour cream
1 cup buttered bread crumbs
¼ cup wine (optional)

Brown onion in the margarine. Add ground beef and brown; season. Cut up cabbage into pieces about 1-inch square; add to the ground beef mixture. Cover and cook slowly until the cabbage turns translucent, about 10 minutes. Add cheese and sour cream; mix thoroughly. Put in greased casserole; top with buttered crumbs. Bake at 375 degrees for about 45 minutes.

Justine Jones

▲ To decrease fat content, use ground round instead of ground beef, lowfat cheese, and replace sour cream with lowfat yogurt or mock sour cream.

Spiced Red Cabbage

"You may want to add a small amount of sugar in the last stage of cooking, but the caloric count in only 45 calories/serving as written."

Serves 6-8

4 cups shredded red cabbage
¼ cup cider vinegar
½ cup water
¼ teaspoon ground allspice
¼ teaspoon ground cinnamon
⅛ teaspoon ground nutmeg
2 tart apples (peeled, cored and diced)

In a saucepan combine all ingredients except the apples. Cover; cook over moderate heat for 15 minutes, tossing several times so the cabbage will cook evenly. Add the apples; toss again. Cover and cook until done. You may need to add a small amount of water, but when the dish is done all moisture should have cooked away.

Joyce Moorman

*Folks say the meal from **Hood's Mill** makes the best cornbread in the county.*

Cabbage or Cauliflower Français

"Fancy up your cabbage or cauliflower with this recipe."

Serves 8

1 green cabbage (½-2 pounds) chopped,
   or 2 small heads cauliflower, cut
3 tablespoons butter
1 cup whipping cream
½ teaspoon salt
⅛ teaspoon red pepper
2 tablespoons butter (for topping)
Parmesan cheese, grated
Water to cover
¼ cup flour
½ cup milk
⅛ teaspoon white pepper
⅛ teaspoon nutmeg
Bread crumbs

Cook cabbage (or cauliflower) in boiling water until tender. Drain well. Melt butter, blend in flour, add cream and milk, slowing stirring constantly until sauce thickens. Stir in salt, white and red pepper and nutmeg. Remove from heat and stir in vegetable. Pour into 1½-quart buttered baking dish, dot with butter and sprinkle with cheese. Bake in 375 degree oven for 20 to 25 minutes.

Pat Perkinson

▲ To decrease fat content, use lowfat margarine, skim/lowfat milk. You may need to use a small amount of cornstarch to thicken the sauce.

Hungarian Cabbage and Noodles

"Foil makes a good cover so the casserole doesn't dry out."

Serves 6-8

3 slices bacon
1½ teaspoons sugar
½ + ¼ teaspoon salt
3 cups chopped cabbage
About ½ cup noodles, fried (may use
   canned or see page 200)
Paprika
Sour cream (if desired)

Cook bacon, remove, then add sugar and salt to drippings in skillet. Add cabbage, stir and cook over medium low heat until tender (about 10 minutes). Combine cabbage, noodles and crumbled bacon. Put in casserole, cover and cook at 325 degrees about 30 to 40 minutes.

Uncover and if you like, spoon sour cream on top and sprinkle with paprika, then back in oven about 5 minutes.

Ella McDonald

Jiffy Baked Beans

"A must when serving hot dogs."

Serves 6-8

2 16-ounce cans pork and beans
¼ cup brown sugar
½ teaspoon dry mustard
½ cup catsup
4 slices bacon (cut in 1-inch strips)
½ cup onion slices

Combine all ingredients. Place in bean pot or casserole. Bake uncovered in moderate oven (350 degrees) for 1 hour.

Van Doyle

Escalloped Eggplant Pyramids

"Lots of fun to prepare - delicious."

Serves 4

1 (1¼-pound) eggplant, cut into ½-inch
   slices
1 large or 2 medium fresh tomatoes, sliced
1 large onion, thinly sliced
¾ cup butter, melted, divided
½ teaspoon salt
½ teaspoon dried basil leaves
¼ pound Mozzarella cheese, sliced
½ cup Italian bread crumbs
2 tablespoons Parmesan cheese, grated

On a medium-sized heatproof platter, arrange
eggplant slices, then stack a tomato slice and
an onion slice on top of each eggplant slice.
Drizzle with ¼ cup butter. Sprinkle with salt
and basil. Bake covered in a preheated 450
degree oven for 20 minutes. Cut Mozzarella
cheese in thirds. Arrange on top of eggplant
pyramids. Stir crumbs into remaining butter
and sprinkle on top. Sprinkle with Parmesan
cheese. Bake uncovered for 10 minutes or
until cheese is bubbly.

Mildred Rawlings

▲ To decrease fat content, use lowfat margarine.

♟ Eggplant Soufflé

"Serve at once after baking."

Serves 3-4

1 eggplant (about 1 pound)
2 teaspoons butter
1 egg, beaten
½ cup soft bread crumbs
¼ cup milk

¼ teaspoon salt
Dash pepper

Peel and slice eggplant. Cook in boiling salted
water until tender. Drain. Mash, adding butter,
salt, pepper, milk, egg and soft bread crumbs.
Pour into a greased baking dish. Sprinkle 2
tablespoons buttered bread crumbs on top.
Bake at 350 degrees for 15 to 20 minutes until
brown on top.

Lucy Heartwell

Green Bean With Dill Casserole

"Use fresh garden dill if it's in season."

Serves 3-4

1 large can green beans, undrained
1 strip bacon
¾ teaspoon dill seed

Sauce
¾ cup milk
½ cup juice from beans
½ teaspoon onion, grated
3 tablespoons flour
3 tablespoons butter
Dash of hot pepper sauce

Cook beans in their own juice with bacon and
dill seed for 20 minutes. Cool in liquid, then
drain, saving the juice. Make sauce. Mix
drained beans with sauce. Put in casserole
with buttered bread crumbs on top. Bake at
350 degrees until bubbly. Add more juice if
beans seem dry.

Connie Stanley

▲ To decrease fat, use bacon bits and
lowfat/skim milk.

Green Bean Casserole

"You can always depend on this one."

2 cans green beans
1 can mushroom soup
¼ cup almonds
1 teaspoon sherry, optional
1 can French fried onion rings

Combine beans, soup, almonds. Place in baking dish. Cook at 350 degrees for 30 minutes. Cover top with onion rings and bake additional 5 minutes.

Lucy Wiley

▲ To lower fat content, use lowfat mushroom soup and fresh onions, sautéed instead of the fried onion rings.

Evelyn's Golden Onion Chip Casserole

"Better if you don't use quite all the potato chips."

Serves 4-6

4 medium sweet onions, peeled and thinly sliced
1 9-ounce bag potato chips, crushed
1 can cream of mushroom soup with ½ can milk
1 cup Cheddar cheese, shredded
Paprika

Simmer sliced onions in 1 cup water until almost tender. Drain. In a 2-quart casserole dish, alternately layer onions, chips, cheese, and soup mixture. Sprinkle top lightly with paprika. Bake at 350 degrees for approximately 30 minutes or till hot and bubbly.

Emily Harrison

Onion Casserole

"Serve with roast beef."

Serves 3-4

½ cup almonds
½ cup corn flake crumbs
4 cups onions, sliced
1 can mushroom soup, undiluted
½ stick melted butter

Mix onions, almonds and mushroom soup. Place in a greased casserole dish. Sprinkle with corn flakes mixed with butter. Bake at 350 degrees for 1 hour.

Isabell Orgain

▲ To decrease fat content, use lowfat mushroom soup and lowfat margarine.

Cream Cheese Potatoes

"Serve with anything."

Serves 6-8

6 large potatoes
1 8-ounce package cream cheese
1 tablespoon chives
1 cup milk
1 teaspoon onion, minced
½ teaspoon salt
Paprika

Dice and cook potatoes until tender, drain. Warm cream cheese and milk to soften cream cheese. Add other ingredients and pour over potatoes that have been placed in a 2-quart casserole dish. Sprinkle with paprika. Bake at 350 degrees for 30 minutes.

Beverly Hudson

▲ To decrease fat content, use lowfat cream cheese and lowfat/skim milk.

Party Potatoes

"Use when you want to be a little more fancy than usual."

Serves 8

8 to 10 medium potatoes, peeled and quartered
2 3-ounce packages cream cheese, softened to room temperature
1 cup sour cream
¼ cup half and half (may substitute milk)
½ teaspoon garlic salt, or to taste
4 tablespoons butter, melted
Paprika

Cook potatoes in water for 30 minutes or until tender, drain well. In a bowl, mash potatoes; add cream cheese, sour cream, half and half and garlic salt, beating (at medium speed) until smooth. Spoon into a greased 2-quart casserole. Drizzle butter over potatoes and sprinkle lightly with paprika. Bake, uncovered, in a moderate oven (350 degrees) for 30 minutes.

Jean M. Clay

▲ To decrease fat content, use lowfat cream cheese, skim milk for half and half, lowfat margarine, and replace sour cream with lowfat yogurt or mock sour cream.

Potato Casserole Supreme

"May be prepared ahead of time and the topping added just before baking."

Serves 10

9 medium baking potatoes
½ cup butter
⅔ cup warm milk
1½ teaspoons salt
¼ teaspoon pepper
1 cup heavy cream, whipped
1½ cups Cheddar cheese, shredded

Peel and boil potatoes until tender. Drain and beat in a large bowl with electric mixer until fluffy, adding butter, seasonings and milk. Turn into a buttered shallow casserole dish. Fold cheese into whipped cream and spread over potatoes. Bake at 350 degrees for about 25 minutes, only until golden brown.

Elnora Caroon

▲ To decrease fat content, use lowfat margarine, skim/lowfat milk, lowfat cheese, and substitute evaporated skim milk, whipped for the heavy cream.

Scalloped Potatoes

"Wonderful for dinner on a cool day."

Serves 6-8

2 pounds potatoes
12 slices bacon, cooked and crumbled
¼ cup green onion, sliced
3 tablespoons butter or margarine
3 tablespoons all-purpose flour
1½ cups milk
¼ teaspoon salt
¼ teaspoon pepper
¼ teaspoon celery seeds
4 ounces sharp Cheddar cheese, shredded (about 1 cup loosely measured)

Peel potatoes and cut into ¼-inch slices; cook in boiling water for 5 minutes. Drain well. Place potatoes in a lightly greased 10 x 6 x 2-inch baking dish; sprinkle with bacon and onion. Melt butter in a heavy saucepan over low heat; add flour, stirring until smooth. Cook 1 minute, stirring constantly. Gradually add milk and cook over medium heat, stirring constantly, till thickened and bubbly. Stir in salt, pepper, celery seeds and remove from heat. Add cheese, stirring until cheese melts. Pour this sauce over potatoes. Cover and bake at 350 degrees for 30 minutes.

Brenda Dennis

Hash Brown Casserole

"Easy to prepare. Great with hamburgers, etc."

Serves 8

32 ounces frozen hash brown potatoes
1 can cream of potato soup
1 can Cheddar cheese soup
1 stick margarine
2 soup cans of milk

Partially thaw hash browns. In a large dish, combine potatoes and 2 soups. Add milk, margarine, and salt and pepper to taste. Cook at 325 degrees for about 1 hour.

Dora Poythress

Festive Sweet Potatoes

"Easy to double for large group. Coconut and pecans are optional in topping."

Serves 6

3 cups sweet potatoes, cooked and mashed
½ cup sugar
¼ cup milk
⅓ cup margarine, melted
1 teaspoon vanilla
2 eggs, beaten
1 cup flaked coconut
1 cup firmly packed brown sugar
⅓ cup flour
⅓ cup margarine, melted
1 cup pecans, chopped

Combine first 6 ingredients, mixing well. Spoon into a lightly greased 8-inch square baking dish. Combine coconut, brown sugar, ⅓ cup flour and ⅓ cup margarine; add pecans and sprinkle over top of sweet potatoes. Bake about 25 minutes or until golden brown.

Ann R. Long

Can be made the day before and refrigerated. Can be cooked in microwave for about 5 minutes.

Rice Au Jambon

"This could also be used as a main dish, just increase the ham to 2 cups."

Serves 8

¼ cup butter or margarine
1 cup cooked ham, cut into ¼-inch cubes
¾ cup minced onion
2 cups uncooked regular rice
4 cups chicken broth

In large saucepan, melt butter and sauté onion until tender. Add ham and rice and sauté a few minutes longer, stirring. Add chicken broth, heat to boiling. Simmer, covered, for 20 minutes or until broth is absorbed by rice and rice is tender. Pour into freezer-proof and oven-proof dish. Cover; seal and freeze.

On day of serving: Remove dish from freezer and thaw about 4 hours. To serve, preheat oven to 350 degrees. Heat, covered, 30 minutes. Fluff rice with a fork. Very good to make ahead for a dinner party.

Cherrill Robertson

▲ To decrease fat content, use lowfat turkey ham.

Spanish Rice

"A nice variation when serving rice."

Serves 6-8

1 cup raw rice (not the instant variety)
½ onion, chopped
1 large can tomatoes
2 or 3 slices bacon
½ green pepper, chopped
1 teaspoon sugar
Salt to taste

Cook rice in boiling, salted water until tender. Cook bacon until crisp. Remove from pan. Sauté onion and green pepper in some of the bacon drippings. Add tomatoes, salt and sugar. Mix all this with rice, add crumbled bacon. Bake in a greased casserole dish, uncovered, at 350 degrees until fairly dry.

Dale Tynes

Spinach Soufflé

"Fast and easy to prepare."

Serves 6-8

2 packages frozen, chopped spinach
1 stick butter or margarine
3 3-ounce packages cream cheese with chives
1 cup herbed stuffing mix

Cook spinach. Mash cream cheese and ½ stick melted butter. Add spinach and put in a greased casserole. Topping is 1 cup crumbs and ½ stick melted butter. Cook at 350 degrees for 20 minutes.

Beth Parker

▲ To decrease fat content, use lowfat margarine and lowfat cream cheese.

Cheesy Broccoli-Spinach Casserole

"The water chestnuts add a crunchy surprise."

Serves 12

2 10-ounce packages frozen chopped broccoli
1 10-ounce package frozen chopped spinach
2 large eggs, beaten
½ cup chopped onion
⅔ cup mayonnaise or salad dressing
1 can cream of mushroom soup or cream of chicken or celery
1 6-ounce can sliced water chestnuts
8 ounces sharp Cheddar cheese, grated

Cook broccoli and spinach separately. Drain well and set aside. Mix together the remaining ingredients, add vegetables. Mix well. Pour into a casserole dish and bake at 350 degrees for 35 to 40 minutes. Let set for 5 minutes prior to serving.

Gladys Wood

▲ To reduce fat, use lowfat/fat-free mayonnaise or salad dressing, lowfat cheese, lowfat soup, and an egg substitute.

Stuffed Squash - Yellow or Zucchini

Instead of white sauce, top with one slice of Mozzarella cheese."

Serves 6-8

2 pounds squash
White sauce

Stuffing
1 tablespoon butter or margarine
1 tablespoon garlic, minced
2 small onions, chopped
½ green pepper, chopped
Seeds of squash if tender (otherwise discard)
1 4½-ounce can deviled ham
2 slices bread dipped in milk
2 eggs, beaten
Parmesan cheese, grated
Grated nutmeg
Salt and pepper

Cook squash in salted water until tender. Drain. Cut lengthwise and scoop out seeds. Make a white sauce and set aside. Make stuffing as follows: Melt butter and cook onions, garlic, green pepper and seeds for a few minutes. Add bread, eggs, ham, cheese, salt, pepper, nutmeg to taste. Stuff squash with mixture. Put in greased casserole. Pour white sauce over stuffed squash and top with Parmesan cheese. Broil until golden brown.

Aida Lipton

▲ To lower fat content, use lowfat deviled ham and an egg substitute.

Squash Casserole

"Freezes well."

Serves 12

2 pounds squash
1 8-ounce carton sour cream
1 can cream of chicken soup
1 can water chestnuts, thinly sliced
1 small jar pimento, diced
1 cup onion, chopped
1 stick margarine, melted
1 small package herb seasoned dressing

Slice and cook squash in salted water, drain thoroughly. Mix together: sour cream, chopped onion, chicken soup, water chestnuts and pimento. Add squash to this mixture. Add melted margarine to herb seasoned dressing; line casserole (9 x 13 inches) with a layer of dressing, add squash mixture, sprinkle rest of dressing mix on top. Bake at 350 degrees for 30 minutes.

Ann R. Long

▲ To decrease fat content, use lowfat soup, lowfat margarine, and replace sour cream with lowfat yogurt or mock sour cream.

Cheese and Squash Casserole

"A nice way to prepare fresh squash."

Serves 6-8

3 pounds squash
2 medium onions, chopped
1 package ranch buttermilk dressing mix
2 eggs, beaten
1 cup sharp Cheddar cheese, grated
1 cup mayonnaise or ½ cup mayonnaise
   plus ½ cup sour cream
12 crumbled saltine crackers

Cook sliced squash and onions in boiling
water until tender. Drain well. Combine all
ingredients (except crumbs); put in casserole
and sprinkle with crumbs dotted with butter.
Bake at 325 degrees until hot.

Louise Frazier

▲ To decrease fat content, use lowfat cheese,
lowfat/no-fat mayonnaise, an egg substitute,
and replace sour cream with lowfat yogurt or
mock sour cream.

Potluck Vegetables

"Take to a 'potluck' party."

Serves 8-10

1 17-ounce can whole kernel corn
1 10-ounce package frozen cauliflower,
   cooked
1 10-ounce package frozen broccoli,
   cooked
1 4-ounce can sliced mushrooms
1 17-ounce can cream corn
2 cups Swiss cheese, shredded
1 can cream of celery soup
2 tablespoons margarine
½ cup bread crumbs

Drain corn, cooked vegetables and mushrooms. Combine cream corn, cheese and soup
and fold into drained vegetables. Sprinkle
bread crumbs tossed in melted butter over
mixture. Bake at 375 degrees for 35 minutes.

Marion Barkley

▲ To decrease fat content, use lowfat cheese
and lowfat soup.

Swiss Vegetable Bake

"So easy to make."

Serves 6

1 16-ounce bag frozen broccoli, carrots
   and cauliflower combination, thawed
   and drained
1 10¾-ounce can condensed cream of
   mushroom soup
1 cup (4 ounces) Swiss cheese, shredded
⅓ cup sour cream
¼ teaspoon ground black pepper
1 2.8-ounce can French fried onions

Preheat oven to 350 degrees. Combine vegetables, soup, ½ cup of the cheese, sour
cream, pepper, and ½ can of French fried
onions. Pour into a 1-quart casserole. Bake,
covered, 30 minutes. Top with remaining
cheese and onions; bake, uncovered, 5
minutes longer.

Emily Peace

Vegetable Medley

"Pretty on a buffet table."

Serves 12

1 head of broccoli, cut into bite-size pieces
1 head of cauliflower, cut into bite-size
  pieces
1 pound package carrots, cook till tender
  but not soft
1 large onion, sliced

Cover overnight with the following marinade:

1 cup vinegar
½ cup oil
1 tablespoon garlic powder
1 tablespoon dill seed
1½ tablespoons sugar
1 tablespoon seasoned salt flavor
  enhancer
Salt and pepper to taste

Dorothy Thomas

Apple Onion Casserole

"Good with roast pork or chicken."

Serves 4 to 6

3 to 4 apples, peeled and sliced as for a pie
2 tablespoons brown sugar
2 to 3 large onions, sliced
½ teaspoon salt
¼ teaspoon pepper
2 tablespoons butter
1 to 2 tablespoons water

Layer apples, sugar, onions, salt and pepper in
casserole dish. Repeat, ending with apples.
Dot with butter. Add water. Cover and bake at
375 degrees for 1 hour.

Kay Outten

Spiced Apples

"Delicious with fried seafood or ham."

Serves 6 to 8

8 large cooking apples, cored
Syrup
2 cups water
1 cup sugar
2 teaspoons cinnamon
1 tablespoon butter
Red food coloring

Boil apples in enough water to cover for 5
minutes. Drain and place in large pot. Combine 2 cups water and remaining ingredients in
saucepan with enough food coloring to make
syrup bright red. Bring to a boil, then pour
syrup over apples. Boil until just tender,
turning apples every few minutes. Let apples
sit in syrup until cool.

Ella Berry

Baked Apple and Carrot Casserole

"Nice accompaniment to pork roast."

Serves 5

5 apples, thinly sliced
2 cups sliced cooked carrots
6 tablespoons sugar
2 tablespoons flour
Salt to taste
¾ cup orange juice

Place half the apple slices in a baking dish and
cover with half the carrots. Mix the sugar, flour
and salt and sprinkle half the mixture over the
carrots. Repeat layers and pour the orange
juice over top. Bake at 350 degrees for 20 to
30 minutes.

Justine Jones

Baked Apples

"Baked apples, sweet potatoes and ham - a sure hit!"

Serves 4 to 6

6 apples, pared and quartered
⅔ cup sugar
½ cup margarine, diced
Cinnamon

Place apples in casserole dish. Add sugar, margarine and sprinkle generously with cinnamon. Cover and cook at 400 degrees approximately 45 minutes or until apples are tender.

Anne Walker

▲ To decrease fat content, use lowfat margarine.

Cranberry Casserole

"Wonderful holiday accompaniment to turkey or ham."

Serves 6

3 cups apples, unpeeled and diced
1 can of whole cranberry sauce
½ cup white sugar
½ cup brown sugar

Topping
½ cup butter or margarine, melted
1½ cups quick cooking oats
⅓ cup flour
½ cup or more broken nuts

Mix apples, cranberry sauce, white sugar and brown sugar well. Pour into a greased flat casserole. Mix topping and sprinkle over top. Bake at 325 degrees for 1 hour or until brown.

Virginia Taylor

Pineapple Casserole

"Great with ham."

Serves 4 to 6

2 15-ounce cans pineapple tidbits, drained
¾ cup sugar
3 tablespoons flour
1 cup Cheddar cheese, shredded
1 tube round buttery crackers
½ stick margarine

Mix first 4 ingredients together and put into a 7 x 9-inch casserole. Crush 1 tube of crackers and sprinkle over top. Melt ½ stick margarine and pour over. Bake at 350 degrees for 20 to 25 minutes.

Isabelle Orgain

▲ To decrease fat content, use lowfat cheese, lowfat margarine, and saltines instead of buttery crackers.

"It seems that a good meal is enhanced by enjoying it in open spaces. Community stews, church picnics, neighborhood barbeques and other settings have provided opportunities for folks to share food and fellowship outside. We often eat outside when the weather permits. The atmosphere surpasses that of the finest restaurants. In this painting, a table is set for breakfast with grainfields and barns in view."

Eldridge Bagley

"BACKYARD BREAKFAST"
Appears through the courtesy of the painting's owner, Mary Graybeal.

Apple Nut Bread

*"Makes great muffins or small loaves for gifts -
remember to adjust baking time."*

Yields 1 loaf

2 cups flour
½ teaspoon salt
½ teaspoon soda
1 teaspoon baking powder
⅓ cup shortening
½ cup sugar
½ cup brown sugar
1 egg
½ cup nuts, chopped
½ cup raisins
1 tablespoon grated orange rind
Juice of 1 orange
1 cup raw apple, chopped

Sift flour. Add salt, soda and baking powder.
Sift together and set aside. Cream shortening
and sugar together. Add egg and beat thoroughly. Add flour mixture and orange juice to
egg mixture, blend well. Add raisins, nuts,
apple and orange rind. Pour batter into a
greased and floured 9 x 5 x 3-inch loaf pan.
Bake at 400 degrees for 45 minutes or until
done.

Pearl Burge

Banana Bread

"Especially delicious buttered and toasted."

Yields 4 mini loaves or 2 big loaves

2½ cups sugar
1 cup shortening
4 eggs
4 cups flour
1 teaspoon salt
1 teaspoon soda
1 teaspoon baking powder
½ cup sour cream
2 teaspoons vanilla
4 to 5 bananas, mashed

Cream shortening and sugar well. Beat in eggs.
Add dry ingredients (which have been stirred
together) alternately with sour cream. Stir in
bananas and vanilla and pour into greased
pans. Bake at 325 degrees for 50 minutes, less
for mini loaves.

Belle Blount

Banana Nut Bread

"Good with cream cheese filling or peanut butter."

Yields 2 loaves

3 ripe bananas
2 eggs
½ cup nuts
Pinch of salt
2 cups flour
½ cup butter
1 teaspoon soda
1 cup sugar

Cream butter and sugar; add mashed bananas,
beaten eggs and flour which has been mixed
with soda and salt. Stir in nuts and pour batter
into 2 well-greased small loaf pans. Bake in a
moderate oven for 50 minutes or until bread
tests done. Cool on rack before slicing.

Mildred Rawlings

Cream Cheese Braids

"These are so good that they should be served only on special occasions."

Yields 4 loaves

Dough
1 8-ounce carton sour cream
½ cup sugar
1 teaspoon salt
½ cup melted butter or margarine
2 packages dry yeast
½ cup warm water
2 eggs, beaten
4 cups all-purpose flour

Cream Cheese Filling
2 8-ounce packages cream cheese
¾ cup sugar
1 egg, beaten
⅛ teaspoon salt
2 teaspoons vanilla extract

Glaze
2 cups powdered sugar
4 tablespoons milk
2 teaspoons vanilla extract

Heat sour cream over low heat; stir in sugar, salt and butter; cool to lukewarm. Sprinkle yeast over warm water in a large mixing bowl, stirring until yeast dissolves. Add sour cream mixture, eggs, and flour, mix well. Cover tightly; refrigerate overnight.

Next day make filling by combining cream cheese and sugar in a small mixing bowl. Add egg, salt, and vanilla, mix well.

Divide dough into 4 equal parts; roll out each part on a well-floured board into a 12 x 8-inch rectangle. Spread ¼ of Cream Cheese Filling on each. Roll up jellyroll fashion, beginning at long sides. Pinch sides together and fold ends under slightly. Place rolls, seam side down, on greased baking sheets. Slit each roll at 2-inch intervals about ⅔ of the way through the dough. Cover and let rise in warm place about 1 hour. Bake in 375 degree oven for 15 minutes. Combine ingredients for glaze, spread on braids while still warm.

Beverly Shearon

*Cakes and confectioneries from **Becky's Bake Shop** are in demand throughout the county.*

Carrot Bread

"Spicy, nutty and delicious."

Yields 1 loaf

⅔ cup oil
1 cup sugar
1½ cups flour
½ teaspoon vanilla
1 teaspoon soda
2 eggs
1 cup carrots, grated and packed
½ cup nuts
½ teaspoon salt
1 teaspoon cinnamon

Beat eggs; add sugar and oil. Mix and fold in dry ingredients; add grated carrots. Bake 1 hour at 350 degrees.

Sara Nabors

English Tea Time Lemon Bread

"Can use 2 small loaf pans."

Yields 1 loaf

1 cup sugar
¼ cup butter
1 tablespoon lemon rind
2 eggs
1½ cups flour
½ teaspoon salt
1 teaspoon baking powder
½ cup milk
½ cup nuts, chopped

Cream sugar and butter together. Add lemon rind. Beat in eggs. Add sifted dry ingredients, alternating with milk. Stir in nuts. Pour into greased 9 x 5 x 3-inch loaf pans. Bake at 325 degrees for 35 to 45 minutes. This loaf is difficult to remove from pan. Line bottom and sides with waxed paper, leaving paper hanging over sides for pulling.

Glaze
¼ cup sugar
Juice of 1 lemon

Mix sugar and lemon juice together and let come to a boil, stirring until dissolved. Pour over hot bread. Cool in pan before removing.

Edith Buford

Mother Sawyer's Oatmeal Bread

"Excellent as toast when stale."

Yields 2 large loaves or 4 small loaves

1 cup quick cooking oats
2 cups boiling water
½ cup molasses
1 tablespoon salt
2 tablespoons corn oil
1 package dry yeast
½ cup lukewarm water
5 cups (or less) flour

Place oats in a large bowl and cover with boiling water. When this is lukewarm, stir in yeast that has been soaking in lukewarm water. Add molasses, salt and corn oil. Add flour, but stay on short side of 5 cups if hard to beat in. Cover with towel and let rise in warm place until doubled. Stir down and pour into pans generously greased with corn oil (not butter). Let rise in pans until doubled. Bake in a preheated 400 degree oven turned down to 350 degrees when bread is put in. Bake 40 minutes for smaller loaves, longer for larger ones. Cool in pans for 10 minutes, then on racks.

Susan Green

Pumpkin Bread

"Serve with cream cheese."

Yields 7 to 8 loaves

1 cup oil
2 cups sugar
½ cup brown sugar
3½ cups flour
2 teaspoons baking soda
½ teaspoon salt
½ teaspoon cloves
½ teaspoon nutmeg
½ teaspoon baking powder
1 can pumpkin (2 cups)
1 cup nuts, chopped
½ to 1 cup dates, chopped

Combine and mix well, the oil and sugars. Sift together the dry ingredients and add to the oil mixture. Add the pumpkin, nuts and dates. Put in greased cans to bake. Will need 7 or 8 the size of pumpkin can. Fill cans ⅔ full. Bake at 300 degrees for 1 hour. Can be wrapped in waxed paper, then foil, then frozen. Slice thin.

Susan Slayton

Orange Bread

"Very light bread and very good as is but may drizzle with sugar icing, if desired."

Yields 2 loaves

2 packages dry yeast
1 cup warm water (105 to 115 degrees)
¼ cup margarine, softened
½ cup sugar
1½ teaspoons salt
1 egg (room temperature)
⅔ cup orange juice (2 small oranges at room temperature)
3 tablespoons orange rind, grated
5¼ cups unsifted flour, save some for kneading

Dissolve yeast in warm water in large warm bowl. Mix in margarine, sugar, salt, egg, orange juice, rind and 2 cups flour. Beat above mixture until smooth. Stir in flour to make soft dough. Knead about 8 to 10 minutes until smooth and elastic. Place in greased bowl and let double in size. Punch down. Divide dough in half, shape into loaves (makes 2 loaves) and bake in greased loaf pans. Cover and let double in size. Bake at 400 degrees for 30 to 35 minutes. If browns too quickly, cover with foil and finish baking. Cool on wire racks.

Icing
1½ cups confectioner's sugar
2 tablespoons milk
½ teaspoon lemon or vanilla extract

Combine and drizzle over warm loaf.

Susan Green and Susan Slayton

Sweet Potato Biscuits

"Stuff with sliced ham or just butter."

Yield 20 small biscuits

1 cup all-purpose flour
3 teaspoons baking powder
½ teaspoon salt
⅓ cup margarine
1 cup mashed, cooked sweet potatoes
3 tablespoons milk, more if needed to make dough

Combine first 3 ingredients. Cut in margarine with two knives or pastry blender. Add potatoes and enough milk to make soft dough. Knead lightly. Roll dough to ½-inch thickness, cut into rounds and place on baking sheet. Bake at 425 degrees for 15 to 20 minutes.

Beth Parker

Angel Biscuits

"Bake ahead of time and freeze, warming in 300 degree oven when ready to serve."

Yields 4 dozen

1 package dry yeast
2 tablespoons lukewarm water
5 cups all-purpose flour
1 teaspoon soda
3 teaspoons baking powder
1 teaspoon salt
¼ cup sugar
1 cup shortening
2 cups buttermilk

Dissolve yeast in warm water. Sift dry ingredients together. Cut in shortening as for regular biscuits. Mix dissolved yeast with buttermilk and add all at once to flour mixture. Stir to form a ball. Knead well and roll to about ¼-inch thickness. Cut, place on ungreased baking sheet and bake in a 375 to 400 degree oven for about 15 minutes or till golden brown. It's not necessary to let dough rise. Dough will keep in refrigerator up to 3 days.

Lorraine Freeman

Sherwood Manor Sweet Potato Angel Biscuits

"Guests at Sherwood Manor love these biscuits."

Yields 7 dozen

3 cups mashed sweet potatoes, warm
3 packages active dry yeast
¾ cup warm water
7½ cups all-purpose flour
1¼ cups sugar
1 tablespoon baking powder
1 tablespoon salt
1½ cups shortening

Combine yeast and warm water in a 2-cup measuring cup. Let stand 5 minutes. Combine flour and next 3 ingredients in a large bowl. Cut in shortening with a pastry blender or fork until mixture is crumbly. Add yeast mixture and warm sweet potatoes, stirring until dry ingredients are moistened. Turn dough out onto a lightly floured surface, knead 5 minutes. Place dough in a lightly greased bowl, turning to grease top. Cover and refrigerate for 8 hours or overnight.

Roll dough out to ½-inch thickness, cut with a cutter. Place on ungreased baking sheet, cover and let rise in a warm place for 20 minutes or until double in bulk. Bake at 400 degrees for 10 to 12 minutes or until lightly browned.

Pat Temple

Buttermilk Cheese Biscuits

"Brush tops with buttermilk and top with cheese."

Yields 16 biscuits

1 tablespoon baking powder
2 cups sifted flour
½ teaspoon salt
¼ teaspoon baking soda
6 tablespoons margarine (or butter)
1 cup buttermilk
1 cup shredded Cheddar cheese
Buttermilk for topping

Sift flour, baking powder, salt and soda together. Cut in butter until mixture is mealy. Stir in buttermilk (with fork) to form a dough. Knead gently on lightly floured surface. Roll and cut in strips or 2-inch rounds. Place on ungreased baking sheet. Brush tops with buttermilk. Sprinkle on cheese. Bake at 450 degrees for 12 to 15 minutes.

Mrs. H. Wilbur Hayes

Virginia Beaten Biscuits

"Plenty of elbow grease is required, whether you do the beating with a mallet and block or with a biscuit 'break' or machine. The latter is much like a clothes wringer. It saves a good deal of labor involved in the original thump-thump method done on a stump or block in the 'old kitchen'. Beaten biscuits by either method is not as hard as it sounds and we speak from experience.... I had beaten biscuits for every main meal during my childhood. It's fascinating to watch the dough grown satiny smooth, and hear the blisters pop and crackle at you!"

Yields 40 biscuits

**1 quart home ground flour, measured
    before sifting***
1 teaspoon salt
¼ pound lard
1 cup cold milk
1 teaspoon baking powder*

After sifting flour, sift and mix in salt and baking powder. Mix in lard with fingers. Make a well in the middle and add ½ the milk. Mix. Add the remaining milk cautiously...enough to make a stiff dough. Let the ball of dough rest in a covered bowl for 15 minutes. Beat with a mallet and block or beaten biscuit roller for 20 to 30 minutes or until the dough is "slick and glossy and full of blisters that pop noisily". It will take 30 minutes to beat them by hand. "200 for home folks and 500 for company." Roll out ¼- to ½-inch thick, cut and prick 3 times with a fork. The pricks should go all the way to the bottom of the biscuit. Bake about 25 minutes in a 400 degree oven.

*Compiled by Mrs. J.B. Barkley for
The Brunswick Times Gazette many years ago.*

*Mrs. Lacy Virginia Harrison, Mrs. Barkley's daughter states she uses unbleached flour when home ground is not available. The addition of baking powder is a newer variation. "One of my mother's hints was to be sure you lifted the dough after rolling before you cut the biscuits."

Buttermilk Biscuits

"Biscuits are much better if the dough is made in advance and allowed to chill thoroughly in refrigerator."

Yields 24 biscuits

2 cups all-purpose flour
1 teaspoon salt
6 tablespoons shortening
2 rounded teaspoons baking powder
¼ teaspoon baking soda
⅔ to ¾ cup buttermilk

Mix dry ingredients. Cut shortening in finely with fork or pastry blender. Stir in buttermilk to make soft dough. Knead lightly on floured surface to round up the dough. Handle as little as possible. Roll dough to desired thickness. Cut with floured biscuit cutter. Bake 10 to 12 minutes at 450 degrees.

Wrap in foil or plastic bag.

Evelyn Black

Beer Muffins

"Fast and easy to make."

Yields 12 to 18 muffins

4 cups biscuit baking mix
1 can beer
4 tablespoons sugar

Mix all ingredients in a bowl until just moist. Grease muffin tins (2 large - 6 each or 3 small - 6 each). Fill ½ to ⅔ full. Bake at 400 degrees about 15 minutes. Leftovers may be frozen.

Nell Catherwood

Raisin Nut Bran Muffins

"A great gift for neighbors and friends."

Yields 48 muffins

1 15-ounce box bran cereal with raisins
5 cups sifted flour
3 cups sugar
2 teaspoons baking soda
2 teaspoons salt
4 eggs, beaten
4 cups buttermilk
1 cup cooking oil
2 cups English walnuts, chopped
  (optional)

In a large bowl, combine the first 5 ingredients, mixing well. Combine eggs, buttermilk and oil; add all at once to the dry ingredients, mixing just until dry ingredients are moistened. Fold in nuts, if desired. Store batter, covered, in a airtight container in the refrigerator for up to 6 weeks. To bake, fill greased muffin pans (2¾ inches in diameter) ⅔ full. Bake in a hot oven (400 degrees) for 15 to 20 minutes or until done and lightly browned.

June Clary

Corn Muffins

"Great to serve with beef stew or seafood."

Yields 12 muffins

1 cup sifted flour
¾ cup yellow or white cornmeal
2½ teaspoons baking powder
½ teaspoon salt
2 tablespoons sugar
1 egg
1 cup skim milk
¼ cup vegetable oil or melted shortening

Preheat oven to 400 to 425 degrees. Sift the flour, cornmeal, salt and baking powder and sugar together into a mixing bowl. Add eggs, milk and oil or melted shortening. Stir lightly until mixed. Do not beat. Dip batter into greased muffin tins, using a metal tablespoon dipped in water. Fill each cup ⅔ full. Bake 20 to 30 minutes or until golden brown.

Betty Fisher

Pocket Bread

"Keep wrapped in foil until cool."

Yields 6

1 package dry yeast
¼ teaspoon brown sugar
1⅓ cups lukewarm water
3 cups flour
1 cup whole wheat flour
1 teaspoon salt
3 tablespoons oil
Cornmeal

Combine yeast and sugar in a bowl and stir in ⅓ cup water. Let sit until yeast proofs. Combine flours and salt in a bowl. Add yeast and sugar, remaining water and oil to flour and mix well. Turn out dough on a floured board and knead until elastic and smooth. Set in a warm place until dough is doubled in bulk. Punch down dough and form into 6 balls. Set on bread board and cover. Let rise 40 minutes, then roll each ball with a rolling pin into a flat 6-inch circle. Dust baking sheets with cornmeal and lay circles on cornmeal, turning once. Let rise 30 minutes while heating oven to 475 degrees.

Bake on lower rack for 6 to 8 minutes or until puffed and brown. Wrap each bread separately in foil immediately out of oven. (This makes air pockets.)

Patricia Samford

Jumbo Popovers

"Remember to make a small slit in each popover to release steam."

Yields 1 dozen

2 cups flour
2 cups milk
6 eggs
1 teaspoon salt
¼ cup plus 2 tablespoons butter or
** margarine, melted**

Combine all ingredients; beat at slow speed of electric mixer until batter is smooth. Fill 12 well-greased, 6-ounce custard cups with batter. Bake at 375 degrees for 50 minutes. Quickly cut a small slit in each popover to release steam; bake an additional 5 minutes. Remove popovers from custard cups and serve warm or cooled completely on wire racks.

Betsy Rawls

Southern Spoon Bread

"Wonderful with ham or pork chops."

Serves 6 to 8

1 cup cornmeal
1½ cups boiling water
1 tablespoon melted shortening
2 eggs
1 cup milk
1 tablespoon baking powder
¼ teaspoon salt

Add the boiling water to the meal and stir until well mixed. Allow to cool. When cool, add the melted shortening, well-beaten eggs, milk, salt and baking powder. Blend thoroughly and pour into a well-greased baking dish about 7 inches in diameter and 3 inches deep. Bake in a 375 degree oven for 30 minutes.

Pattie Prince Turnbull

Spoon Bread

"A favorite for breakfast, lunch or dinner."

Serves 6 to 8

2 cups cold water
1 teaspoon salt
3 well-beaten eggs
1 cup white cornmeal
1 cup milk
2 or 3 tablespoons melted shortening

Mix water, cornmeal, and salt together and boil for 5 minutes, stirring constantly. Stir in milk, eggs and lastly the melted shortening. Mix well and pour into a heated, well-greased casserole dish. Bake in a 400 degree oven for 50 minutes or until top is firm and brown.

Ann Peebles

Corn Spoon Bread

"Serve with plenty of butter."

Serves 5 to 6

1 7-ounce can cream style corn
¾ cup cornmeal
¾ teaspoon salt
1½ cups milk, scalded
2 tablespoons butter or margarine
¾ teaspoon baking powder
3 eggs, separated

Stir cornmeal and salt into the hot milk over medium heat. Beat hard until it is the consistency of thick mush. Blend in butter, corn and then baking powder. Beat egg yolks well and beat into the corn mixture. Beat egg whites until stiff, but not dry, and fold in gently. Pour mixture into a well-buttered medium casserole dish and bake in a 375 degree oven for 35 minutes or until puffy and firm in the center.

Delma Patsell

Corn Bread

"Some folks who use this recipe cut back on the butter to ½ stick."

Serves 8

1 heaping cup cornmeal
¼ teaspoon salt
1 beaten egg
1 stick butter or margarine
2 teaspoons baking powder
1 tablespoon sugar
1¼ cups milk

Mix dry ingredients. Add milk and beaten egg. Melt butter in baking dish or iron skillet. Pour half of butter in cornmeal mixture and mix well. Pour mixture in container and bake at 475 degrees for about 20 minutes.

Sara Bishop

Angel Corn Sticks

"Makes a very light corn stick."

Yields 3 dozen

1½ cups cornmeal
1 cup all-purpose flour
1 package dry yeast
1 tablespoon sugar
1 teaspoon salt
1½ teaspoons baking powder
½ teaspoon baking soda
2 eggs, beaten
2 cups buttermilk
½ cup vegetable oil

Combine first 7 ingredients in a large bowl. Combine eggs, beaten; buttermilk and oil. Add to dry ingredients, stirring until smooth. Spoon batter into well-greased cast iron corn stick pans, filling half full. Bake at 450 degrees for 12 to 15 minutes.

Nita Lane Fleshood

Low Cholesterol Rolls

"Health conscious - just the rolls for you!"

Yields 3 dozen

1 package dry yeast
¼ cup warm water
2 egg whites, lightly beaten
½ cup corn oil
1 teaspoon salt
¼ cup sugar
1 cup warm water
4 cups all-purpose flour

Dissolve yeast in ¼ cup warm water. Combine egg whites and oil in a large bowl. Add yeast mixture. Stir in salt and sugar. Add warm water. Add flour and mix until smooth, adding a small amount of flour if dough is too soft. Chill dough at least 12 hours. Make into rolls and place in a greased baking pan. Let rise for 2 hours. Bake in a 400 degree oven until lightly browned.

Virginia Elmore

*Everyone turned out for the dedication of the **Bryan School**, named for William Jennings Bryan, that opened in 1901.*

Rolls

"Rolls freeze well when buttered or keep well in refrigerator for several days."

Yields 3 dozen

3 rounded tablespoons sugar
¾ cup shortening
1½ cups hot water
4 full cups flour (slightly rounded)
1 tablespoon salt
½ cup warm water
1 large egg

Put sugar, shortening and hot water in large mixing bowl. Set aside to allow shortening to soften. Meanwhile measure the flour and salt and sift together. Put yeast in ½ cup warm water to dissolve. Beat egg in small bowl until very light. Add egg to the softened shortening mixture, then yeast and half of the flour. Beat hard. Gradually add balance of flour. Dough should be soft, but not sticky, may add more flour. Store in covered bowl in refrigerator until ready to make.

When ready to make rolls, turn dough onto a lightly floured surface and knead a few strokes. To shape into turnovers, grease hands, pinch off small amount of dough and roll into ball the size of a walnut. Flatten ball with the palm of hand on a lightly floured surface, fold flattened round into turnover, pinch edges lightly. Put rolls on a greased cookie sheet, cover and let rise in a warm place.

Bake at 400 degrees until rolls begin to brown. Brush with melted shortening, continue baking until brown.

Edith Buford

Madison Rolls

"This recipe was used by my mother for many years."

Yields 4 dozen

1 medium white potato
1 cup potato water
1 package dry yeast
¼ cup warm water to dissolve yeast
⅓ cup sugar
Pinch of ginger (optional)
¼ cup butter or margarine
2 teaspoons salt
2 eggs, well-beaten
5 or 6 cups flour, sifted

Cook potato (reserve 1 cup water from cooking potato). Dissolve yeast in ¼ cup of warm water. Mash hot potato adding butter, salt and sugar. When the potato water is lukewarm add the dissolved yeast, pinch of ginger (optional) and ½ teaspoon of sugar to the potato water. When the potato mixture is lukewarm add the yeast mixture and the beaten eggs all together. Using mixer on low add 2 cups flour slowly. Then turn on floured board and knead in more flour. When dough is satiny put in a greased bowl and turn over once so that top of dough is also greased. Cover with a damp towel. Let rise until double in size (2 hours). Roll out to ½-inch and cut with biscuit cutter, place in pan - sides not touching. Let rise until doubled in size (1 hour). Bake at 400 degrees for 15 to 20 minutes. If dough is to be refrigerated let rise once, push down, then refrigerate. When ready to use, make into rolls and let rise about 2 hours.

Van Doyle

Alta's Yeast Rolls

"This recipe doubles well, keeps well in refrigerator for several days or baked rolls are wonderful for freezing."

Yields 3 dozen

1 package dry yeast
½ cup shortening
¼ cup sugar
½ teaspoon salt
½ cup cold or warm water
1 egg, beaten
½ cup hot water
3 to 4 cups sifted flour
Melted butter or margarine

Dissolve yeast in cold or warm water. Cream shortening, salt and sugar with electric mixer. Pour hot water over mixture. Set aside to cool to lukewarm (105 to 115 degrees). Add dissolved yeast and egg to mixture; mix well; add 1 to 2 cups flour and beat with mixer until bubbly. Add remaining flour until you can handle the dough as for biscuits. Shape into ball, place in greased bowl; then turn once. Cover; let rise in a warm place until double in bulk (about 1 hour in oven with light on). Punch down. At this time the dough can be stored covered in the refrigerator or made into shapes desired. For Parker House rolls, on a slightly floured surface roll out dough to ¼-inch thickness, cut with round cutter, make an off-center crease in each round with the back of the knife. Brush with melted butter, fold so large half overlaps slightly; slightly press edges together. Place on lightly greased baking sheet (large half up). Bake at 425 degrees for 10 to 12 minutes. When rolls begin to brown, brush with melted butter, continue baking.

Alta Brown

Sally Lunn

"A Southern Favorite."

Many years ago in the 18th century, a young girl used to go up and down the streets of Bath, England, selling hot crusty rolls. With a basket full of the tasty buns, she would call out, "Sol et Lun" over and over again. These were the French words for "Sun and Moon." She spoke in French since Bath was the most fashionable health spa in all of England.
The buns were golden on top and had pale bottoms, so this may be why she called them sun and moon. When the English colonists settled in North Carolina and Virginia over 200 years ago, they brought the recipe for these buns with them. But they called this warm crumbly bread "Sally Lunn" which sounds like "Sol et Lun" and baked it in a fancy mold instead of in individual cakes. It's even listed in Webster's dictionary as "a slightly sweetened, yeast-raised tea bread."
With the Sally Lunn, it's nice to serve a fruit salad. When fresh fruit is in season, that's what tastes best. But at other times, canned or frozen fruit will do.

Yields 1 tube pan or 18 muffins

1 package dry yeast
1 cup warm milk
3 tablespoons shortening
3 tablespoons sugar
2 eggs
3½ cups flour
1½ teaspoons salt

Pour warm milk over yeast. Cream shortening and sugar. Add eggs and mix well. Add milk and yeast. Sift flour and salt together and add to mixture. It is important that this is well beaten.

Cover and let rise until double. Beat again and put into a greased tube pan or 18 muffin tins. Let rise until double. Bake in a preheated oven. If using a tube pan bake at 300 degrees for 1 hour. For muffin tins bake at 350 degrees until muffins are done.

"Snooze" Barkley

Icebox Rolls

"Brush tops with melted shortening after they begin to brown."

Yields 3 dozen

1 yeast cake
½ cup warm water
1 teaspoon sugar
1 egg, beaten
3½ cups flour
1 cup milk
1 teaspoon salt
¼ cup sugar
3 tablespoons shortening

Mix yeast with ½ cup warm water and 1 teaspoon sugar. Scald milk, pour over salt, ¼ cup sugar and shortening; let cool. Add beaten egg to yeast mixture. Add 2 cups of flour and beat with mixer until bubbles form. Stir in 1½ cups flour last. Let rise in refrigerator at least 2 hours; overnight is better. On a lightly floured surface, roll out ⅜-inch thick. Cut with 2½-inch biscuit cutter. Brush lightly with melted butter or margarine. Fold over, press folded edges. Let rise until rolls double in bulk. Cook in a 400 degree oven for 10 minutes.

Emily Harrison

Yeast Rolls for Freezing

"Just the bread to serve for folks who like to entertain, but are short on time."

Yields 4 dozen

2 tablespoons sugar
6 tablespoons shortening
1 cup boiling water
1 egg, slightly beaten
1 teaspoon salt
1 package dry yeast, dissolved in ¼ cup warm water
4 cups flour
Pan of melted butter

Combine sugar, shortening and boiling water. Cool. Then add egg, salt and yeast. Beat in flour, 2 cups at a time, using slotted spoon. Turn dough out onto a floured pastry cloth and knead 4 times quickly. Roll out and cut rolls using a round biscuit cutter. Dip rolls into melted butter and place on baking pan. Fold over into Parker House rolls. The faster you work at this stage, the lighter the rolls. Put the entire pan uncovered into freezer just until dough is frozen. Remove from freezer. Cover lightly with foil and replace in freezer until 3 hours before serving time. Place pan in warm spot for rising. Bake at 425 degrees for about 15 minutes.

Anna Delbridge

Wheat Bread

"Very healthy bread."

Yields 4 loaves

4 cups warm water
3 packages dry yeast
⅓ cup honey
4 teaspoons salt
⅓ cup cooking oil
1¾ cups nonfat dry milk
10 cups (approximately) whole wheat flour

Stir yeast into warm water. Add honey, salt, oil, powdered milk and enough flour to reach the kneading stage. Use the rest of the flour to sprinkle on hands and board. Knead for 8 to 10 minutes. Place in a greased bowl and turn dough over. Cover and let rise in warm place until doubled in bulk. Knead lightly, divide into 4 portions, cover, let rise 10 minutes. Shape into loaves and place in 4 greased 8½-inch loaf pans. Let rise until doubled in bulk. Bake in 350 degree oven about 1 hour.

Lucy Heartwell

Swift Creek Mill Bread

"Serve at any dinner party."

Yields 1 tube pan

½ cup shortening
½ cup sugar
1½ cups water
1 teaspoon salt
1 package yeast
2 eggs, beaten
5 to 6 cups flour, enough to make soft
   batter

Heat water to simmering and pour over sugar and shortening. Add salt and stir. Let cool slightly. Add yeast, eggs, and flour. Let rise in bowl until double in size. Beat down and spoon batter into a greased tube pan. Let rise again until 1 inch from top of pan. Bake at 325 degrees for 1 hour.

Waffles

"Freeze leftovers."

Yields 4 to 5 waffles

2¼ cups flour
2½ teaspoons baking powder
½ teaspoon baking soda
1 teaspoon salt
3 eggs
2 cups buttermilk
¼ cup salad oil or melted shortening

Preheat waffle iron. Stir together dry ingredients. With an electric mixer, set on high, beat eggs till thick, about 3 minutes. Then at low speed beat in flour mixture alternately with buttermilk. Then stir in salad oil. When waffle iron is preheated, pour 1 cup batter back and forth across grid. Close and cook according to grill instructions. Serve hot with butter and syrup.

Jenny Showalter

Fly-Off-The-Plate Pancakes

"Use club soda instead of milk, you may like them even better."

Yields 8 to 10 pancakes

1 cup all-purpose flour
¼ teaspoon salt
1 tablespoon sugar
1 tablespoon baking powder
1 egg
1 cup milk
2 rounded tablespoons dairy sour cream
2 tablespoons butter, melted (at room
   temperature)

Sift dry ingredients into mixing bowl. In another bowl, mix egg, milk and sour cream; pour this into dry ingredients and beat with wire whisk to keep from lumping. Add butter and beat until smooth. If batter is too thick, add more milk until right consistency. Bake on a hot grill.

Orpha Steed

Quick Cheese Wafer

"Great with dips. Particularly good with hot crab dip."

1 loaf of bread
Melted butter or margarine
Parmesan cheese

Cut crust off bread slices and cut into triangles or cut with cookie cutters into any shape. Dip into melted butter or margarine and roll in Parmesan cheese. Bake in 250 degree oven for 40 minutes. These can be stored in a plastic bag in the freezer.

Joyce Moorman

"It only takes a brief reflection to realize how many childhood memories are associated with cakes. I especially remember the birthday cakes my mother made. A fall favorite was the applesauce cake made with the apples and walnuts gathered from trees on our farm. In addition, there were the 'no special occasion' cakes indulged in after school or while taking a break from the fields."

Eldridge Bagley

"HOME PLATE"
Appears through the courtesy of the painting's owners, Dr. and Mrs. James C. Gussett.

Fresh Apple Cake

"A wonderful moist cake!"

1 cup oil
2 cups sugar
3 eggs
3 cups plain flour
2 cups apples, chopped
1 teaspoon salt
1 teaspoon baking soda
1 teaspoon vanilla

Topping
1 stick butter
1 cup brown sugar
1 teaspoon vanilla

Mix all cake ingredients together and mix well. Bake in a greased and floured tube pan for approximately 1 hour at 350 degrees.

Mix and heat all topping ingredients until it comes to a boil (good boil). Boil about 2 or 3 minutes. Pour over hot cake.

Annie Laura Valentine

Aunt Nellie's Applesauce Cake

"This recipe has been in our family for several generations. Christmas just isn't the same without it."

4 cups applesauce
2 cups sugar
1 cup margarine
1½ boxes raisins
1 cup black walnuts
1 package figs, cut into pieces
1 teaspoon nutmeg
1 teaspoon cinnamon
2 eggs
4 cups flour
4 level teaspoons soda

Flour raisins, nuts and figs by shaking in a bag with a small amount of flour; then put in a colander and shake off excess flour; set aside. Heat applesauce until it is hot, then melt margarine in the applesauce. Allow applesauce mixture to cool. Stir in well-beaten eggs and sugar. Add flour, soda, nutmeg and cinnamon. Mix well, then add figs, nuts and raisins. Bake in a greased and floured 10 x 4-inch tube pan in a 350 degree oven for about 1½ hours. (It may be necessary to cover top of cake with loose foil to keep the top from getting too brown while the middle cooks completely.) Cake is done when knife inserted in middle comes out clean. This makes a large cake. May be baked in several loaf pans.

Joyce Moorman

Brazil Nut Cake

"Adjust cooking time according to the size pan used."

1½ cups brazil nuts (½ pound)
1 cup chopped pecans
1 6-ounce package chopped dates
1½ cups drained maraschino cherries
¾ cup flour
¾ cup sugar
½ teaspoon baking powder
½ teaspoon salt
3 eggs
1 teaspoon vanilla

Combine nuts, dates and cherries. Stir together flour, sugar, baking powder and salt. Beat eggs and vanilla until foamy; stir in flour mixture. Pour over nut mixture. Mix well. Turn into greased, papered 9 x 5 x 3-inch loaf pan or several small loaf pans (4). Bake 1 hour 30-40 minutes in 300 degree oven. Cool, wrap in cheese cloth moistened with wine.

Van Doyle

Cracker Cake

"Uneeda Biscuits are not always easy to find; you may use unsalted cracker crumbs."

2 eggs
1 teaspoon almond extract
1 cup sugar
1 teaspoon baking powder
1 cup pecans, chopped
1 cup Uneeda Biscuit crumbs

Beat eggs and almond extract together. Stir baking powder into cup of sugar, beat this into eggs and extract. Add chopped nuts and cracker crumbs. Lightly butter a medium size baking dish or a pie dish. Pour in mixture. Bake at 275 degrees for 25 minutes.

Virginia Taylor

Carrot Cake

"For a spicier taste, increase the cinnamon to 2 teaspoons. You can use just two cake pans for the layers."

3 cups carrots, grated
2 cups all-purpose flour
2 cups sugar
2 teaspoons baking soda
1 teaspoon baking powder
½ teaspoon salt
1 teaspoon ground cinnamon
4 eggs, well beaten
1¼ cups vegetable oil
1 teaspoon vanilla extract
Cream Cheese Frosting (below)

Combine first 7 ingredients; stir in eggs, oil and vanilla, mixing well. Spoon batter into 3 greased and floured 9-inch round cake pans. Bake at 350 degrees for 30 minutes or until a wooden pick inserted in center comes out clean.

Cream Cheese Frosting
1 16-ounce package powdered sugar
1 8-ounce package cream cheese, softened
½ cup butter or margarine
1 teaspoon vanilla extract
1 cup pecans, chopped

Cream first 4 ingredients together until well blended; stir in pecans. Spread frosting between layers and on top of cake while still warm.

Brenda Dennis

Chiffon Cake

"To serve, sprinkle with confectioner's sugar or frost with whipped cream."

2 cups cake flour
1½ cups sugar
1 tablespoon baking powder
1 teaspoon salt
¾ cup water
1 teaspoon vanilla extract
¼ teaspoon almond extract
½ cup salad oil
5 large egg yolks
7 large egg whites
½ teaspoon cream of tartar

Preheat oven to 325 degrees. In a large bowl, stir flour with sugar, baking powder and salt until combined. Add water, extracts, oil and egg yolks, stir just until smooth.

In a large bowl of an electric mixer, beat egg whites with cream of tartar until stiff. Gradually add batter to beaten egg whites, mixing just until combined. Pour into an ungreased 10-inch tube pan, bake 65 minutes. When cake is done, let it cool in the pan, upside down, loosen cake from side of pan with a spatula. If cake doesn't drop out of the pan easily, give it a good whack on the bottom. It won't hurt the cake a bit.

Brenda Tucker and Rachel Hayes

Two Step Cake

"Easy and fast to prepare."

1½ cups rolled oats
1 cup brown sugar
1 teaspoon soda
1½ cups flour
¾ cup butter or margarine

Cream butter and sugar. Mix flour, oats and soda and add to creamed mixture. Spread half the mixture in a well-greased 13 x 9-inch sheet cake pan and spread filling over it.

Filling
½ pound dates, chopped
1 cup cold water
½ cup brown sugar

Boil all ingredients until dates are soft. Cool. Spread over cake mixture. Cover with remaining cake mixture and bake at 325 degrees for about 30 minutes or until brown. Serve plain or warm with whipped cream. May be frozen after baking. Can be used well with other fruits, too.

Kitty Daniel

▲ To decrease fat content, use lowfat margarine.

Amaretto Cheese Cake

"Depending upon your oven, you may need to bake longer in the first step. Wonderful cheese cake, but don't attempt to freeze! The sour cream will get runny."

Crust
2 cups graham cracker crumbs
¼ pound butter, melted
¼ cup sugar

Mix together and press into the bottom of a 10-inch springform pan.

Filling
4 8-ounce packages cream cheese
1 tablespoon amaretto
1½ cups sugar
1 teaspoon vanilla
1 teaspoon almond extract
Pinch of salt
4 eggs

Blend cream cheese, amaretto, sugar, vanilla extract and salt together. With mixer on lowest speed, add eggs, one at a time, mixing as little as possible. Pour into prepared crust and bake at 350 degrees for 30 minutes. Remove from oven and let stand for 10 minutes before adding topping. When done, a one inch area in the center will jiggle slightly.

Topping
2 cups sour cream
1 teaspoon almond extract
¼ cup sugar
½ cup sliced almonds, toasted

In a plastic bowl, using a rubber spatula, blend sour cream, almond extract and sugar together. Pour mixture on top of filling and bake for 10 minutes at 350 degrees. Remove from oven, sprinkle with almonds and put directly into the refrigerator.

Kim Lucy

▲ To lower fat content, substitute lowfat cream cheese in filling and mock sour cream in topping.

Lois's Cheese Cake

"Worth the trouble."

Cookie Dough Crust
1 cup flour
Rind of lemon
½ cup butter, softened
½ cup sugar
1 egg yolk

Mix flour and sugar. Add other ingredients. Mix and chill. Line bottom of springform pan with dough (9-inch pan). Bake at 400 degrees till light brown. Cool. Now line sides with dough. Add filling.

Filling
5 8-ounce packages cream cheese
3 tablespoons flour
Grated rind of 1 lemon
5 eggs
1¾ cups sugar
¼ teaspoon salt
Grated rind of 1 orange
1 cup half and half

Have ingredients at room temperature. Mix flour, sugar and salt. Set aside. Beat cheese until fluffy. Gradually add flour mixture, keeping smooth. Add rinds, then eggs, one at a time, beating well after each, but not too long. Then add half and half; mix again and turn into pan lined with cookie dough crust. Bake at 475 degrees for 15 minutes, then turn to 200 degrees for 1 hour. Turn oven off and let set 15 minutes.

Marilyn Creamer

▲ To lower fat content, substitute lowfat cream cheese and try nonfat evaporated milk instead of half and half in the filling.

Gingerbread

"Serve with lemon or wine sauce or topped with whipped cream."

½ cup shortening
2 eggs
2 cups flour, sifted
1 teaspoon soda, dissolved in ¾ cup hot water
1 teaspoon ginger
½ cup sugar
1 cup molasses
1 teaspoon cloves
1 teaspoon cinnamon
1 teaspoon salt

Cream shortening and sugar. Add eggs, one at a time, and beat well. Blend in molasses, flour and spices. Add ¾ cup hot water with soda dissolved in it. Bake in a greased and floured oblong pan or 2 square cake pans at 350 degrees until firm (as you would cook a sheet cake).

Lemon Sauce
1 stick margarine
2 cups sugar
2 eggs, well beaten
6 tablespoons hot water
Juice of 2 lemons
Dash of nutmeg

Mix all ingredients together in a heavy saucepan. Cook, stirring constantly until thick and transparent-looking, and all the foam has disappeared. Add a dash of nutmeg.

This keeps well in the refrigerator for a week or two and can be warmed by setting jar in hot water. Serve on warm gingerbread.

Edith Buford

▲ To lower fat content, use lowfat margarine and an egg substitute.

Fresh Coconut Cake

"An especially nice treat at Easter."

1 cup butter, softened
1½ cups sugar
1⅔ cups sifted cake flour
5 large eggs
1 teaspoon vanilla

Cream butter with sugar until fluffy. Alternately add flour and eggs, blending well after each addition. Add vanilla. Continue beating on medium speed until batter is smooth. Pour into three 8-inch greased and floured cake pans. Bake at 350 degrees for 20 to 30 minutes. Cool on racks.

Filling
1 coconut
1 cup sugar
1 cup milk

Reserve coconut juice. Finely grate coconut meat. Reserve small amount for garnish. In a saucepan, mix remaining coconut, coconut juice, sugar and milk. Cook slowly over low heat for 20 minutes. The mixture will be thin. Spread mixture over layers, stacking the layers as each is covered. Use all the liquid. The cake will absorb all the liquid and be very moist. Cover and allow to mellow in refrigerator for 24 to 72 hours. Cake may be frozen at this point and frosted before serving.

Seven Minute Frosting
2 unbeaten egg whites
1½ cups sugar
2 teaspoons light corn syrup
⅓ cup cold water
Dash of salt
1 teaspoon vanilla

Beat egg whites, sugar, corn syrup, water and salt in top of a double broiler for 1 minute. Place the mixture over, but not touching boiling water. Beat constantly while cooking until soft peaks form (about 7 minutes). Use a timer. Do not overcook. Remove from heat. Add vanilla. Beat until blended (about 2 minutes). Frost sides and top of cake. Garnish with remaining coconut. Store in refrigerator.

Joyce Moorman

Gooey Butter Cake

"This may be served as a dessert or a morning coffee cake."

1 stick butter or margarine
4 eggs
1 8-ounce package cream cheese
1 box white or yellow cake mix
1 box powdered sugar

Preheat oven to 350 degrees. Grease and flour a 9 x 13-inch cake pan. Mix 1 box white or yellow cake mix with 1 stick butter or margarine and 2 eggs. Pat this mixture evenly in prepared pan. Then mix together the cream cheese, powdered sugar (1 box) and remaining 2 eggs. Pour this mixture over cake mixture in pan. Sprinkle with nuts if desired. Bake 35 to 40 minutes until brown. When slightly cool, sprinkle with powdered sugar.

Betty A. Vaughan

▲ To lower fat content, use lowfat margarine and lowfat cream cheese, and substitute 2 egg yolks and 4 egg whites for the 4 eggs.

Butterscotch Coffee Cake

"Raisins may be substituted for nuts. Better made a day ahead."

1 package yellow cake mix
1 package vanilla instant pudding
1 package butterscotch instant pudding
4 eggs
1⅓ cups water
½ cup oil
1 teaspoon vanilla

Topping
1 cup brown sugar
½ cup nuts
1 teaspoon cinnamon

Mix topping and set aside. In another bowl, mix cake mix, puddings, eggs, oil and water. Grease and flour a 13 x 9-inch pan. Alternate layers of batter and topping. Bake at 350 degrees for 20 minutes; reduce heat to 325 degrees and bake 20 minutes more.

Gertrude W. Cole

Merk's Coffee Cake

"Sunday morning treat."

½ cup shortening
¾ cup sugar
1 teaspoon vanilla
3 eggs
2 cups flour
1 teaspoon baking powder
1 teaspoon baking soda
1 cup sour cream

Filling and Topping
1 cup firmly packed brown sugar
6 tablespoons butter or margarine

2 teaspoons cinnamon
1 cup nuts, chopped (optional)

To make batter, cream first 3 ingredients thoroughly. Add eggs, one at a time, beating well after each. Stir together the dry ingredients and add to creamed mixture alternately with sour cream. Spread half of this batter in a 10-inch tube pan that has been greased and lined with waxed paper. Now make filling by creaming 6 tablespoons butter and brown sugar together with cinnamon. Add nuts, if desired. Dot ½ of this mixture over the batter in the pan. Cover with remaining batter and top with rest of filling mixture dotted evenly on top. Bake at 350 degrees for about 50 minutes. Cool 10 minutes before removing from pan.

Orline White

Angel Cake

"Yummy and easy."

Serves at least 16

1 large angel food cake, broken into bite-size pieces
1 8-ounce (large) package cream cheese
½ cup sugar
½ cup milk
1 12-ounce package prepared whipped topping
Cherry or blueberry pie filling

Soften cream cheese; add sugar and milk. Fold in whipped topping and cake pieces. Spread in large casserole and chill. Add pie filling as a topping. Keeps well in refrigerator.

Allene Barkley

▲ To lower fat content, use lowfat cream cheese, lowfat skim milk and lowfat whipped topping.

Cocoa-Cola Cake

"Very good - very rich!"

2 cups flour
2 cups sugar
2 sticks butter or margarine
3 tablespoons cocoa
1 cup cola drink
½ cup buttermilk
2 eggs, beaten
1 teaspoon soda
1 teaspoon vanilla extract
1½ cups small marshmallows

Combine sugar and flour in bowl. Heat butter, cola drink and cocoa to boiling; pour over flour mixture and mix thoroughly. Add milk, eggs, soda, vanilla extract and marshmallows. Bake in a large flat pan, greased and floured, at 350 degrees for 30 to 35 minutes.

Icing
1 stick butter or margarine
3 tablespoons cocoa
6 tablespoons cola
1 box powdered sugar
1 cup pecans, chopped
1 teaspoon vanilla extract

Combine butter or margarine, cocoa and cola and heat to boiling. Pour mixture over sugar and beat smooth. Stir in vanilla and nuts. Spread over hot cake. Leave in pan and cut in small squares.

Angela Coltrane

▲ To lower fat content, use lowfat margarine, skim buttermilk and egg substitute.

Do Nothing Cake

"After baking this cake, you sit down to eat it and 'do nothing'."

2 cups plain flour
2 cups sugar
2 eggs
1 teaspoon baking soda
½ teaspoon salt
1 teaspoon vanilla
1 1-pound, 4-ounce (large) can crushed
pineapple

Mix all ingredients together until well blended. Pour into a greased and floured 13 x 9-inch pan. Bake at 350 degrees for 25 to 40 minutes. Cool in pan on cake rack for 10 minutes before icing.

Icing
1 stick margarine
1 cup sugar
⅔ cup evaporated milk (small can)
1 cup nuts, chopped
1 cup coconut

Mix together and cook 5 minutes, the margarine, sugar and milk; stir constantly. After it boils, stir in nuts and coconut. Pour over cake.

H. Lenwood Wright

▲ To lower fat content, use lowfat margarine and substitute skim evaporated milk for the milk in the icing.

Fudge Cake

"Chocolate lovers delight!"

Makes 12 servings.

¾ cup butter or margarine
2¼ cups sugar
1½ teaspoons vanilla
3 eggs
3 1-ounce squares unsweetened chocolate, melted
3 cups sifted cake flour
1½ teaspoons baking soda
¾ teaspoon salt
1½ cups ice water
Date Cream Filling (recipe follows)
Fudge Frosting (recipe follows)

Cream together butter and sugar in mixing bowl, until light and fluffy, at medium speed of electric mixer. Beat in vanilla. Add eggs, one at a time, beating well after each addition. Blend in chocolate. Sift together cake flour, baking soda and salt. Add dry ingredients alternately with water to creamed mixture, beating well after each addition. Pour batter into 3 greased 8-inch round cake pans. Bake at 350 degrees for 30 to 35 minutes or until cake tests done. Cool in pans on racks 10 minutes. Remove from pans; cool on racks.

Date Cream Filling
1 cup milk
½ cup dates, chopped
1 tablespoon flour
¼ cup sugar
1 egg, beaten
½ cup walnuts, chopped
1 teaspoon vanilla

Combine milk and dates on top of double broiler. Heat mixture over low heat. Combine flour and sugar in small bowl. Add eggs; beat until smooth. Stir into hot milk mixture; place over simmering water. Cook, stirring constantly, until thick. Cool. Stir in walnuts and vanilla.

Fudge Frosting
2 cups sugar
¼ teaspoon salt
1 cup light cream
2 tablespoons light corn syrup
2 1-ounce squares unsweetened chocolate

Combine all ingredients in a 2-quart saucepan. Cook over low heat, stirring constantly until sugar dissolves. Cover saucepan; cook 2 minutes. Remove cover and cook to 234 degrees (soft ball stage). Remove from heat. Beat with wooden spoon to spreading consistency. Add a little hot water if frosting becomes too stiff or confectioner's sugar if it becomes too thin.

Brenda Adcock

The **White's Family Inn** *has been receiving travelers and providing them with wholesome meals since 1798.*

Texas Chocolate Cake

"This cake is very convenient for bake sales, youth suppers, etc., in place of brownies."

2 cups sugar
2 cups flour
1 cup butter or margarine
½ cup cocoa
1 cup water
½ cup buttermilk
2 eggs
1 teaspoon soda
1 teaspoon vanilla

Mix flour and sugar. Combine in saucepan the butter, cocoa and water and bring to a boil. Pour over sugar and flour and blend well. Add rest of ingredients. Pour in greased jelly roll pan (11 x 17 inches) and bake at 375 degrees for 20 minutes.

Frosting
½ cup butter or margarine
5 tablespoons milk
¼ cup cocoa
1 box 10-x sugar
1 teaspoon vanilla
1 cup nut meats (optional)

Make frosting while the cake is in the oven. Bring to a boil over medium heat, the margarine, milk and cocoa. Pour over 1 box 10-x sugar in bowl. Mix to form smooth frosting. Add vanilla and nuts. Spread on warm cake and refrigerate.

Maureen Harris and Wilma Edmonds

▲ To lower fat content, use lowfat margarine, skim buttermilk and egg substitute.

Turtle Cake

"Great sheet cake - very rich!"

1 box German chocolate cake mix
1 14-ounce bag caramels
¾ cup butter
1 small can evaporated milk
1 cup chocolate chips
1 cup pecans, chopped

Prepare the cake batter per package instructions. Pour half the batter into 9 x 13-inch pan and bake at 350 degrees for 15 minutes. Meanwhile, melt the caramels with the butter and milk in a saucepan over low heat. Stir constantly. Pour over the hot half baked cake. Top with chocolate pieces and pecans, then pour remaining batter over all. Finish baking at 350 degrees for another 20 minutes.

Alice B. Samford

Variation: Same ingredients as above except use 1 cup evaporated milk instead of 1 small can. Mix together cake mix, melted butter and ⅔ cup evaporated milk. Batter will be very thick, spread half of batter on greased 9 x 13-inch pan. Bake at 350 degrees for 10 to 15 minutes. Meanwhile, melt caramels in ⅓ cup evaporated milk, spread this over baked layer and sprinkle with nuts and chocolate chips. Spread rest of batter over all. Sprinkle with additional nuts if desired. Bake 15 to 20 minutes more. Cut in squares when cool.

Isabelle Orgain

▲ To lower fat content, use nonfat evaporated milk.

Grandmama's Jam Cake

"If you use a tube pan for cake, simply cut through the cake with a long knife to make two layers. Put a generous amount of icing on bottom layer, replace top of cake and pour icing so that it overflows the top and drips down the sides."

1 cup butter or margarine (or combination of both)
2 cups sugar (I use a bit less)
4 eggs, separated
4 cups flour
1 cup jam (seedless blackberry jam or preserves is best)
2 level teaspoons baking soda dissolved in 1 cup buttermilk
1 teaspoon each cinnamon, ground cloves, nutmeg, allspice

Cream shortening and sugar thoroughly. Beat yolks and beat into creamed mixture. Stir flour and spices together and add alternately with buttermilk-soda to creamed mixture. Beat well but don't overbeat. Beat in jam and finally fold in egg whites which have been beaten stiff but not dry. Bake in 3 greased and floured 9-inch layer cake pans for about 30 minutes in a 325 or 350 degree oven or in a well-greased and floured tube pan for about 1 hour or till center tests done.

Icing
6 level tablespoons flour
1½ cups sugar
1 stick margarine
1½ cups milk
1 teaspoon vanilla
1 cup raisins
1 cup pecans, broken

In a medium saucepan mix sugar and flour well. Add milk and stick margarine and cook on medium burner, stirring constantly, until mixture thickens. Remove from heat and add raisins, vanilla and pecans. When cake is cool, ice generously. I sometimes make another ½ batch of icing to make sure there's enough as the icing makes the cake!

Jenny Showalter

*It is said that the bricks at **St. Mark's Chapel** show the wear of generations of families who have worshipped there.*

Hummingbird Cake

"May bake in tube pan at 325 degrees for 1 hour and 20 minutes."

3 cups flour
2 cups sugar
1 teaspoon salt
1 teaspoon ground cinnamon
3 eggs, beaten
1½ cups oil
1½ teaspoons vanilla
1 8-ounce can crushed pineapple,
    undrained
1 cup nuts, chopped
2 cups bananas, chopped

Combine dry ingredients, eggs and salad oil in a large bowl and stir until dry ingredients are moistened. Do not beat. Stir in vanilla, pineapple, bananas and nuts. Spoon into 3 well-greased and floured 9-inch cake pans. Bake at 350 degrees 25 to 30 minutes. Cool in pans 10 minutes after removing from oven. Remove from pans and cool completely before frosting. Frost with Cream Cheese Frosting. When baking in tube pan reduce frosting by half.

▲ To lower fat content, substitute 1 yolk and 3 whites for the 3 eggs.

Cream Cheese Frosting
2 8-ounce packages cream cheese, softened
1 cup butter
2 pounds powdered sugar
2 teaspoons vanilla
1 cup pecans (optional)

Combine cream cheese and butter and cream until smooth. Add powdered sugar, beating until fluffy and light. Add vanilla and nuts.

Barbara Slayton

▲ To lower fat content, use lowfat cream cheese and lowfat margarine.

Snowball Cake

"Very pretty and easy!"

1 angel food cake (broken into bite-size
    pieces)
2 packages unflavored gelatin
1 cup boiling water
Juice of 1 lemon
2 packages prepared dry whipped topping
2 tablespoons cold water
1 cup sugar
1 large can crushed pineapple
1 can coconut

Sprinkle a layer of cake pieces in bottom of oblong Pyrex dish. Dissolve gelatin in cold water. Add hot water and sugar. When cool, add pineapple and lemon juice and let set until it begins to congeal. Prepare whipped topping per package instructions. Fold whipped topping into gelatin mixture. Cover first layer of cake pieces with part of gelatin mixture, then sprinkle with coconut. Make another layer (cake, gelatin, coconut). Allow to age in refrigerator 24 hours.

Carolyn Sykes

Try using 1½ packages of lemon gelatin instead of unflavored gelatin and lemon juice. To make cake look like a snowball, spray large mixing bowl with Pam, crumble cake and place in bowl loosely, pour gelatin and whipped topping mixture over cake. Press firmly with back of spoon so all of cake will be covered. Be sure you have saved some whipped topping for frosting. Turn onto cake plate. Frost bowl-shaped cake with prepared whipped topping, sprinkle on coconut and garnish with cherries if desired. Chill overnight.

Sour Cream Pound Cake

"Try serving with fudge sauce."

1 cup butter or margarine
3 cups sugar
6 eggs
1 cup sour cream
¼ teaspoon baking soda
¼ teaspoon baking powder
¼ teaspoon salt
3 cups sifted flour
1½ teaspoons lemon extract
1½ teaspoons almond extract

Preheat oven to 300 degrees. Cream butter, add sugar, one cup at a time, beating at high speed after each addition. Add eggs, one at a time, beating well at medium speed. Add sour cream, beating well. Add soda, baking powder and salt to flour. Add dry ingredients, one cup at a time, mixing well after each addition. Add flavorings. Pour into a well-greased tube pan and bake for 1½ hours. Let stand 10 minutes before removing from pan.

Frances S. Wholey

Dot's Pound Cake

"Serve with lemon sauce or ice cream."

2 sticks margarine
3 cups sugar
½ cup milk
1½ cups flour
1 teaspoon vanilla
½ cup vegetable shortening
1½ cups cake flour
4 eggs
½ cup milk
1 teaspoon lemon

Cream 2 sticks margarine with ½ cup vegetable shortening until very fluffy. Add 3 cups

sugar gradually, cream until grains disappear. Add 1½ cups cake flour, ½ cup milk and blend. Add 4 eggs, one at a time, and add additional 1½ cups flour and ½ cup of milk. Add 1 teaspoon of vanilla, 1 teaspoon of lemon. Pour into a large tube pan that is well greased. Put into a **cold** oven. Bake for 1 hour at 325 degrees, then raise the temperature to 350 degrees. Bake another 30 minutes. Do not open oven until cake is done.

Dot Peebles

Pound Cake

"Be sure your oven light is working. Read instructions to understand why."

3 cups sugar
1 cup butter
½ cup shortening
6 eggs
2 tablespoons lemon flavoring
2 tablespoons vanilla flavoring
3 cups sifted cake flour
½ teaspoon baking powder
½ teaspoon salt
1 cup whole sweet milk

Cream sugar and shortening (butter and shortening) well. Add eggs, one at a time, beating well each time to mix. Add flavoring.

Sift flour, salt and baking powder together. Add alternately with milk to creamed mixture. Mix well.

Bake in a large tube pan which has been greased well. Line sides and bottom with waxed paper after greasing. Bake at 300 degrees for 1 hour and 50 minutes to 2 hours. Do not open oven until ready to take cake out.

Dorothy Daniel

Five Flavor Pound Cake

"A recipe exchanged between two former First Ladies of Virginia, Mrs. Mills Godwin and Mrs. Albertis Harrison."

2 sticks butter
½ cup vegetable shortening
3 cups sugar
5 eggs, well beaten
3 cups all purpose flour
½ teaspoon baking powder
1 cup milk
1 teaspoon coconut extract
1 teaspoon rum flavoring
1 teaspoon butter extract
1 teaspoon lemon extract
1 teaspoon vanilla

Cream the butter, shortening and sugar until light and fluffy. Add eggs. Combine flour, baking powder and add this to the creamed mixture alternately with the milk. Stir in the 5 flavors. Spoon the mixture into a 10-inch greased, floured tube pan. Bake at 325 degrees for 1½ hours or until the cake tests done. Add glaze to warm cake. Let cool before turning out.

Glaze
½ cup sugar
¼ cup water
½ teaspoon lemon extract
½ teaspoon coconut extract
½ teaspoon rum flavoring
½ teaspoon butter extract
½ teaspoon vanilla

Combine all ingredients in saucepan and bring to a boil. Stir until the sugar is melted. Spoon very slowly over hot cake in pan. Let the cake sit until cool.

Katherine Godwin
(Submitted by Lacy Harrison)

Red Velvet Pound Cake

"Pretty cake for a luncheon or holiday."

3 cups sugar
¾ cup shortening (butter or margarine)
7 eggs
¼ teaspoon salt
3 cups flour
1 cup milk
1 ounce red food coloring
1 teaspoon vanilla

Cream sugar and shortening together. Add eggs one at a time while beating with electric mixer. Add vanilla and salt. Add flour and milk alternately beginning and ending with flour. Add food coloring; beat batter until smooth. Bake in a greased and floured tube pan for approximately 1½ hours at 325 degrees until done. Let cake rest on a cooling rack in the pan for 10 minutes. Turn cake from the pan on the cooling rack and let it cool. Frost with a cream cheese frosting.

Icing
1 pound box powdered sugar
3 ounces cream cheese, softened
1 stick margarine, softened
3 tablespoons milk

Cream cheese and margarine together; add milk and powdered sugar slowly. Beat well.

Peggy Martin

Red Velvet Cake

"Give your sweetheart a Red Velvet Cake for Valentine's Day!"

½ cup shortening
1½ cups sugar
2 eggs
2 tablespoons cocoa
2 ounces red food coloring
2¼ cups flour
1 teaspoon salt
1 cup buttermilk
1 tablespoon vanilla
1 teaspoon soda
1 tablespoon vinegar

Cream shortening with sugar; add eggs. Combine cocoa and food coloring to make a paste. Stir into creamed mixture. Sift flour and salt together; with electric mixer at medium speed, add alternately with buttermilk to mixture. Blend well; add vanilla. Combine vinegar and soda and while still foaming, add to batter. Do not beat; instead stir gently. Bake in two 9-inch layer cake pans in 350 degree oven for 30 to 35 minutes.

Icing
3 tablespoons flour
1 cup milk
1 cup granulated sugar
½ pound (2 sticks) butter
1 teaspoon vanilla

Cook flour and milk over medium heat until thick; stirring constantly; cool. Add sugar, butter and vanilla. Beat at high speed until smooth and creamy. Spread on cooled cake. Icing will take a long time to set; it resembles whipped cream when completely set.

Mayme Darden

Down South Yam Cake

"Cake freezes well."

Serves 16

2 cups sugar
1 cup margarine or butter, softened
1½ teaspoons vanilla
5 eggs
1 16-ounce can cut yams, drained
3 cups self-rising flour (see note)
2 teaspoons cinnamon
½ teaspoon baking soda
½ teaspoon nutmeg
1 cup pecans, chopped
1 cup raisins
1 8¼-ounce can crushed pineapple, well drained
1 15.75-ounce container coconut-pecan frosting

Heat oven to 325 degrees. Grease and flour 10-inch tube pan. In large bowl, cream sugar, margarine and vanilla until light and fluffy. Add eggs, one at a time, beating well after each. Cut up yams, add to creamed mixture, beating until well mixed. Level off cups of flour and add to creamed mixture. Fold in pecans, raisins and drained pineapple. Spoon thick batter into prepared tube pan and spread evenly. Bake at 325 degrees for 60 to 70 minutes or until toothpick inserted in center comes out clean. Cool in pan 10 minutes. Invert onto serving plate.

In saucepan, heat frosting over medium heat just until melted, stirring constantly. Spoon over cooled cake allowing to run down sides.

Ruth P. Baynard

Note: To substitute all-purpose flour increase baking soda to 2 teaspoons and add 2 teaspoons baking powder and 1 teaspoon salt to 3 cups flour.

Prune Cake

"Moist and delicate cake!"

3 eggs
1 cup vegetable oil
2 cups flour
1½ cups sugar
1 cup buttermilk
1 cup cooked and chopped prunes
1 cup chopped black walnuts
1 teaspoon soda
1 teaspoon cinnamon
1 teaspoon nutmeg
1 teaspoon allspice
1 teaspoon vanilla
½ teaspoon salt

Mix sugar and oil; add eggs. Add dry ingredients which have been sifted together alternately with buttermilk. Add vanilla, nuts and prunes. Pour into greased tube pan or standard sheet cake pan. Bake at 350 degrees for 45 minutes to one hour. When brown, take from oven and add icing while the cake is still hot.

Icing
1 cup sugar
½ cup buttermilk
½ teaspoon soda
1 teaspoon white corn syrup
¼ cup butter
½ teaspoon vanilla

Mix all ingredients and boil together until a drop forms a ball in cold water. Pour over cake while still hot. It soaks the cake a little, but cake does not become soggy, only moist and delicate.

Betty Fisher

▲ To lower fat content, use skim buttermilk.

Mandarin Orange Cake

"Pretty, fast and yummy!"

1 box Butter Recipe cake mix
1 11-ounce can mandarin oranges (juice also)
4 eggs
½ stick margarine

Bake cake by package instructions for layer cake. Do not add any liquid except juice from oranges. Let completely cool.

Icing
1 9-ounce container prepared whipped topping
1 #2 can crushed pineapple
1 box instant vanilla pudding mix
Handful of coconut

Stir all ingredients by hand until completely mixed. Frost cake and refrigerate.

Lori Moorman

Date Nut Cake

"For color, add ½ cup of green and red maraschino cherries."

1 pound pitted dates
1 cup flour, sifted 3 times
2 teaspoons baking powder
4 eggs, separated
1 pound English walnuts
½ teaspoon salt
1 cup sugar
1 teaspoon vanilla

Add whole dates and walnuts to flour and then add sugar (mix by hand). Beat egg yolks very lightly. Add to flour mixture. Add vanilla. Next, add stiffly beaten egg whites, folding in by hand. Bake for 1 hour at 350 degrees in a loaf pan lined with aluminum foil, oiled. Cool in pan before removing. Store in cloth dipped in wine.

Nora Peterson

Apricot Nectar Cake

"Easy and moist pound cake."

1 package Lemon Supreme cake mix
½ cup sugar
¾ cup cooking oil
1 cup apricot nectar
4 eggs

Icing
1 cup 4x powdered sugar, sifted
Juice and grated rind of 1 lemon

Combine cake mix and sugar, mix thoroughly. Add oil, mix thoroughly. Add nectar, mix thoroughly. Add 1 egg at a time, beating well after each. Bake in tube pan (two thicknesses of wax paper at bottom of pan), grease well, but not sides of pan. Bake at 350 degrees for 45 minutes or until cake springs back after touching.

While cake bakes, mix icing ingredients thoroughly. After cake bakes and while still warm, make small holes in top of cake with toothpicks. Spread icing over warm cake.

Mayme Darden

Icebox Fruitcake

"Absolutely no cooking!"

1 cup pecans
1 cup walnuts
½ box golden raisins
1 pound marshmallows
1 can shredded coconut
1 pound round buttery crackers
1 pound candied cherries
½ pound candied pineapple
1½ cups evaporated milk
1 package dried mixed fruit

Cut marshmallows in small pieces, melt marshmallows in milk in double broiler. Crumble crackers and add to milk mixture. Blend well. Add remaining ingredients. Put in tube or loaf pan. Put in refrigerator to chill until firm enough to slice.

Eleanora Clary

▲ To lower fat content, use skim evaporated milk.

White Fruitcake

"Makes a large cake. Halve recipe for smaller cake. Omit the coconut - the cake will last longer."

1 pound shelled almonds, blanched
1½ pounds crystallized cherries
1 pound citron
1 coconut, grated
1 pound eggs, usually a dozen
1 pound sugar
1 cup white wine, rum or brandy
** (or whiskey)**
1½ pounds crystallized pineapple
1½ pounds white raisins
¼ pound crystallized lemon and orange
** peel, mixed**
1 pound butter
1 pound flour sifted with 2 teaspoons
** baking powder**

Cream butter (room temperature) and flour. Separate eggs and beat yolks well. Add sugar and beat more. Mix with flour and butter mixture. Beat whites and add to mixture. Then add coconut. Add wine and then fruit, cook very slowly for 2 hours, testing with a broom stick straw. May take longer than 2 hours.

Helen Nelson

Variation: 1 teaspoon lemon extract, 1 teaspoon nutmeg, 2 tablespoons white syrup.

Wright's Special Light Fruitcake

"See beverage section for homemade grape wine recipe."

Makes a 7- to 8-pound cake

1½ cups butter or margarine, softened
1½ cups sugar
1 tablespoon vanilla
8 eggs, separated
3½ cups sifted flour
¼ teaspoon salt
2 tablespoons strained honey
2 cups red and green candied cherries, cut up
2 cups red and green candied pineapple, cut up
1 cup mixed fruits, cut up
1 cup golden raisins
1 cup dark raisins
3 cups pecans, chopped
½ cup homemade grape wine (light)

Line a 10-inch tube pan, bottom and sides, with brown paper greased with margarine and set aside. Cream butter, sugar, vanilla, salt, honey and wine until light and fluffy. Beat in egg yolks alternately with 3 cups sifted flour in a large bowl. In another large bowl, mix fruits, raisins and nuts with remainder of sifted flour until well coated. Beat egg whites to a soft peak, stir into the batter, alternately with mixture of fruits, nuts, etc. using a small amount of the egg whites at a time until well mixed with all ingredients. Spoon batter into the greased pan, decorate the top with red and green cherries cut in half and whole pecans. Cook 4 hours at 250 degrees. Take cake from oven and brush well with homemade grape wine while cake is hot. When cake cools turn out of pan, brush again with wine and wrap with cloth. Store in plastic container and brush with wine again in a few days. Rum/Brandy may be substituted for wine if desired.

Willie Wright

Fruitcake

"Makes one 5-pound cake."

1 cup cooking oil
4 eggs
3 cups flour
1½ cups candied cherries
1 cup candied pineapple, chopped
1 cup seedless raisins
3 cups nuts, chopped
1 teaspoon cinnamon
1 teaspoon cloves
1½ cups brown sugar
1 cup figs, chopped
1½ cups citron, sliced
2 teaspoons salt
1 teaspoon baking powder
2 teaspoons allspice
1 cup orange juice

Combine oil, sugar, and eggs, beat 2 minutes. In a large bowl, combine 1 cup flour with fruits and nuts. Sift remaining flour with baking powder and salt and spices. Stir into cooking oil mixture alternately with orange juice. Pour batter over fruit mixture, blend well. Turn into a tube pan lined with greased brown paper. Place a pan of water on lower oven rack. Bake in 275 degree oven for 2½ to 3 hours. Cool on wire rack. Remove from pan. Wrap in cloth damp with wine or brandy, then in foil. Chill for easy slicing.

Alice Samford

"The trees that produce sour red cherries, commonly called 'May cherries', are found growing in many farmyards. Their tartness, which makes them unappealing to many people for eating fresh, nevertheless contributes to delicious pies and cobblers. This painting features a table covered with the makings of a cherry pie in progress."

Eldridge Bagley

"MAY CHERRIES"
Appears through the courtesy of the painting's owners, Mr. and Mrs. Gregory S. Hooe.

Stratford Hall Ice Cream Pie

"Lovely finish to a special meal."

Yields 2 pies

1 cup flour
1 stick butter
2 quarts vanilla ice cream
¼ cup brown sugar
½ cup pecans, chopped

Mix together flour, sugar and pecans. Add melted butter and mix well. Reserve about ¼ of this for topping and crumble in a shallow pan. Bake slowly at 325 degrees until brown. Pat remaining mixture on sides and bottom of two 8- or 9-inch pie pans. Brown slowly at 325 degrees and cool. Slightly soften 2 quarts vanilla ice cream, spreading 1 quart in each crust. Sprinkle topping over this and refreeze.

Justine Jones

▲ To lower fat content, use lowfat butter and lowfat ice cream.

Brown Sugar Pie

"A traditional favorite."

Yields 2 pies

1 1-pound box light brown sugar
6 eggs
2 teaspoons vanilla
1 cup white sugar
1 stick butter
⅛ teaspoon salt
2 unbaked pie shells

Mix all ingredients together and bake in an unbaked pie shell at 350 degrees for 30 to 35 minutes.

Lavonia Abernathy

▲ To decrease fat content, use lowfat margarine and an egg substitute.

Damson Preserves Pie

"Tried and proven delicious."

Yields 1 pie

½ cup sugar
½ cup butter
½ cup damson preserves
½ cup milk
2 eggs, separated
1 teaspoon vanilla
1 unbaked pie shell

Cream sugar and butter. Add preserves, beaten egg yolks, milk, and vanilla. Fold in stiffly beaten egg whites. Bake in an unbaked pie shell at 350 degrees for 30 minutes.

Georgia K. Hammack

▲ To decrease fat content, use lowfat margarine and lowfat/skim milk.

Southern Transparent Pie

"Center should be slightly shaky."

Yields 2 pies

1 1-pound box light brown sugar
1 stick butter or margarine, melted
5 whole eggs
1 teaspoon vanilla extract
2 unbaked 8-inch pie shells

Blend sugar and butter. Add eggs, one at a time, blending well after each addition. Add vanilla. Pour into 2 unbaked pie shells and bake at 400 degrees for 10 minutes. Reduce heat to 300 degrees and bake until firm, about 35 to 40 minutes.

Pat Temple

▲ To decrease fat content, use lowfat margarine and an egg substitute for half the amount of eggs.

Buttermilk Meringue Pie

"The meringue adds something extra."

Yields 1 pie

⅔ cup sugar
1 tablespoon flour
3 teaspoons lemon juice
2 egg yolks (reserve whites)
1 cup buttermilk
½ tablespoon butter or margarine
⅛ teaspoon salt
1 unbaked pie crust

Combine sugar, flour and margarine. Add buttermilk, lemon juice, salt and slightly beaten egg yolks. Mix thoroughly. Pour into unbaked pie crust. Bake in hot oven (425 degrees) until inserted knife comes out clean.

Cover with meringue made of 2 egg whites and 2 tablespoons sugar. Bake in a slow oven for 20 minutes or until browned.

Myrtle S. Brockwell

▲ Using skim buttermilk will decrease the fat content.

Buttermilk Pie

"Always good."

Yields 2 pies

3¾ cups sugar
½ cup flour
¼ teaspoon salt
6 eggs
1 full cup butter or margarine
1 cup buttermilk
1 tablespoon vanilla
2 unbaked pie shells

Combine sugar, flour and butter or margarine. Add salt and slightly beaten eggs. Pour in buttermilk. Mix up well, but do not overbeat. Pour into 2 unbaked 9-inch pie shells and bake in a 350 degree oven for 35 to 40 minutes, or until brown in center.

Mabel E. Brewer

▲ To decrease fat content, use an egg substitute for ½ the eggs, use lowfat margarine and skim buttermilk.

Lemon Meringue Pie

"Superb!"

Yields 1 pie

2 egg yolks
Juice from 2 lemons
1½ cups sugar
4 teaspoons flour
2 cups milk
1 tablespoon butter

Mix sugar and flour in top of double broiler. Beat egg yolks, milk and lemon juice together and add to sugar and flour mixture. Cook until very thick, stirring constantly. Add butter and cool. Pour into baked pie shell and cover with meringue.

Meringue
3 egg whites
3 heaping tablespoons sugar
⅛ teaspoon cream of tartar

Place egg whites in bowl; add cream of tartar and beat until foamy. Add sugar and continue beating until mixture will stand in peaks. Bake in 300 to 325 degree oven until brown.

Lottie M. French

▲ To decrease fat content, use skim/lowfat milk.

Lemon Meringue Pie

"Your family will love this."

Yields 1 pie

1 cup sugar
2 heaping tablespoons flour
3 egg yolks, beaten
Juice of 1 large lemon
⅛ teaspoon salt
1 cup hot water
1 tablespoon butter
1 baked pie shell or graham cracker crust

Mix sugar and flour in top of double broiler. Beat egg yolks until very light. Add water, lemon juice and salt. Add liquid to sugar and flour. Cook over hot water until very thick, stirring constantly. Add butter and set aside to cool. Pour into a baked pie shell or graham cracker crust.

Meringue
3 egg whites
3 heaping tablespoons sugar

Beat egg whites until foamy. Gradually add sugar and beat until soft peaks form. Brown meringue in a very slow oven (300 to 325 degrees).

Edith Buford

Lemon Cake Pie

"I found this recipe among some of my grandmother's which she had collected over forty years ago."

Yields 1 pie

1 cup sugar
¼ cup flour
¼ cup margarine
⅛ teaspoon salt
2 eggs

2 lemons, grated peel and juice
1 cup milk
1 9-inch pie crust, unbaked

Combine sugar, butter, salt, flour and egg yolks. Beat in lemon juice and peel. Add milk, beating slowly. Beat egg whites stiff but not dry; fold in. Bake pie shell at 350 degrees for 5 minutes. Pour in filling. Bake 40 minutes or until filling is firm. When cut there will be a delicate cake on top of the pie filling.

Virginia Ruff

▲ To decrease fat, use lowfat/skim milk.

Lemon Chess Pie

"Travels well, good for carrying to church suppers."

Yields 2 pies

2 cups sugar
½ cup butter
Juice of 2 lemons
⅛ teaspoon salt
3 tablespoons flour
4 eggs
1 teaspoon lemon rind
½ cup sweet milk
2 pie shells, unbaked

Cream sugar, butter and flour. Add salt. Add eggs, one at a time, beating until blended. Add milk, slowly blending. Remove beaters, then dribble in lemon juice and rind, stirring. Bake in unbaked pie crusts at 350 degrees for 25 to 30 minutes.

Christine Hall

Lemon Chess Pie

"A family favorite with all generations."

Yields 1 pie

1 cup sugar
3 eggs, separated
¼ cup lemon juice
¼ cup butter
1 pie shell, unbaked

Cream sugar and butter and add beaten egg yolks; add lemon juice. Beat egg whites and fold in. Pour into uncooked pie shell and cook in a 300 degree oven for 45 minutes or until golden brown.

Pat Temple

Pineapple-Coconut Pie

"Top with whipped cream, if desired."

Yields 2 pies

5 eggs
1 cup sugar
3 tablespoons butter
1 teaspoon vanilla
1 cup light corn syrup
2 tablespoons flour
⅛ teaspoon salt
2 cans angel flake coconut (8 ounces)
1 large can crushed pineapple
2 pie shells, unbaked

Beat eggs. Add sugar, butter, vanilla, flour, salt and syrup. Beat these ingredients for 1 minute. Add pineapple and coconut and mix well. Cook in unbaked pie shells. Bake at 450 degrees for 10 minutes, then at 350 degrees for 1 hour.

Alta Brown

Pineapple Chess Pie

"For pineapple lovers this is a tasty treat."

Yields 1 pie

3 tablespoons butter
1 cup sugar
⅛ teaspoon salt
3 tablespoons flour
2 large eggs, separated
1 cup crushed pineapple
1 pie shell, unbaked

Cream butter and sugar (add a little juice if needed). Add flour and salt. Separate eggs. Add yolks; beat whites separately. Add pineapple and egg whites. Cook in moderate oven for about 40 minutes (350 degrees).

Ella MacDonald

Pineapple Nut Pie

"Terrific Company Treat."

Yields 2 pies

1 can sweetened condensed milk
6 tablespoons lemon juice
1 9-ounce carton prepared whipped topping
1 20-ounce (large) can crushed pineapple, drained
1 package nuts - pecans, etc.
2 graham cracker crusts

Add lemon juice to condensed milk and mix. Fold in whipped topping and pineapple. Pour into 2 graham cracker crusts. Sprinkle nuts on top of pies. Refrigerate until firmly set.

Lucy Wiley

Pineapple-Coconut Pie

"Great combination."

Yields 2 pies

1 stick margarine
4 eggs
2 cups sugar
1 8-ounce (small) can crushed pineapple,
do not drain
1 7-ounce package angel flake coconut
1 teaspoon vanilla
2 tablespoons flour (optional)
2 pie shells, unbaked

Mix all ingredients and pour into 2 unbaked pie shells. Bake at 325 degrees until lightly browned, about 1 hour.

Viola B. Jones and Bertie Mae Fleshood

▲ To decrease fat content, use lowfat margarine and an egg substitute.

Impossible Pie

"This pie makes its own crust."

Yields 1 pie

½ stick butter or margarine, melted
4 ounces canned coconut
2 eggs
1 cup milk
1 cup sugar
1 teaspoon vanilla or lemon extract
¼ cup self-rising flour
¼ teaspoon salt

Beat eggs and sugar together. Add flour and beat, add other ingredients and pour into a 9-inch greased pie plate. Cook at 350 degrees for 30 minutes or until firm.

Millie Bendall

Exquisite Pie

"So easy and delicious."

Yields 2 pies

2 cups sugar
5 eggs
1 cup raisins
¼ teaspoon cinnamon
2 tablespoons vinegar
2 sticks butter
1 cup coconut
1 cup nuts
¼ teaspoon allspice
2 pie shells, unbaked

Beat sugar and butter. Add beaten eggs, vinegar, spices, coconut, nuts and raisins. Put in unbaked pie shell and bake about 35 to 40 minutes at 400 degrees.

Myrtilla Pierce

▲ To decrease fat content, use lowfat margarine.

The Randolph Place *is a two-story house flanked by twin chimneys that sits atop a ridge in the White Plains section of the county.*

Old-Fashioned Coconut Pie

"Coconut lovers' delight."

Yields 1 pie

3 eggs, beaten
1¼ cups sugar
2 tablespoons margarine or butter, melted
1 teaspoon flour
½ cup water
½ cup undiluted evaporated milk
1½ cups coconut
1 teaspoon vanilla
1 pie shell, unbaked

Mix eggs and sugar well. Add flour and margarine. Mix milk and water and add to mixture, then add vanilla and coconut.

If you wish, mix milk and pour over coconut and let stand while mixing other ingredients. This helps prevent coconut from rising to top of pie. Bake at 350 degrees, until golden brown, about 45 minutes.

Marian Connell

▲ To lower fat, use skim evaporated milk.

"Mother's" Crusty Coconut Pie

"A very special recipe."

Yields 2 pies

14 ounces coconut
1 large can evaporated milk
½ cup butter, melted
2 cups sugar
6 eggs
2 teaspoons vanilla
Pinch of salt
2 deep dish pie shells, unbaked

Pour milk over coconut to soak while you prepare the other ingredients. Beat 6 eggs and stir in the sugar, butter, vanilla and a dash of salt. Add the coconut and milk mixture. Pour into pie shells and bake at 350 degrees for approximately 30 minutes, or until set.

Sarah Bishop

▲ To decrease fat content, use skim evaporated milk, lowfat margarine, and replace 3 of the eggs with an egg substitute.

At **Peebles & Purdy Co.** *shoppers can find "the best values that can be had for hard cash in everything to wear and to eat for man and beast".*

Toasted Coconut-Pecan Pie

"Garnish with whipped cream and pecan halves."

Yields 1 pie

3 eggs, beaten
1½ cups sugar
½ cup (4 ounces) butter or margarine,
melted
2 teaspoons lemon juice
1 teaspoon vanilla
1 3½-ounce can flaked coconut
½ cup pecans, coarsely broken
1 unbaked 9-inch pie shell

Preheat oven to 350 degrees. Thoroughly combine eggs, sugar, butter or margarine, lemon juice and vanilla. Stir in coconut and pecans. Pour into pie shell. Bake at 350 degrees for 45 to 50 minutes or until filling is set. Cool. Garnish with sweetened whipped cream and pecan halves, if desired.

Pecan Pie

"Always a favorite pie, sells well at bake sales."

Yields 1 pie

¾ cup granulated sugar
1 cup dark corn syrup
3 eggs, slightly beaten
1 teaspoon vanilla
1 cup pecans, broken
4 tablespoons butter or margarine
1 pie shell, unbaked

Preheat oven to 350 degrees. Boil sugar and syrup for about 2 minutes. Pour slowly over slightly beaten eggs, stirring vigorously. Add butter or margarine, vanilla and nut meats. Pour into unbaked or frozen pie shell. Bake for 50 to 60 minutes. Serves 6 to 8.

Sue Meredith

Kentucky Pecan Pie

"Allow to cool before slicing."

Yields 1 pie

1 cup white corn syrup
1 cup dark brown sugar
½ teaspoon salt
⅓ cup butter or margarine, melted
1 teaspoon vanilla
3 large eggs, slightly beaten
1 heaping cup shelled pecans
1 pie shell, unbaked

Combine syrup, sugar, salt, butter, vanilla and mix well. Add slightly beaten eggs. Pour into a 9-inch unbaked pie shell. Sprinkle pecans over all. Bake in a preheated 350 degree oven for approximately 45 minutes, until center is firm.

Barbara Warriner

Southern Pecan Pie

"Old fashioned and delicious."

Yields 1 pie

½ cup sugar
1 cup brown sugar (not firmly packed)
1 tablespoon flour
2 tablespoons milk
1 teaspoon vanilla
2 eggs
7 tablespoons margarine
1 cup pecans, broken if desired
1 unbaked pie shell

Mix all ingredients except butter and pecans. Melt butter and add to mixture. Add pecans and pour into pie shell. Bake at 350 degrees for 30 to 35 minutes.

Ressie Roberts

Quick Chocolate Pie

"Goes together quickly."

Yields 1 pie

2 eggs, beaten
2 tablespoons flour
2 tablespoons cocoa
½ teaspoon vanilla
1¼ cups sugar
¼ teaspoon salt
2 tablespoons butter or oleo
½ cup milk

Beat the 2 eggs lightly and add sugar, flour, salt, cocoa, butter, vanilla and milk. Beat all at one time and bake at 375 degrees for about 35 minutes or until set.

Jane Sebrell

Chocolate Meringue Pie

"A much requested recipe."

Yields 2 pies

6 egg yolks
6 heaping tablespoons flour
1 12-ounce can evaporated milk mixed
  with 1 can water
3 cups sugar
6 tablespoons cocoa
⅛ teaspoon salt
2 teaspoons vanilla
2 pie shells, baked

Sift dry ingredients together and mix. Scald milk and add to dry ingredients. Gradually add to well-beaten egg yolks. Add butter last. Place over boiling water and cook until thickened. You may use heavy saucepan over direct medium heat and stir constantly. Cool, add vanilla and pour into 2 baked pie shells. Top with meringue made with egg whites.

Meringue
6 egg whites
¼ teaspoon cream of tartar
2 teaspoons cold water
12 teaspoons sugar

Place 3 egg whites in each bowl and add 1 tablespoon cold water and ⅛ teaspoon cream of tartar to each. Whip until foamy and add 2 teaspoons sugar for each egg white. Beat until mixture stands in peaks. Spread over pies, being sure that meringue covers all of filling, sealing to the crust. Bake in a 350 degree oven for 10 to 15 minutes.

Bettie Sue Neal

Kentucky Pie

"A chocolate chip pie."

Yields 1 pie

1 cup sugar (may use ½ cup brown
  plus ½ cup white)
½ cup flour
1 teaspoon vanilla
1 cup pecans, chopped
½ bag chocolate chips (1 cup)
2 eggs
¼ pound margarine, melted
1 pie shell, unbaked

Mix sugar and flour. Add eggs, beaten slightly. Melt butter and add to mixture. Stir well. Add vanilla, nuts and chocolate chips. Pour into unbaked pie shell. Bake at 325 degrees for 35 minutes and then serve warm. Whipped cream or ice cream make a delicious topping.

Susan O. Tucker

For an extra kick add an ounce or so of good old Kentucky Bourbon.

Beth Sullivan

Chocolate Chess Pie

"This can make 3 regular size pies, shorten cooking time."

Yields 2 pies

4 squares unsweetened chocolate
2 sticks margarine
6 eggs
3¾ cups sugar
1 12-ounce can evaporated milk
1 tablespoon vanilla
2 deep dish 9-inch pie shells, unbaked

Melt chocolate and margarine, then add sugar and eggs and beat well by hand. Add milk and vanilla and stir well. Pour mixture into 2 deep dish 9-inch pie crusts and bake at 325 degrees for 45 minutes.

Jessie S. Daniel

Chocolate Silk Pie

"Very important to add eggs one at a time and beat well."

Yields 1 pie

1 stick butter or margarine, softened
2 squares, unsweetened chocolate, melted
2 eggs
¾ cup sugar
1 teaspoon vanilla
1 pie shell, baked

Cream margarine and sugar. Add eggs, one at a time, beating at least 3 minutes after each addition. Add melted chocolate and vanilla, beating well. Pour into baked pie shell and chill. May be garnished with whipped cream and shavings of bitter chocolate.

Helen Fleshood

Chocolate Chess Pie

"Good for taking to potluck suppers."

Yields 2 pies

2½ cups white sugar
⅔ cup or 5-ounce can evaporated milk
4 tablespoons butter
1 teaspoon vanilla
4 eggs
4 tablespoons cocoa
¼ teaspoon salt
2 pie shells, unbaked

Mix all ingredients together and pour into unbaked pie shells. Bake at 350 degrees for 45 minutes.

Anne Lewis

Fruit Cobbler

"For peach cobbler, add ½ teaspoon almond extract."

Serves 8

1 cup sugar
2 teaspoons baking powder
¾ cup milk
1 cup flour
⅛ teaspoon salt
1 stick butter or margarine
1 quart or less sweetened berries or fruit
(may substitute canned fruit)

Melt butter or margarine in baking pan - 2-quart size. Combine dry ingredients and stir in milk and melted butter. Pour mixture into buttered pan. Pour berries or fruit in middle of batter, do not stir. Bake at 350 degrees for 45 to 60 minutes. Batter will rise over fruit.

Angela Coltrane and Orline White

▲ To decrease fat content, use lowfat/skim milk and lowfat margarine.

Orangey Peach Cobbler

"Especially good served warm, but good cold too."

Serves 8

1 1-pound, 5-ounce can peach pie filling
¼ cup water
¼ teaspoon nutmeg
1 tablespoon lemon juice
¼ cup chopped nuts
¼ cup raisins
1 package refrigerator orange Danish rolls

In saucepan, combine pie filling, water, nutmeg, lemon juice, nuts and raisins. Heat to boiling. Pour into 9-inch round ovenware cake dish. Top hot peaches with rolls, cut side up. Bake at 400 degrees for 20 minutes. Remove from oven and spread tops of rolls with icing that comes in the orange roll package.

Justine Jones

Strawberry Pie

"Easy and delicious."

Yields 1 pie

1 cooled, baked pastry shell
1 cup water
4 tablespoons strawberry gelatin
1 cup sugar
1 pint strawberries
3 tablespoons cornstarch
3 to 4 drops red food coloring

Combine sugar, cornstarch and water and cook until clear. Remove from heat and add red food coloring and powdered gelatin. Stir until gelatin is well dissolved. Add strawberries, mix well and pour into pie shell. Chill thoroughly.

Helen Manson and Hilda Anderson

Easy Strawberry Yogurt Pie

"Folks ask for more."

Yields 1 pie

2 8-ounce containers strawberry yogurt
½ cup fresh strawberries (or frozen)
1 8-ounce container frozen whipped
  topping, thawed
1 graham cracker crust

Combine fruit and yogurt in bowl. Fold in thawed whipped topping mix. Spoon into graham cracker crust and freeze 4 hours.

Margaret Andrews

▲ To lower fat, use lowfat yogurt and lowfat whipped topping.

Strawberry Pie

"A springtime treat."

Yields 1 pie

2 cups strawberries, chopped,
  unsweetened
1 cup sweetened condensed milk
1 12-ounce (large) carton prepared
  whipped topping
1 cup nuts, chopped
⅓ cup lemon juice
2 pie shells, baked

Mix milk and lemon juice together. Stir in nuts and berries. Fold in whipped topping and pour into baked pie shells. Refrigerate for 2 or 3 hours before serving.

Lucy Clary

Blueberry Pie

"Fun for July 4th. Use cherry pie filling in half of pie and blueberry filling in the other half— red, white and blue."

Yields 2 pies

1 cup pecans, finely chopped
2 regular pie crusts
2 envelopes whipped topping mix
1 8-ounce package cream cheese
1¼ cups confectionary sugar
1 teaspoon vanilla
2 cans blueberry pie filling

Allow pie crusts to slightly thaw. Push chopped pecans into the pie crusts. Bake crust according to instructions. Mix the whipped topping according to package instructions. Combine softened cream cheese, sugar and vanilla. Blend whipped topping into cream cheese mixture. Spread on top of cooked pie crusts. Refrigerate for several hours. Put 1 can blueberry pie filling on top before serving.

Evelyn Carpenter

▲ To lower fat content, use diet whipped topping mix and lowfat cream cheese.

Sherry Chiffon Pie

"Chill thoroughly before serving."

Yields 1 pie

1 tablespoon plain gelatin
1½ tablespoons cold water
½ cup evaporated milk
¼ cup water
2 well-beaten egg yolks
⅓ cup sugar
Pinch of salt
3 or 4 tablespoons sherry wine
4 egg whites
5 tablespoons sugar
1 pie shell, baked

Soak gelatin in 1½ tablespoons water; set aside. Mix together and cook until thick milk and the ¼ cup water, the egg yolks, sugar and salt. When done add gelatin into hot custard to dissolve. Remove from heat, add sherry wine. Beat egg whites stiff with 5 tablespoons sugar. Fold whites into cooked custard. Put into a large baked pie shell and chill. To make coconut, omit sherry, add 1 teaspoon vanilla and fold in 1 cup fresh coconut.

Edith Buford

Limeade Pie

"Summertime flavor anytime of the year."

Yields 1 pie

1 small can frozen limeade
1 9-ounce carton prepared whipped topping
1 can sweetened condensed milk
1 graham cracker crust

Mix limeade, milk and whipped topping together, blend well. Pour into crust and refrigerate at least 1 hour before serving.

Marion Barkley

Jell-e-O Pie

"Top with whipped cream."

Yields 2 pies

1 package strawberry gelatin
1 cup sugar
1 cup pineapple juice
2 eggs
1 12-ounce can evaporated milk, chilled
2 graham cracker crust pie shells

Mix gelatin, sugar, eggs and juice. Bring to a boil, remove from heat. Beat chilled milk and mix well with gelatin mixture. Pour in graham cracker crust and chill 2 hours. Top with whipped cream before serving.

Brenda Ray

"Snowfall, or even the prediction of a snow, has always seemed to be welcomed by school children. Of course, it could mean more time to do inside chores. But it often means time for listening to favorite music, working on a model car kit, taking part in a cookie-baking project, or taking a long walk in the falling snow. For many children and adults alike, the words 'snow day' evoke a thrill. Snow changes much more than the landscape."

Eldridge Bagley

"SNOW DAY"
Appears through the courtesy of the painting's owners, Joyce and Mike Moorman.

Bourbon Fruit Cookies

"An alternative to fruit cake."

Yields 9 dozen

1 pound red candied cherries, chopped
1 pound green candied pineapple, chopped
1 pound pecan halves, chopped
1 15-ounce package golden raisins
3 cups all-purpose flour, divided
1 teaspoon baking soda
1 teaspoon ground cinnamon
1 teaspoon ground nutmeg
1 teaspoon ground cloves
½ cup butter or margarine, softened
½ cup firmly packed brown sugar
4 eggs
½ cup bourbon
3 tablespoons milk

Combine cherries, pineapple, pecans, raisins and ½ cup flour; toss well to coat. Set aside. Combine remaining flour and next 4 ingredients; set aside.

Cream butter, gradually add sugar, beating until fluffy. Add eggs and beat well. Add dry ingredients, bourbon, and milk, mix well. Stir in fruit mixture. Drop dough by teaspoonfuls onto lightly greased cookie sheets. Bake at 300 degrees for 20 minutes.

Harriette Newsom

Elegant Chocolate Chip Cookies

"Always a favorite."

Yields 4 dozen

1½ cups all-purpose flour
½ teaspoon soda
⅓ teaspoon salt
⅔ cup soft butter or half shortening
½ cup granulated sugar
½ cup brown sugar, packed
1 teaspoon vanilla
1 large egg or 2 small
1 tablespoon cream
½ cup chopped nuts
1 6- or 7-ounce package chocolate chips

Grease baking sheets lightly. Start oven 10 minutes before baking; set to moderate (375 degrees). Sift flour, measure and add soda and salt; resift 4 times with soda and salt. Cream butter until smooth and shiny, add sugars and cream well. Stir in vanilla, then beat in egg until fluffy. Add flour in 2 portions, mixing, until smooth after each. Stir in cream, then nuts and chocolate chips. Drop level spoonfuls onto prepared sheets 2½ inches apart; bake about 10 minutes or until delicately browned. Remove from oven; let stand a minute, then remove cookies to cake racks.

Virginia Waite Lucy

Black-Eyed Susans

"Pretty as a picture."

Yields 3 dozen

¾ cup stick margarine, softened
½ cup sugar
1 teaspoon vanilla extract
12 drops yellow food coloring
1 egg
1 3-ounce package cream cheese, softened
2 cups flour
35 deluxe chocolate baking pieces

In a large bowl, beat margarine, sugar, vanilla, food coloring, egg and cream cheese until well mixed. Stir in flour until thoroughly blended. Cover and refrigerate until firm, about 2 hours.

Preheat oven to 375 degrees. Shape dough into 1¼-inch balls. Place about 2 inches apart on ungreased baking sheets. Using scissors and cutting about three-fourths through, cut each ball into 6 wedges. Spread wedges apart slightly. (Cookies will flatten as they bake.) Bake until set and edges just begin to brown, 10 to 12 minutes. Immediately press a chocolate piece in center of each cookie. Remove to cool completely on wire rack.

Lois W. Outten

Raisin Oatmeal Cookies

"So good."

Yields 32 large cookies

1½ cups raisins
1½ cups water
2 eggs
1½ teaspoons vanilla extract
1 cup shortening
¾ cup plus 2 tablespoons granulated sugar
1⅓ cups brown sugar, packed
2 cups flour

1⅛ teaspoons salt
½ teaspoon baking soda
½ teaspoon baking powder
3¾ cups oats

Cover raisins with warm water and soak 10 minutes. Drain thoroughly and set aside. Combine eggs, 2 tablespoons water, vanilla, shortening and sugars in mixer bowl. Sift together flour, salt, baking soda and baking powder. Add to egg mixture and beat at low speed 2 to 3 minutes or until smooth. Add oats and raisins and mix until blended. Form into 2-inch thick rolls. Wrap in waxed paper and chill. Slice rolls into ½-inch slices and place on baking sheets. Flatten slightly. For thin cookies, flatten to ¼-inch thickness. Bake at 375 degrees for 10 to 12 minutes.

Brenda Adcock

Cowboy Cookies

"Great oatmeal cookie."

Yields 4 dozen

1 cup granulated sugar
2 cups raw oatmeal
2 eggs
1 teaspoon baking soda
½ teaspoon baking powder
1 cup brown sugar
2 cups flour
1 cup shortening or margarine
¾ teaspoon salt
Nuts (optional - black walnuts especially
   good)

Blend all ingredients. Drop on ungreased cookie sheet by teaspoonfuls. Bake at 325 degrees for about 12 minutes on top shelf.

Annie Ruth Clarke

Oatmeal Molasses Crisps

Yields 3 dozen

1 cup flour
1 cup sugar
1 teaspoon salt
1 teaspoon soda
1 teaspoon cinnamon
¼ teaspoon ginger
½ teaspoon nutmeg
½ cup shortening
¼ cup molasses
1 egg
1½ cups oatmeal

Mix first 7 ingredients, add remaining 4 ingredients and mix well. Drop from teaspoon onto lightly greased cookie sheet and bake at 325 degrees for about 12 minutes.

Mary Tucker

Raisin Cookies

"It doesn't seem like Christmas until I smell these baking in my kitchen."

Yields 8 dozen

1 cup water
2 cups raisins
1 teaspoon baking soda
1 cup butter or margarine
2 cups sugar
1 teaspoon vanilla
2 eggs, well beaten
4⅓ cups all-purpose flour
1 teaspoon baking powder
½ teaspoon salt
1 teaspoon cinnamon
¼ teaspoon nutmeg
1 cup nut meats, chopped

Combine raisins and water in small saucepan. Bring to a boil and boil briskly for 5 minutes. Let cool, then stir in baking soda and allow to stand.

Cream together the shortening, sugar, vanilla and eggs. Add the raisins and juice to the creamed mixture. Sift together the flour, baking powder, salt, cinnamon and nutmeg. Add to creamed mixture along with the nut meats, mixing well. Drop onto greased cookie sheet. Bake in 350 degree oven for 8 to 10 minutes or until lightly brown on top.

Linda Kirchman

Indian Nut Cookies

"The secret is the finely chopped nuts. These brownies melt in your mouth."

Yields 3 dozen

2 cups sugar
½ pound butter, melted
1 cup flour
½ cup cocoa
4 eggs, slightly beaten
½ cup nuts, finely chopped
2 teaspoons vanilla

Pour melted butter over sugar and stir. Then add ingredients in the following order: cocoa, vanilla, eggs, flour and nuts. Stir after each addition, do not beat. Pour into buttered 7 x 11½-inch pan. Cook at 325 degrees for 25 minutes. Batter will still be moist in center when tested. Let cool then cut into small squares. Roll squares in confectionary sugar. If the squares should lose their shape just gently press back into shape of square.

Virginia Outten

Sugar-Coated Molasses Cookies

Yields 4 dozen

¼ cup shortening
4 tablespoons molasses (dark)
2 cups flour
1 teaspoon cinnamon
1 teaspoon ginger
1 cup sugar
1 egg
2 teaspoons soda
1 teaspoon cloves
½ teaspoon salt

Mix ingredients. Roll in small balls and dip in sugar. Flatten with bottom of a glass and bake at 350 degrees for 12 minutes.

Joanna Hayes

Noel Chews

"A Christmas treat."

Makes 16

2 tablespoons butter
2 eggs, slightly beaten
1 cup firmly packed brown sugar
⅛ teaspoon soda
1 cup nut meats
5 tablespoons flour
1 teaspoon vanilla

Melt butter in a 9-inch square pan. In a mixing bowl combine all remaining ingredients, mixing well. Pour this batter into pan over the melted butter, do not stir. Bake for 15 to 20 minutes in 350 degree oven. Cut into squares when slightly cool.

Mary Lough

Crackly Orange and Ginger Cookies

"These keep for months in a closed container or freeze very well."

Yields 6 dozen

¾ cup shortening or margarine
1 cup brown sugar
½ cup dark molasses
1 egg
3 tablespoons fresh grated orange rind
2½ cups flour (or more)
1 tablespoon ground ginger
1 teaspoon cinnamon
2 teaspoons baking soda
½ teaspoon salt
½ cup sugar

Mix together the shortening and brown sugar. Add to this the molasses, egg and 2 tablespoons of the orange rind, reserving the remaining orange rind for later. Combine the flour, ginger, cinnamon, baking soda and salt in a separate bowl. After mixing dry ingredients well, combine all. Batter should be stiff; if not add a little more flour. Mix the remaining orange rind and sugar together. Make balls of the cookie dough about the size of walnuts. Roll in the sugar and orange rind mix. Put on a greased baking sheet and bake 9 to 12 minutes in a 350 degree oven. Take out when surface crackles.

Susan Neale

Hello Dolly Cookies

"Also known as Seven Layer Cookie."

Yields 18 cookies

1 stick margarine
1 cup graham cracker crumbs
1 cup coconut (or 1 cup crispy rice cereal)
1 cup chocolate bits
1 package butterscotch bits
1 cup pecans, chopped
1 can sweetened condensed milk
2 tablespoons rum, optional

Melt margarine in a 9 x 9-inch pan. Sprinkle graham cracker crumbs over this evenly. Add in layers, coconut, chocolate, butterscotch bits and pecans, spreading each evenly. Over this pour the can of sweetened condensed milk and 2 tablespoons rum. Bake at 350 degrees for 35 minutes or until browned. Mark off squares while warm. Cut when cool. Freezes beautifully.

Ann Mathews and Nell Lashley Knight

Chinese Chews

"Coconutty and chewy."

Yields 2 dozen

1 stick butter
1 box light brown sugar
2 cups flour
3 eggs
1 cup coconut
1 teaspoon baking powder
½ teaspoon salt
1 teaspoon vanilla
1 cup nuts

Mix all ingredients. Place in a 13 x 9-inch oblong pan, greased. Bake for 25 minutes at 350 degrees. Cut in squares.

Willie B. Abernathy

Date Pinwheels

"Really good."

Yields 8 dozen

½ cup margarine
½ cup brown sugar
½ cup granulated sugar
1 egg
½ teaspoon vanilla
2 cups all-purpose flour
½ teaspoon baking soda
½ teaspoon salt
1 recipe date filling

Thoroughly cream butter and sugar. Add egg and vanilla; beat well. Sift dry ingredients. Stir into other mixture. Chill. Divide dough in half. On a lightly floured surface, roll 1 part 12 x 18-inch rectangle about ¼-inch thick. Spread surface with half of date filling, beginning at long edge and roll up like a jellyroll. Repeat with other batch. Wrap in waxed paper, chill well. Slice ¼-inch thick. Bake at 400 degrees for approximately 8 minutes.

Date filling
1 pound dates, cut up
½ cup sugar
½ cup water
½ cup nuts (optional)

Combine dates, sugar and water. Cook and stir until boils and thickens slightly. Cool before spreading. Add nuts just before spreading on dough.

Beth Parker

Date Nut Bars

"Don't overcook. Cooking time will depend on size of pan you use."

Yields 5 dozen

¾ cup butter or margarine
3 eggs
2 teaspoons baking powder
1 8-ounce package pitted dates, chopped
1 pound light brown sugar
2¾ cups flour
1 cup nuts, chopped
1 teaspoon vanilla
½ teaspoon salt

Melt margarine or butter; add sugar and beaten eggs. Mix well. Sift flour, baking powder, and salt. Add to sugar mixture. Stir until blended. Add nuts, dates and vanilla. Mix well. Spread in well-greased jellyroll pan. Batter will be very stiff. Bake for 25 to 30 minutes in a 350 degree oven. Cool, cut into small squares.

Virginia Elmore

Congo Squares

"Delicious."

Yields 3 dozen

¾ cup shortening or margarine
3 eggs
2½ teaspoons baking powder
1 cup broken nuts
1 pound light brown sugar
2¾ cups flour
½ teaspoon salt
1 6-ounce package semisweet chocolate
  morsels

Melt the shortening in a large saucepan. Add brown sugar and mix well. Cool slightly. Add eggs, one at a time, beating well after each addition. Sift together the flour, baking powder and salt. Add the flour mixture to mixture in the saucepan; mix well. Add broken nut meats and chocolate morsels. Pour into 2 greased 7½ x 11 x 1½-inch pans. Bake at 325 to 350 degrees for 25 to 30 minutes. When almost cool, cut into squares.

Pat Temple

Pecan Pie Surprise Bars

"A special treat."

Yields 3 to 4 dozen

1 18½-ounce package yellow cake mix
½ cup melted butter
4 eggs
½ cup firmly packed brown sugar
1½ cups dark corn syrup
1 teaspoon vanilla flavoring
1 cup pecans, chopped

Combine ⅓ of the cake mix (reserve remainder for later use) with the melted butter and 1 egg. Mix with a fork until crumbly, press this mixture into a greased 13 x 9 x 2-inch pan. Bake at 350 degrees for 15 to 20 minutes or until lightly brown.

Then combine the remainder of the cake mix with 3 eggs, brown sugar, corn syrup and vanilla in a bowl. Beat for 1 to 2 minutes at medium speed with mixer. Pour over the partially baked crust then sprinkle with pecans. Return to oven and bake for 30 to 35 minutes. Cool and cut into bars.

Bertie Fleshood

Brownies

"Do not overcook."

Yields 2 dozen

2 sticks margarine
1 cup flour
2 cups sugar
4 squares chocolate
4 eggs
1 teaspoon vanilla
1 cup pecans, chopped (optional)

Melt chocolate and butter; add sugar and flour and mix well. Add 4 eggs and 1 teaspoon vanilla and nuts if desired. Spread into a 9 x 13-inch greased and floured pan and bake at 325 degrees for about 25 minutes. Do not overcook. Take out when center still seems soft. Cut into squares when almost cool.

Ann R. Long

Chocolate Mint Party Squares

"So pretty for a party."

Yields 2 dozen

1 package brownie mix
2 cups powdered sugar
2 tablespoons crème de menthe liqueur
½ cup margarine
1 cup semisweet chocolate chips
6 tablespoons margarine

Mix brownies according to instructions. Bake in a 13 x 9-inch pan at 350 degrees for 15 minutes. Cool. Beat together powdered sugar, crème de menthe liqueur and ½ cup margarine. Spread like icing over brownies and chill thoroughly. Melt chocolate chips and 6 tablespoons margarine in double boiler. Spread over icing layer and refrigerate until set. Cut into small squares. May be frozen.

Ann Peebles

Lemon Squares

"Use jellyroll pan."

Yields 32

1 cup melted butter
2 cups flour
½ cup sugar

Mix together; press with hands into 9 x 13-inch pan. Bake at 350 degrees for 15 to 20 minutes or until a light golden. Meanwhile, prepare the following:

4 eggs
2 cups sugar
4 tablespoons flour
Rind and juice of 2 lemons

Beat eggs and add sugar, flour, lemon juice and rind. Pour over the cooked crust and return to oven for 15 to 20 minutes. Cool and cover with confectioner's sugar. Cut and serve in squares. Keeps well in refrigerator.

Kay Outter

*The bay window at **The Wilson House** is filled with flowers and their fragrance blends with the holiday fragrances that fill the home.*

Cinnamon Sticks

"Simply good."

Yields 3 dozen

1 cup all-purpose flour
1 cup sugar
2 teaspoons cinnamon
1½ sticks butter or margarine
1 egg, separated
½ teaspoon vanilla
1 cup pecans, finely chopped

Sift together flour, sugar and cinnamon. Cream butter, then work in flour mixture. Add egg yolk and vanilla and mix well. Spread to ¼-inch thickness on a lightly greased jellyroll pan. Brush egg white on with pastry brush. Sprinkle liberally with pecans. Bake at 325 degrees for 30 minutes, or until light brown. Cut into rectangles. Remove to wire rack to cool.

Justine Jones

Country Crisp Sugar Cookies

"Roll thin, use appropriate cookie cutter for the season."

Yields 6 dozen

½ cup butter or margarine
1 cup sugar
1 egg
1 tablespoon heavy cream
   (or evaporated milk)
1 teaspoon vanilla
2 cups sifted all-purpose flour
½ teaspoon salt
1 teaspoon baking powder
Colored sugar for tops

Cream butter or margarine with sugar in mixing bowl until light and fluffy. Add egg, cream and vanilla. Beat well. Sift flour with salt and baking powder. Add to creamed mixture beating until well combined. Chill dough overnight. When ready to bake, start oven at 350 degrees. Grease 2 or more cookie sheets lightly. Dust with flour. Roll out small amount of dough at a time, very thin, on lightly floured board. Cut with desired shaped cutter. Sprinkle cookies lightly with sugar. Bake for about 5 minutes, or until done. Makes 6 dozen small cookies.

Joyce Moorman

Old Fashioned Tea Cakes

"Keeps very well in tight container."

Yields 6 dozen

2 eggs
1 cup sugar
3 cups flour
3 teaspoons baking powder
1 teaspoon salt
1 teaspoon vanilla
1 cup shortening

In mixing bowl, sift the flour, salt and baking powder. Rub shortening into flour with fingertips.

Beat eggs until very light, add sugar and vanilla to beaten eggs and mix well. Pour this liquid into flour and make a soft dough. Wrap dough in waxed paper and put in icebox until chilled enough to handle.

Roll out dough on lightly floured board; sprinkle top with sugar and cut into cookies. Bake in preheated oven at 350 degrees until lightly browned. Keep in container with tight top.

Edith Buford

Snickerdoodles

"Children will love them, you can stick a chocolate candy kiss in center before baking for an additional treat."

Yields 6 dozen

1 cup shortening
1½ cups sugar
2 eggs
2¾ cups flour
2 teaspoons cream of tartar
1 teaspoon soda
½ teaspoon salt

Mix shortening, sugar and eggs. Cream until smooth. Sift flour, cream of tartar, soda and salt together and add to creamed mixture. Refrigerate for several hours for easier handling.

Roll dough into small balls, then in mixture of granulated sugar and cinnamon. Place on ungreased cookie sheet. Bake in a 400 degree oven for 8 to 10 minutes.

Ann Peebles

Sand Tarts

Yields 6 dozen

1 cup butter or margarine
4 tablespoons powdered sugar
2 cups flour
1½ teaspoons baking powder
½ teaspoon salt
1 tablespoon vanilla
1 cup pecans, finely chopped (optional)

Cream butter and sugar. Sift together flour, baking powder and salt. Gradually add flour mixture to creamed mixture. Add vanilla and nuts. Drop 1-inch balls onto a greased cookie sheet and then mash slightly flat. Bake at 375 degrees until brown.

Frosting
1½ cups confectioner's sugar
2 tablespoons cocoa
2 tablespoons hot water
½ teaspoon vanilla

Combine sugar and cocoa; add hot water and vanilla. Spread on cooled cookie. Top with almond half.

Kaye Samford

Welsh Cookies

"Christmas cooking together for Mother and Father."

1 cup butter or margarine
1 cup shortening
2 cups sugar
3 eggs, beaten
¼ cup milk
7½ cups sifted flour
1 teaspoon salt
1 teaspoon nutmeg
1 teaspoon cream of tartar
1 teaspoon baking soda
2 teaspoons baking powder
1 pound box of currants

Cream butter and shortening. Add sugar and cream together well. Add beaten eggs and milk. Sift together the dry ingredients and add to the above mixture. Stir in currants. Roll on a lightly floured board about ¼-inch thick and cut with a cookie cutter. Fry on an ungreased griddle over low heat. Turn when brown. Be sure that cookies are only turned once.

Rev. Richard Handley

Chocolate Mexican Wedding Cookies

"The addition of chocolate to this traditional cookie works well."

Yields 5 dozen

¾ **cup each: firmly packed brown sugar, softened butter**
3 **1-ounce squares unsweetened baking chocolate, melted**
1 **teaspoon vanilla extract**
2 **cups flour**
1 **cup finely chopped pecans**
½ **teaspoon salt**
Confectioner's sugar

Preheat oven to 350 degrees. In a large bowl with electric mixer at medium speed, beat brown sugar and butter, scraping down sides of bowl often, until light and fluffy, 1 to 2 minutes. Add chocolate and vanilla. Continue beating and scraping 2 minutes longer.

Reduce speed to low and add flour and nuts. Beat until well mixed, 1 to 2 minutes. Shape dough into 1-inch balls. Place 2 inches apart on ungreased baking sheets. Bake just until set, 8 to 10 minutes. Cool 5 minutes on cookie sheets. Remove to wire racks and cool 5 minutes longer. While still warm, roll in confectioner's sugar. Cool completely then roll in confectioner's sugar again.

Carolyn Berry

Mexican Wedding Cookies

"Also known as Swedish Wedding Cookies or Pecan Puffs."

Yields 6 dozen

½ **pound butter**
7 **tablespoons confectioner's sugar**
1 **teaspoon vanilla**
2 **cups sifted flour**
1½ **cups pecans, finely chopped**
Pinch of salt

Cream butter. Add sugar, vanilla, flour and nuts; mix well. Shape into small fingers. Bake in a 325 degree oven on an ungreased cookie sheet for about 25 minutes. Roll warm cookies in confectioner's sugar. Roll in sugar again when cool.

Anne Walker

Orange Blossoms

"Make several days before serving to let juices soak in well."

Yields 80

1 **box yellow cake mix**
Juice and rind of 3 oranges
Juice and rind of 3 lemons
1½ **boxes confectioner's sugar**
1 **teaspoon vanilla**

Mix cake according to directions. Bake in miniature muffin tins. Combine juices, rinds, confectioner's sugar and vanilla. Stir well until dissolved. Place hot cakes into juice mixture, turn over and cover well, and then put on waxed paper to drain. Will make at least 80 small cakes. Better made at least 1 day ahead. Freezes well.

Betty Vincent

Pecan Tea Tassies

"Freeze well."

Yields 2 dozen

Pastry
1 3-ounce package cream cheese
½ cup butter or margarine
1 cup sifted all-purpose flour

Cream cheese and butter, softened at room temperature, then blend and stir in flour. Chill about an hour in refrigerator. Shape 2 dozen 1-inch balls and place in ungreased small muffin tins. Press dough in bottom and sides of pan to shape pastry.

Filling
¾ cup brown sugar
1 tablespoon butter or margarine
1 teaspoon vanilla
1 egg
Dash of salt
⅔ cup pecans, coarsely broken

Stir together the beaten egg, butter, vanilla, salt, brown sugar and beat until smooth. Divide pecans in half. Put few pecans in each pastry shell and add egg mixture. Top with remaining pecans. Bake in a 325 degree oven for 25 minutes or until filling is set. Cool before removing from pans.

Irene Kirchman

Mini Chocolate Cherry Tarts

"If you don't have small heart-shaped muffin tins you can use regular mini muffin tins."

Yields 3½ dozen

Pastry Crust
1½ cups flour
½ cup sugar
¼ cup unsweetened cocoa
½ cup butter or margarine
1 to 2 tablespoons water
Cherry or raspberry pie filling

Lightly spray small heart-shaped muffin tin with vegetable pan spray. In a small bowl combine flour, sugar and cocoa. Cut in butter or margarine until pieces are the size of small peas. Sprinkle with water, tossing until moistened. Form into 1-inch diameter log. Divide pastry into 40 balls. Press balls into muffin tins, making an even shell. Fill with cream cheese mixture. Bake at 350 degrees for 10 to 15 minutes or until cheese filling is firm but not brown. Remove from pan and cool completely. Top each with teaspoon of pie filling.

Cream Cheese Mixture
2 8-ounce packages cream cheese, softened
1 cup sugar
2 eggs
2 teaspoons vanilla

Beat cream cheese until light and creamy; gradually add sugar; mix well. Add eggs, one at a time, mixing well after each addition. Stir in vanilla.
Hint: I find that half of this recipe is enough to fill the tarts.

Alta Brown

Thumbprint Cookies

"Use any jam or jelly you prefer."

Yields 2½ dozen

¼ **cup each: packed brown sugar,**
   shortening, softened stick margarine
½ **teaspoon vanilla extract**
1 **egg, separated**
1 **cup flour**
¼ **teaspoon salt**
1 **cup finely chopped walnuts, pecans,**
   almonds or peanuts
7½ **teaspoons jam or jelly**

Preheat oven to 350 degrees.

In a large bowl, beat sugar, shortening, margarine, vanilla and egg yolk until well blended. Stir in flour and salt. Shape dough into 1-inch balls.

In small bowl, beat egg white slightly. Dip each ball in egg white then roll to coat in nuts. Place about 1 inch apart on ungreased baking sheet. Press thumb deeply in center of each. Bake until light golden brown, about 10 minutes. Quickly remake indentions with end of wooden spoon if they've risen during baking. Remove to wire rack. Fill each with ¼ teaspoon jam or jelly.

Joan Mitchell

Fade-A-Ways

"These look pretty on a tea table."

Yields 4 dozen

2 **small packages cream cheese**
2 **cups flour**
Orange marmalade
½ **pound butter**
Dash of salt
Powdered sugar

Cream together cream cheese and butter. Add flour and salt. Roll thin and cut into small squares or rounds. Place small amounts of orange marmalade on each. Fold over and pinch into triangles or puffs. Bake for 10 minutes at 350 to 375 degrees on cookie sheet. Sprinkle with powdered sugar as they come from oven.

Ruth Anderson

Ugly Cookies

"You won't believe how good these are - ignore the name."

Yields 3 dozen

1 **cup raisins**
1 **cup nuts, chopped**
1 **can sweetened condensed milk**
Round buttery crackers

Cook combined ingredients, stirring until thick, over medium heat. Spread on crackers. Bake on ungreased cookie sheet at 350 degrees for 10 minutes. Cool.

Topping
½ **stick butter or margarine**
1 **cup 4-X sugar**

Mix thoroughly and spread on top.

Edith Marcuson

Peanut Butter Cookies

"I have never found a better peanut butter cookie recipe."

Yields 8 dozen

1 cup creamy peanut butter
1 cup granulated sugar
1 cup brown sugar
1 cup margarine or butter
2 eggs, beaten
3 cups flour
2 teaspoons baking soda
½ teaspoon salt
1 teaspoon vanilla

Cream together the sugar and shortening until light and fluffy. Add soda, salt and eggs, continue blending. Add peanut butter and vanilla and mix well. Beat in flour till well blended. Roll in balls the size of a walnut and place on greased cookie sheet. Press flat with fork. Cook at 375 degrees for 8 to 10 minutes.

Sue Browning

Strawberry Chews

"A pretty and delicious dessert for a tea or reception."

Yields 2 dozen

1 pound coconut (ground fine in a meat grinder)
¼ pound ground almonds (meat grinder)
Dash of salt
1 6-ounce package strawberry gelatin, minus 2 tablespoons
Red food coloring, as desired
1 tablespoon sugar
1 can sweetened condensed milk
½ teaspoon vanilla
1 3-ounce package strawberry gelatin for rolling

Add food coloring to milk and add to all the remaining ingredients, except the 3-ounce package of gelatin. Mix well and then shape in berry shapes with your hands. Roll in the 3-ounce package of gelatin plus the 2 tablespoons from the above 6-ounce package. Use a tube of green icing (made for cake decorating) to make green leaves and a stem on each berry.

Peggy Martin

Robin's Ginger Snaps

"Wonderful fall treat, especially nice on Halloween."

1 cup sugar
¾ cup vegetable shortening
1 egg
¼ cup molasses
2 cups flour
2 teaspoons baking soda
½ teaspoon salt
1 teaspoon cinnamon
1 teaspoon ginger
1 teaspoon cloves
Granulated sugar (for rolling)

Cream together the sugar and shortening. Add the egg. Beat and add molasses. Sift the dry ingredients together and add to the creamed mixture. Chill at least 20 minutes (or overnight). Shape into balls and roll in granulated sugar. Bake on greased cookie sheet at 350 degrees for 10 to 15 minutes. Cool on a rack.

Beth Bagley

Gingerbread Men

"I like them spicy, so I use full, rounded measures of the spices."

Yields 3 dozen

¼ cup margarine
½ cup brown sugar
   (packed, but not firmly)
½ cup molasses
3½ cups flour (I use whole wheat flour
   for a small portion of this)
1 teaspoon soda
¼ teaspoon ground cloves
½ teaspoon cinnamon
1 teaspoon ginger
½ teaspoon salt
About ¼ cup water

Blend margarine and sugar till creamy. Beat in molasses. Stir dry ingredients together and add to batter alternately with water in about 3 additions. I find I need to add a bit more than ¼ cup of water to mix in all flour. Roll dough out on a lightly floured board or waxed paper to thickness you desire. I make some thin and some thick. Cut with gingerbread man cutter and press raisins into dough for eyes, buttons, shoes, etc. Bake on lightly greased cookie sheet at 350 degrees for 8 minutes or more according to thickness. They're done when they spring back when touched lightly with your finger. You can make an icing with confectioner's sugar and a few drops of water, but I never use it. All the cookies rise when you cook them. The thinner ones will be crisper, the fatter ones, more cake-like. They're delicious both ways.

These also make charming Christmas tree decorations which will save from year to year if well stored. Just make a small hole at the top of the head before baking so that a threaded needle will pass through it without crumbling your gingerbread man, tie off the threads, and hang on tree. Hang them far enough back on branch to support their weight and high enough so that pet dogs or cats don't nibble them!

Jenny Showalter

Divinity

"Should be made in very dry weather."

Yields 3 dozen

2 cups sugar
½ cup light corn syrup
½ cup water
Dash of salt
2 egg whites, stiffly beaten
1 teaspoon vanilla

In a large saucepan, stir sugar into corn syrup, water and salt until dissolved. Boil to soft ball stage (240 degrees). Slowly pour ⅓ of syrup over egg whites, beating constantly.

Cook remaining syrup to very hard ball stage (265 degrees). Slowly pour remaining syrup over egg mixture and beat at high speed about 8 minutes, until divinity loses its gloss and holds shape. Add vanilla. Drop by teaspoons onto buttered cookie sheet.

Myrtle Brockwell

Microwave Fudge

"The magic of microwave."

Yields 24 pieces

1 pound powdered sugar
½ cup cocoa
¼ cup milk
¼ teaspoon salt
½ cup margarine (1 stick)
½ to 1 cup nuts, chopped (optional)

Mix first 4 ingredients in microwave or glass bowl. Cut margarine in small pieces and stir into mixture. Microwave on high for 2 minutes. Remove and stir in nuts. Put into a greased pie plate or 8 x 8-inch casserole dish. Cool before cutting.

Maureen J. Harris

Chocolate Fudge

"Everybody wants some."

1 cup nuts
1 teaspoon vanilla
1 6-ounce package semisweet chocolate chips
¼ pound butter or margarine
1 6-ounce can evaporated milk
2 cups sugar
10 large marshmallows

In a large bowl, add nuts, vanilla, chocolate and butter. Set aside. In saucepan, add milk, sugar, marshmallows. Bring to boil. Boil 6 minutes, stirring constantly. Pour over chocolate mixture in bowl. Mix until chocolate dissolves. Pour into a greased shallow pan.

Sara Nabors

$500 Fudge

"This is superb."

Yields 2 dozen

4½ cups sugar
1 12-ounce can evaporated milk
2 sticks margarine or butter (1 cup)
3 6-ounce packages chocolate chips
3 teaspoons vanilla
Nuts, if desired

Bring sugar and milk to a rolling boil that cannot be stirred down. Boil for 6 minutes (time this), stirring constantly. Remove from heat and add margarine, chocolate chips and vanilla, stir until melted; add nuts, if desired.

Pour into a 13 x 9-inch buttered pan, let stand 6 hours (preferably overnight) before cutting. Use larger pan if thinner fudge is desired.

Store in tight container and it will keep for weeks and stay creamy.

Kitty Daniel

Traditional Fudge

"We used to make this at slumber parties."

Yields 1½ dozen

3 cups sugar
6 tablespoons cocoa
4 tablespoons corn syrup
1 cup canned cream (undiluted)
3 tablespoon butter
1 teaspoon vanilla

Put sugar, cocoa, corn syrup, cream into pan and stir until it is all mixed well. Place on medium heat stirring constantly until it starts to boil. When it starts to boil, cover for 2 minutes, after 2 minutes uncover and stir occasionally until it forms a firm ball in cold water. Remove from heat, add butter and vanilla and beat until it is ready to pour. Pour on buttered plate. It is ready to pour when the shine leaves and the consistency changes.

Irene Kirchman

Peanut Brittle

"Crackling, crunchy, good."

Yields 1 cup

1 cup roasted peanuts
1 cup sugar
1 teaspoon vanilla
Dash of salt

Melt sugar and salt in iron frying pan. Add peanuts and vanilla. Pour into greased dish. Let cool.

Virginia Vaughn

Holiday Fudge

"A Christmas treat."

Yields 2½ dozen

2 6-ounce packages semisweet chocolate pieces
1 14-ounce can sweetened condensed milk
1 cup nuts, coarsely chopped
¼ cup mixed candied fruit, coarsely chopped

Line 9 x 5 x 3-inch loaf pan with waxed paper, let paper hang over the sides. Butter lightly.

In top of double boiler over hot water, not boiling water, melt chocolate. Add milk, nuts, and fruit. Mix well.

Turn into prepared pan. Refrigerate several hours or until firm. To turn out of pan, grasp paper and remove in one block. Cut into 32 1-inch squares. Makes 2 pounds.

Chum Morehead

Candy Peanuts

"It's hard to eat just one!"

Yields 3 cups

1 cup sugar
¼ cup water
1 tablespoon red food coloring
3 cups raw peanuts

Combine sugar, water, and food coloring. Heat in iron frying pan on low heat until sugar is dissolved. Add peanuts, stirring constantly until peanuts are coated. Pour peanuts on cookie sheet and place in a 300 degree oven for 35 minutes.

Alice Samford

Peanut Butter Cups

"A toothpick is helpful for dipping balls into chocolate."

Yields 6 dozen

2 boxes confectioner's sugar
2 sticks margarine
1 quart peanut butter
1 tablespoon vanilla
2 large packages chocolate chips
½ block paraffin wax

Mix sugar, margarine, peanut butter and vanilla. Blend well and roll into small balls and chill for a while.

Melt in a large double boiler, the chocolate chips, add paraffin and melt. After all is melted dip each ball into chocolate mixture and place on waxed paper to cool. Keep refrigerated.

Peggy Vaughan

Peanut Butter Strips

"These seem to go fast."

Yields 3 dozen

7 slices bread
7 tablespoons peanut butter
7 tablespoons corn oil
1 tablespoon brown sugar
Graham cracker crumbs

Leave crust on bread slices or cut it off. Cut in narrow strips. Place on cookie sheet and toast for 1 hour in a 200 degree oven. Should be dry but not brown.

Combine peanut butter, oil and brown sugar in a saucepan. Melt and mix well. Dip cold toasted bread strips in peanut mixture and roll in graham cracker crumbs. Store in tight container.

Edith Marcuson

Christmas Turtles

"Arrange in glass container for Christmas giving."

Yields 18

Pecan halves
1 large package caramels (unwrapped)
1 12-ounce package semisweet chocolate bits
1 tablespoon paraffin

Place 2 pecan halves side by side - touching on an ungreased cookie sheet. Place a caramel on top of the pecan halves. Continue until caramels are used up. Place in a 175 degree oven until caramels are soft, about 15 minutes. Remove from oven and mash on caramel to flatten. Cool. Then melt chocolate and paraffin over low heat and carefully spoon over caramels. Allow turtles to cool completely. Store in airtight containers.

Ann Peebles

Chocolate Covered Peanut Balls

"Great for gift giving."

Yields 3 dozen

2 sticks margarine
1 cup peanut butter
1 box powdered sugar
2 cups graham crackers, finely crushed
1 cup coconut
1 cup nuts, chopped
1 6-ounce package chocolate bits
1 4-ounce stick paraffin

Melt margarine. Stir in peanut butter and sugar; mix well. Add graham crackers, coconut and nuts. Roll into small balls.

Melt chocolate and paraffin. Dip balls into chocolate mixture and set on rack to cool.

Pat Hardy

Easter Egg Nests

"Any type of egg shaped candy can be used for the nest. I prefer the peanut candy coated chocolate pieces in pastel colors."

Yields 12 nests

1 7-ounce jar marshmallow cream
¼ cup creamy peanut butter
2 tablespoons melted margarine
1 5-ounce can chow mein noodles
1 cup crushed (pastel colored) plain
    candy-coated chocolate pieces

Mix the marshmallow cream, peanut butter and margarine together. Add the noodles and candy pieces. Mix well with hands. Chill briefly to make it easier to work with. Separate into ¼-cup portions and shape into nest. Make an indentation for the "eggs". Refrigerate until ready to use.

Beth Bagley

Caramel Popcorn

"Keeps well in plastic bags."

Yields 10 cups

1½ cups uncooked popcorn
2 cups brown sugar
2 sticks margarine
1 teaspoon salt
½ cup white corn syrup
2 cups raw peanuts
1 teaspoon vanilla
½ teaspoon soda

Pop 1½ cups popcorn. Mix together the sugar, margarine, salt, corn syrup and raw peanuts. Bring to a boil. Boil 5 minutes over low heat - not stirring. Remove from heat and add vanilla and soda, stir in. Pour over popcorn in a very large container (a large roasting pan) sprayed with Pam. Bake 1 hour at 250 degrees, stirring every 15 minutes. When cool, break apart quickly.

June Clary

Candied Grapefruit Peel

"Sugar may be repeatedly sprinkled on the hot peel until there is a good sugar coating."

Yields 4 cups

**4 cups grapefruit peel, cut in thin strips
   (3 medium grapefruit)
2 cups sugar
1 cup water**

Cut peel from 3 medium-sized grapefruit, then cut into thin strips, using a sharp pointed knife (you should have about 4 cups). Be sure to keep your fingernails out of the way.

Now add enough cold water to cover strips of peel. Cover the pan and bring to boiling point. Boil 5 minutes. Drain and repeat 3 times. This removes the bitter bitterness.

Add 2 cups sugar and 1 cup water to drained peel. Bring to boil and boil gently over low heat until syrup is thick and almost all absorbed by the peel, stirring occasionally.

Drain peel on soft paper - brown paper. Roll in sugar while still hot, so sugar will stick on.

Sugar may be sprinkled on the hot peel spread on the paper, and repeated several times, until there is a coating of sugar.

Elizabeth Connelly

Liz Turnbull's Mints

"This must be 'pulled' similar to taffy. Be sure to grease your hands and allow to cool."

Yields 6 dozen

**1 pound sugar
¾ cup water
1 stick butter (not margarine)
24 drops oil of peppermint**

Put sugar, water, butter in pan and stir over low heat until thoroughly dissolved. Bring to boil (do not stir after it begins to boil). Cook to 260 degrees (from boil stage). Pour into a shallow greased pan. Add immediately 24 drops oil of peppermint.

When cool enough to handle, pull (grease hands) until light and fluffy. Pull out into strips and cut with scissors to mint size.

Nora Peterson

"In creating this painting, I recalled memories of gathering this luscious fruit from the orchards of an uncle and a great-uncle. In earlier years, my parents had a small orchard which produced a modest cash crop and provided our family with Elbertas, Red Havens and 'Georgia Belles.' Often though, frosts and freezes took their toll and wiped out the entire peach crop. I remember riding by the orchard in August, with the car windows rolled down, inhaling the aroma of tree-ripened peaches."

Eldridge Bagley

"PEACH BOWL"
Appears through the courtesy of the painting's owners, Dr. and Mrs. Lawrence G. Miller, III.

Apple Crisp

"This was Mother's recipe, but I continue using it often. Especially nice for a wintertime bridge luncheon."

Serves 6 to 8

8 medium apples, sliced
1 cup flour
1 cup sugar
½ teaspoon salt
1 teaspoon baking powder
1 egg, beaten
Cinnamon and butter

Lay apples in 6 x 9-inch pan. Combine flour, sugar, salt, baking powder and egg. Sprinkle over apples, then top with cinnamon and slivers of butter. Bake at 350 degrees for 40 minutes. Delicious just as is or good with a lemon sauce.

Nancye Lashley

Cinnamon Baked Apples

"Serve as a side dish to ham or as a dessert and topped with whipped cream."

6 to 8 apples, peeled and cored
2 cups sugar
½ cup water
⅓ cup cinnamon hearts
½ stick margarine

Mix all above ingredients except apples and bring to boil. Stir until cinnamon hearts melt. Pour over about 6 or 8 apples, quartered. Bake at 400 degrees until done.

Miss Virginia Stanley

▲ To lower the fat content, use lowfat margarine.

Dried Apple Dumplings

"Great with ice cream, too!"

Serves 8

1½ cups dried apples
1 quart water
1 quart sifted flour
1 cup buttermilk
½ cup shortening
2½ quarts boiling water
3 cups milk
Allspice to taste

Cut up apple into small pieces; put in bowl and cover with 1 quart water. Allow to stand for 1 hour. Drain off water. Combine apples, flour, milk and shortening. Stir until well mixed and stiff. Shape into small balls about the size of an egg. Drop into boiling water and cook until done (15 to 20 minutes). Remove from water and serve with milk that has been sweetened with some sugar and flavored with allspice or whipped cream.

Lottie M. French

▲ To lower the fat content, use skim buttermilk and replace the 3 cups milk with lowfat/skim milk.

Pineapple-Strawberry Ambrosia

"A pretty, cool and simple dessert."

Serves 4

1 can crushed pineapple
1 pint frozen strawberries
2 pints lime or orange sherbet
1 cup coconut

Chill fruit together overnight (may be sweetened). Place sherbet in serving dishes. Spoon fruit over sherbet and top with coconut. This is a very cool and refreshing make-ahead dessert.

Loretta C. Young

Brown Sugar Bread Pudding

"Delicious as is or top with whipped cream."

Serves 6 to 8

2 cups bread cubes
½ cup brown sugar
¼ teaspoon salt
1 teaspoon cinnamon
1 teaspoon vanilla
2½ cups milk
½ cup raisins
2 slightly beaten eggs
½ cup walnuts, chopped
2 tablespoons butter

Combine bread cubes with brown sugar, salt and cinnamon; add vanilla, milk, raisins, eggs and walnuts. Pour mixture into a well-greased 1-quart baking dish; dot with butter. Bake at 325 degrees for 45 minutes or until knife comes out clean.

Evelyn W. Carpenter

▲ To lower fat content, use lowfat/skim milk and an egg substitute.

Banana Pudding

"The children and grandchildren always look forward to this dessert when they come home."

Serves 15

1 large box vanilla wafers
6 large bananas
¾ cup to 1 cup sugar (I use ¾ cup)
Pinch of salt
3 rounded tablespoons flour
1 quart milk
4 eggs, separated (save whites for meringue)
1½ teaspoons vanilla

Mix sugar, flour and salt in top of double boiler. Add just enough milk to smooth the mixture, then add rest of milk. Cook over boiling water till milk gets hot. Add a little of hot milk mixture to beaten egg yolks, then pour egg mixture into milk mixture, stirring constantly to keep from lumping, and cook till mixture thickens. Remove from heat and add vanilla. Meanwhile, in an oblong Pyrex baking dish put a layer of vanilla wafers and a layer of bananas and another layer wafers. Pour custard over all (you may want to stick a knife down through layers to help custard penetrate well). Now spread over all a meringue made of 4 egg whites, pinch of salt and 4 teaspoons sugar, whipped till stiff (just before egg whites are finished, whip in another teaspoon sugar). Place in a 350 degree oven and bake till brown. Serve right away. Refrigerate any leftovers.

Lorraine Freeman

▲ To lower fat content, use lowfat/skim milk.

Baked Custard

"A wonderful old-fashioned dessert."

Serves 8

4 eggs, beaten slightly
½ cup sugar
¼ teaspoon salt
2¾ cups milk, scalded
1 teaspoon vanilla
¼ teaspoon nutmeg

Blend eggs, sugar and salt in a small mixing bowl. Slowly stir in milk. Add vanilla. Pour into a 1½-quart casserole dish. Sprinkle with nutmeg. Bake at 350 degrees in a large baking pan of hot water for 45 to 50 minutes, or until knife inserted in center comes out clean.

Pat Temple

▲ To lower fat content, use lowfat/skim milk.

Boiled Custard

"Serve warm over pound cake!"

Serves 6 to 12

1 quart milk
4 eggs
1 cup sugar
1 teaspoon vanilla

Put milk in double boiler and heat. In a bowl, beat eggs; add sugar to eggs and stir well. Pour about ½ cup of hot milk into the egg mixture, then slowly add this egg mixture to the hot milk in the double boiler. Cook until thick, stirring constantly. Remove from heat and add vanilla.

Julia Lee Harris

▲ To decrease fat, use lowfat/skim milk.

Lemon Bisque

"Light and refreshing! Top with a sprig of mint."

Serves 12

1 13-ounce can evaporated milk
1 package lemon gelatin (small)
1½ cups boiling water
½ cup sugar
⅛ teaspoon salt
½ cup lemon juice (fresh is recommended)
Grated rind of 1 lemon
2 cups graham cracker crumbs

Chill milk, dissolve gelatin in hot water. Add sugar, salt, lemon juice and rind; when partially congealed, whip evaporated milk and then whip the congealed mixture into it. Spread ½ of crumbs into a 10 x 13-inch dish. Spoon mixture into it and top with the remaining graham cracker crumbs. Chill at least 3 hours prior to serving or overnight. Keeps well in the refrigerator for several days (if it lasts that long!). You can put a small amount of whipped topping on top if you desire.

Virginia Hylton

▲ To lower the fat, you can use skim evaporated milk.

Lemon Delicacy

"My son Tommy's favorite when he comes home."

Serves 6

1 tablespoon butter
¾ cup sugar
Juice and grated rind of lemon
1 cup milk
2 tablespoons flour
2 eggs, separated

Cream butter and sugar. Add the egg yolks, juice and rind of lemon and flour to the creamed mixture. Mix thoroughly; add milk and blend. Fold in stiffly beaten egg whites. Bake in a greased casserole placed in pan of hot water for 45 minutes in a 350 degree oven, or until brown. Spoon into dessert dishes to serve or bake for a shorter length of time in individual custard dishes. Serve lightly warm or better served cold.

Vi Epperson

▲ To lower fat content, use lowfat/skim milk.

Lemon Pudding

"Lemon dessert like your grandmother used to make."

1 cup sugar
2 heaping tablespoons flour
Pinch of salt
Juice and grated rind of 1 lemon
2 egg yolks, well beaten
1 cup milk
2 egg whites, beaten stiff and folded in
  lightly

Mix in order given. Pour into a greased pan or baking dish and place in pan of hot water. Bake in slow oven of 325 degrees for about 40 minutes or until browned lightly.

Serve from baking dish into fruit saucers. Can also be served in sherbet glasses topped with whipped cream that has been sweetened and flavored.

Elfie Meredith

▲ To lower fat, use lowfat/skim milk.

Sweet Potato Pudding

"This was my mother's recipe and Governor Harrison's absolute favorite!"

Serves 8 to 10

2 pints grated raw sweet potato
3 eggs, well beaten
1 cup milk
1½ cups sugar
1 teaspoon cinnamon
1 teaspoon allspice
1 teaspoon cloves
½ cup butter or margarine

To well-beaten eggs add milk, sugar, spices and sweet potatoes. Melt butter in iron frying pan; to this add the other ingredients. Cook this until brown on bottom, starting with a hot skillet and gradually reducing heat - you want to brown not burn. Now stir and cook again the same way until almost done. Place in Pyrex baking dish in a 350 degree oven for 15 to 20 minutes to finish cooking. The pudding can actually be completely cooked in skillet but finishing in oven avoids overbrowning. Also good for making ahead of time to the point of putting in the oven and then finishing when ready to serve.

It can be topped with damson preserves, meringue or served with a slice of cheese.

Lacey Virginia Harrison

Orange Sweet Potato Pudding

"Adapted from an 1828 recipe."

Serves 8 to 10

**1 pound sweet potatoes, cooked and
  peeled
1 cup sugar
6 eggs, well beaten
1 cup orange juice
½ cup butter, melted
1 tablespoon lemon rind, grated
¼ teaspoon mace (or nutmeg)**

Rub the potatoes through a sieve, or mash
with potato masher, or put in blender. Add
sugar and melted butter, then other ingredients, blending well. Pour into a well-greased
3-quart baking dish. Bake at 350 degrees for
about 1 hour.

Georgia Hammack

Warm Fruit Mélange

"Wonderful brandied fruit."

Serves 8

**2 1-pound jars light sweet cherries
1 large can Bartlett pears
1 large can apricots
2 to 3 tablespoons brown sugar
⅓ cup brandy
8 whole cloves
2 to 3 cinnamon sticks
1 teaspoon lemon peel, shredded**

Drain and mix juices. Pour about 1 cup of
juices in a saucepan and add 2 to 3 tablespoons brown sugar, 2 to 3 cinnamon sticks
(broken up), 8 whole cloves, 1 teaspoon
shredded lemon peel, ⅓ cup brandy. Heat.
Add fruit, heat and serve.

Peggy Valdrighi

Heavenly Plum Kuchen

*"The sweet crumb base and the tart plums make for
an unusually good combination."*

Serves 9

**½ cup margarine, softened
1 cup sugar
1¼ cups sifted flour
½ teaspoon salt
½ teaspoon cinnamon
¼ teaspoon baking powder
5 plums - washed, halved and pitted
1 egg
1 cup whipping cream (do not whip)**

Cream margarine and sugar. Measure dry
ingredients into sifter and sift into creamed
mixture, blending until crumbly. Measure out
⅓ cup, pressing remaining mixture in an
ungreased 8 x 8-inch or 9 x 9-inch pan.
Arrange 9 plum halves, rounded side up,
sprinkle with reserved mixture. Bake at 375
degrees for 15 minutes. Meanwhile, beat egg
slightly and stir in cream. Pour over plums and
bake 25 to 30 minutes longer or until custard
is set.

Beth Bagley

Christmas Tipsy Cake

"Spoon into dessert dishes, top with whipped cream and serve after church on Christmas Eve."

5 eggs, separated
1 cup sugar
1 teaspoon vanilla
1 cup flour
1 teaspoon vinegar
Parched almonds
1 cup sherry
3 cups boiled custard flavored with
  bourbon
Whipping cream, whipped

Beat yolks well and add sugar gradually. Add other ingredients except whites. Beat whites stiff and fold them in last. Pour into ungreased shallow pan. Bake at 350 degrees for about 30 minutes.

Piece cake generously with almonds. Pour sherry over cake, then the custard generously flavored with bourbon. Let stand in refrigerator, preferably overnight. When ready to serve, top with whipped cream.

Lucy Heartwell

Chocolate Éclair Cake

"Children will love this dessert. All their favorite ingredients!"

Serves 12

1 box graham crackers
2 3½-ounce packages instant French
  vanilla pudding
3 cups cold milk
1 8-ounce carton prepared whipped
  topping
Butter or margarine

Frosting
1 cup sugar

⅓ cup cocoa
¼ cup milk
¼ cup butter
1 teaspoon vanilla

In a buttered 9 x 13-inch baking dish, put 1 layer of whole graham crackers. Blend pudding and 3 cups milk on low speed in a mixing bowl. Let stand for a minute; fold in whipped topping until well blended. Pour ½ of pudding mixture over crackers. Add another layer, pour in rest of pudding mixture. Put on third layer of crackers. Top with frosting.

Boil sugar, cocoa and ¼ cup milk for 1 minute; add butter and vanilla. Let cool. Pour over cake.

Refrigerate cake overnight or several hours.

Susan W. Myers

▲ To lower fat content, use diet pudding, lowfat/skim milk and diet whipped topping.

Meringues

"Nice to make ahead and freeze. Take out to thaw and top with fresh fruit, ice cream, etc."

Serves 8 to 12

3 egg whites, beaten stiff
1 cup sugar
Pinch of cream of tartar
1 teaspoon vanilla

Heat oven to 450 degrees. Beat egg whites until they form soft peaks. Add the sugar with cream of tartar gradually. Then fold in vanilla. Drop meringues on brown paper lined cookie sheet. Make a little "scoop" in the middle for fruit or ice cream. Put in oven and turn oven off. Leave overnight. Do not open door. Do not make on a damp day.

Lacy Virginia Harrison

Chocolate Velvet Dessert

"Can be doubled easily for larger groups."

Serves 8 to 10

1½ cups vanilla wafers, finely crushed
⅓ cup butter or margarine
1 8-ounce package cream cheese
½ cup sugar
1 cup heavy cream (or you may substitute
  2 cups prepared whipped topping)
1 teaspoon vanilla
2 eggs, separated
1 6-ounce package chocolate chips, melted

Crust
Combine 1½ cups finely crushed vanilla wafers with ⅓ cup melted margarine. Press into bottom and sides of 8 or 9-inch rectangular pan. Chill.

Filling
Combine 8 ounces softened cream cheese, ¼ cup sugar, 1 teaspoon vanilla (be generous if you like vanilla) and blend well. Stir in 2 beaten egg yolks. Add package chocolate chips, melted. Beat 2 egg whites to soft peaks. Gradually add ¼ cup sugar. Fold into chocolate mixture. Fold in 1 cup heavy cream, whipped (you may substitute 2 cups prepared whipped topping, easy and just as good). Pour into crumb crust. Top generously with chopped nuts. Freeze.

Decorate with whipped topping before serving. Can be made ahead of time about a week or just a day.

Jean Cyrus

▲ To lower fat content, use lowfat margarine, lowfat cream cheese, and diet whipped topping.

Butterscotch Dessert

"A very rich and yummy dessert."

Serves 12

First Layer
1 cup flour
1 stick margarine
¾ cup nuts, chopped

Combine softened margarine, flour and nuts. Press into 9 x 13-inch pan. Bake at 350 degrees for 15 minutes. Cool

Second Layer
1 8-ounce package cream cheese
1 cup powdered sugar
1 large carton prepared whipped topping
  (use 1 cup)

Mix cream cheese with 1 cup of whipped topping and add powdered sugar. Spread on cooled pastry.

Third Layer
2 3½-ounce packages instant butterscotch
  pudding
3 cups milk

Mix butterscotch pudding mix with 3 cups milk, mixing until thick. Spread over top of cream cheese layer. Spread remaining whipped topping on top. Sprinkle with chopped nuts. Let refrigerate overnight. Cut into squares and serve.

Ann Burke

▲ To lower fat content, use lowfat margarine, lowfat cream cheese, diet whipped topping, diet pudding, and lowfat/skim milk.

Chocolate Pudding Layer Cake

"Death by way of chocolate!"

Serves 10

First Layer
1 stick margarine
1 cup flour
1 cup pecans, chopped (or less)

Melt margarine, then mix with pecans and flour. Press into bottom of a 9 x 13-inch pan. Bake at 350 degrees for 20 to 30 minutes. Watch closely as it burns easily. Cool.

Second Layer
1 8-ounce package cream cheese
1 cup powdered sugar
1 8-ounce container prepared whipped topping

Beat cream cheese with powdered sugar, then beat in 1 container whipped topping. Spread over crust.

Third Layer
1 3½-ounce package instant vanilla pudding
1 3½-ounce package instant chocolate pudding
3 cups milk
1 8-ounce container prepared whipped topping

Mix vanilla and chocolate pudding with milk until thick. Pour over cream cheese layer. Top with container of whipped topping. Attractive to decorate top with chocolate shavings. Keep refrigerated.

Ann Peebles and Helen T. Manson

▲ To decrease fat, use lowfat margarine, lowfat cream cheese, diet whipped topping and puddings and lowfat/skim milk.

Chocolate Sandwich Cookie Refrigerator Cake

Serves 10

1 1¼-pound package dark chocolate sandwich cookies
2 sticks margarine
2 8-ounce packages cream cheese
2 cups confectioner's sugar
2 8-ounce containers prepared whipped topping
1 6-ounce package chocolate pudding mix

Crush cookies, reserve ½ cup. Pour melted margarine over cookies. Press this into a 13 x 9-inch dish. Refrigerate 15 minutes. Mix cream cheese, 1 8-ounce container whipped topping and confectioner's sugar. Spread this over cookie crumb crust, refrigerate. Prepare pudding per directions on box. Cool and spread over cream cheese layer. Let set 15 minutes or longer. Spread the other container of whipped topping over pudding. Sprinkle remaining ½ cup crushed cookies on top layer. Cover tightly and refrigerate.

Jackie Browder

Butterscotch Sauce

"Great over ice cream or pound cake."

Yields 1½ cups

1 cup dark brown sugar, packed
½ cup granulated sugar
⅔ cup evaporated milk
¼ cup butter
2 tablespoons light corn syrup
¼ teaspoon salt
½ to 1 teaspoon vanilla, to taste

Mix all ingredients except vanilla in saucepan. Bring to a boil over medium heat, stirring constantly. Reduce heat and add vanilla.

Charlotte Matthews

Lemon Sauce

"The nutmeg enhances the flavor."

Yields 2 to 3 cups

1 cup sugar
1 tablespoon cornstarch
1 cup cold water
¼ stick margarine
1 whole egg, beaten
Juice and grated rind of 1 lemon
Nutmeg for garnish

Add cornstarch to sugar, then add next 3 ingredients. Cook in double broiler until mixture coats a spoon. When cool, add lemon juice and grated rind.

Use on ice cream, pound cake or gingerbread.

Maxine Rodgers

Hot Fudge Sauce

"For all chocolate lovers."

Serves 6

1 tablespoon butter or margarine
1 1-ounce square chocolate
⅓ cup boiling water
1 cup sugar
2 tablespoons corn syrup
½ teaspoon vanilla
⅛ teaspoon salt

Melt butter in saucepan. Add chocolate and stir over low heat until chocolate is melted. Add boiling water gradually, stirring constantly. Heat to boiling. Add sugar and syrup, stirring until dissolved. Simmer 5 minutes, add vanilla and salt.

Margaret Andrews

Thick Lemon Sauce (Curd)

"Can be refrigerated 3 to 6 months."

Yields 3 to 4 cups

4 lemons, washed and dried
2 cups sugar
¾ cup (1½ sticks) butter or margarine
4 eggs, slightly beaten

Grate finely the yellow rind of lemons. Squeeze and strain juice. Place lemon juice, rind, sugar and butter in saucepan and cook over low heat until butter is melted and sugar dissolved. Remove from heat.

Stirring vigorously, slowly blend in beaten eggs. Return to low heat and cook, stirring constantly until mixture coats the back of a metal spoon. Pour into jar.

Can be used as filling for tarts; will fill 12 bought and cooked tart shells. Serve warm or cold over ice cream or pound cake.

Barbara Warriner

The **Brunswick County Library** *is constructed of bricks made from local clay, hand-fashioned in a traditional style.*

"One of the benefits of rural life is the opportunity to watch wildflowers make their annual appearance on the landscape. Springing up in unpredictable places, their color, design and fragrances please the senses. Black-eyed Susans in a stone pitcher are the focal point of 'Porch Morning'. This porch provides a welcome shelter from the scorching sun and a glass of icy lemonade offers refreshment."

Eldridge Bagley

"PORCH MORNING"
Appears through the courtesy of the painting's owner, Julia J. Norrell.

Bread and Butter Pickles

"Folks love a gift of homemade pickles on any occasion."

Yields 4 to 6 pints

30 cucumbers (1-inch in diameter)
10 medium onions
4 tablespoons salt
5 cups vinegar
2 teaspoons celery seed
2 teaspoons ground ginger
4 cups sugar
1 teaspoon turmeric
2 teaspoons white mustard seed

Slice cucumbers and onions, sprinkle with salt. Let stand 1 hour. Drain. Make a spiced vinegar with the remaining ingredients. Let spiced vinegar come to a boil. Add cucumbers and onions and bring to boiling point. Simmer for 10 minutes. Seal in sterilized jars.

Lollie Butler

Sweet Pickle Chunks

"Delicious and crisp."

Yields 4 pints

10 medium cucumbers
8 cups sugar
2 tablespoons pickling spice
5 teaspoons coarse salt
4 cups vinegar

Cover cucumbers with boiling water. Let stand until next morning. Drain, repeat this procedure for the next 3 days. On the fifth day drain and slice in 2-inch pieces. Combine remaining ingredients, bring to a boil and pour over cucumbers. Let stand for 2 days. On third day, heat to boiling and seal in clear jars.

Justine Jones

Russ Meredith's Cucumber Pickle

"A great recipe endeavor for men because there is a lot of lifting."

Yields 4 to 6 pir

3½ pounds cucumbers, sliced
1 gallon cold water with ½ cup slack lime
3 pounds sugar
1 quart vinegar
Pickling spices (remove red pepper)

Soak cucumbers in water with lime for 24 hours. Drain. Soak in clear water 4 hours, changing water each hour. Drain.

Make syrup of sugar, vinegar; add spices with pepper removed (tie spices in several small cheesecloth bags). Pour over cucumbers and let stand overnight. Next morning cook 45 minutes or till cucumbers are clear. Put in sterilized jars and seal.

This recipe may be doubled. The pickles are superb and make wonderful gifts.

Sue Meredi

Glazed Pickles

"I use a 32-ounce jar of sliced dill pickle and cut down on the sugar, vinegar and water."

Yield 1 j

6 large dill pickles (46-ounce jar), sliced
2 cups sugar
1 cup water
½ cup vinegar

Combine sugar, water and vinegar in saucepan and bring to a boil. Boil until it is a syrup. Ad sliced pickles and heat. Put in a jar and let stand in a cool place to season.

Lacey Virginia Harrison

Yellow Squash Pickles

You can also use cucumbers in place of squash in this recipe.

Yields 4 to 6 pints

4 quarts yellow squash (very small),
   thinly sliced
5 medium white onions, thinly sliced
¼ cup medium-coarse salt
   (regular salt can be used)
5 cups white sugar
1 tablespoon turmeric powder
1½ teaspoons celery seed
1½ tablespoons mustard seed
5 cups cider vinegar

Slice squash thin; add onions and salt; stir thoroughly, cover with cracked ice and let stand 3 hours. Drain off liquid; combine sugar, turmeric, celery seed, mustard seed and vinegar. Pour over squash mixture. Heat to a boil. Place at once in hot sterilized jars and seal.

Jane Roberts

Squash and Pepper Pickle

"Makes a pretty jar of pickle."

Yields 8 pints

4 sliced bell peppers (part green, part red)
8 cups sliced tender summer squash
2 cups sliced onion
¾ cup salt
Crushed ice
2 cups vinegar
2 cups sugar
2 tablespoons celery seed
2 tablespoons mustard seed

Cover squash and onion with salt and crushed ice. Let soak for 1 hour. Rinse and drain. Add bell peppers, sliced.

Bring vinegar, sugar, celery seed and mustard seed to a boil. Pour this hot liquid over other ingredients and let the entire mixture simmer for 2 minutes. Put in hot jars and seal.

Lola Woodroof

Pickled Beets

"A special side dish for any meal."

Serves 5-8

½ cup cider vinegar
½ cup beet juice (liquid from can)
1 tablespoon apple juice concentrate,
   thawed
2 cloves
3 peppercorns
¼ bay leaf
2½ cups canned sliced beets
2 small green onions, sliced

Boil vinegar and beet juice. Add juice and spices to boiling. Pour over beets and then chill well.

Kelly Stokes

Crisp Watermelon Pickles

"Store in dark cool place for two weeks before opening."

Yields 6 to 8 pints

1 large watermelon rind, cut up
4 quarts cold water and 4 tablespoons salt
4 quarts cold water and 3 tablespoons powdered alum
5½ pounds (or 11 cups) sugar
2 cups white vinegar
1½ tablespoons whole cloves
1 stick cinnamon (broken in small pieces)
¼ teaspoon ground mace

Soak rind in 4 quarts water and 4 tablespoons salt overnight. Drain and rinse in cold water. Add 4 quarts cold water and the 3 tablespoons powdered alum. Bring to a rolling boil and simmer 30 minutes. Drain and rinse in cold water. Add 4 more quarts cold water and simmer till tender, about 45 minutes. Add sugar and simmer 45 minutes more (until rind is transparent). Add vinegar and simmer 25 minutes. Add spices and simmer 5 minutes only. Pack in hot sterilized jars and seal. Store in refrigerator after opening.

Jane Smith

Dill Pickles

"Season two weeks before serving."

Yields 4 to 6 pint

Cucumbers
1 quart vinegar
3 quarts water
1 cup salt
2 bunches fresh dill
Garlic

To 1 quart vinegar add 3 quarts water, 1 cup salt and 2 bunches of fresh dill. When mixture comes to a boil, add well-scrubbed cucumbers and turn burner to low. Do not let pickle come to a boil. When pickle begins to turn yellow and lose green color, pack in sterilized jars with sprig of fresh dill and ¼ clove of sliced garlic. Pour vinegar mixture over pickles and seal in sterile jars.

Doris Baker

Pickled Peaches

"Taken from a 1935 Rumford cookbook."

Yields 8 pints

4 quarts peaches
2 pounds brown sugar
1½ pints vinegar
3 to 4 sticks cinnamon
Cloves

Make a syrup with the sugar, vinegar and cinnamon, cooking them together for 20 minutes. Remove the skin of the peaches by dipping them for a moment in boiling water, then rubbing with a cloth. Stick 2 cloves in each peach and then cook in the syrup until tender. Do not cook too many peaches at a time. Boil syrup 10 minutes after fruit is done. Pack peaches in sterile jars and pour sugar mixture over the peaches. Seal.

Ethel Edwards

Pickled Okra

"Southern cooks love okra, especially pickled."

Yields 5 pints

2 pounds young okra pods
5 1-pint screw top jars
1 teaspoon dill seed
1/2 teaspoon alum
1 clove garlic
1 small pod hot pepper

Wash okra, leaving small stem. Pack in 5 jars. Add remaining ingredients in amount as above to each jar. Place jars in large pot and heat water to boiling. Make a syrup of 3 cups white vinegar, 1 cup water, and 6 teaspoons salt. Bring vinegar, water and salt to boil; pour hot over okra. Be sure jars are filled with vinegar syrup. Seal.

Kay Outten

Corn Relish

"Best if stored 3 to 4 weeks prior to using."

Yields 6 pints

2 quarts fresh corn (about 1½ ears)
1 cup minced yellow onions
1 cup minced sweet green pepper
1 cup minced sweet red pepper
1 cup minced celery
3 cups cider vinegar
1½ cups sugar
1 tablespoon pickling salt
1 tablespoon mustard seed
2 teaspoons turmeric
1 teaspoon celery seed

Mix all ingredients in a large kettle. Cover and simmer 20 minutes. Ladle into sterile jars, wipe rims and seal with sterile closures. (Cover to ⅛-inch of top - be sure liquid covers the vegetables).

Beth Parker

Chow-Chow

"Old fashioned way to use the bounty of the garden in season."

Yields 24 to 30 pints

6 quarts finely chopped cabbage
2 quarts finely chopped green tomatoes
6 peppers, red and green
2 quarts vinegar
8 large onions, chopped
2 big handfuls salt
8 cups sugar

Mix all of the above together and let stand for 2 hours, covered. Prepare sterile jars and closures. Keep jars hot while waiting for chow-chow to cook. Drain off the liquid from the vegetables. Prepare the following mixture: 8 cups of vinegar and 8 cups of sugar. Let come to a boil and simmer for 15 minutes. Add vegetables and simmer, uncovered for 10 minutes. Ladle boiling hot chow-chow into sterile jars.

Emma Hensley

Pepper Relish

"Store in a cool dark place for 3 to 4 weeks before using."

Yields 6 pints

1 dozen sweet green peppers
1 dozen sweet red pepper
2 cups minced yellow onions
1 cup minced celery
3 cups white vinegar
1½ cups sugar
1 tablespoon pickling salt
1 tablespoon mustard seed
1 teaspoon celery seed

Sterilize jars and closures, stand them on a baking sheet and keep warm in a 250 degree oven until needed. Core, seed and mince peppers. Mix all ingredients in a large, heavy enamel or stainless-steel kettle, cover and simmer for 15 minutes. Ladle into jars, filling to within ⅛-inch of tops and making sure the liquid covers the vegetables. Wipe rims and seal.

Nellie Wood

Strawberry Jam

Yields 4 to 6 jelly jars

1 quart strawberries
8 cups sugar
2 cups water
2 packages powdered fruit pectin

Hull and chop strawberries. Stir in sugar until it dissolves. Bring water to a boil. Add pectin and let dissolve. Let cool and stir in berry mixture. Pour into jars and seal with paraffin.

Pat Hardy

Pear-Orange Marmalade

"Good way to use green pears prior to frost."

Yields 4 to 6 jelly jar

10 hard green pears
6 small oranges
1 lemon
1 teaspoon soda
6 cups sugar (or more - to taste)

Peel and cut up pears. Slice oranges and lemon fine, peels and all. Fill blender ½ full of fruit. Add 1 cup water; chop for 20 seconds. Put in a big saucepan, simmering while you continue blending the balance of the fruit.

When all is in the pan, add quart water and 1 teaspoon soda. Simmer 2 hours. Add sugar. Boil 15 minutes or more until sticky. Cool. Put in boiled jars and seal with wax.

Gaye Neale

Peach Preserves

For spiced peach preserves, tie loosely in cheesecloth bag spices of choice and cook with peaches, discarding bag after peaches are cooked."

Yields 4 to 6 pints

4 pounds ripe peaches
3 pounds sugar
Juice of 2 lemons

Peel and cut peaches into eighths. Place in large pot or kettle. Add sugar and lemon juice. Let stand 4 to 6 hours. Simmer very slowly and cook until syrup becomes thick (about 1 hour depending on peaches). Stir occasionally with wooden spoon to prevent sticking. Skim foam when necessary. Pour into sterilized jars and seal.

Gladys Wood

Tomato Preserves

"Delicious and different."

Yields 4 pints

5 pounds tomatoes
3 cups sugar
1 lemon
1 orange

Peel and quarter tomatoes. Thinly slice lemon and orange. Cover all with sugar. Let stand overnight. Drain off syrup and boil to "spin a thread" (until syrup is a thick consistency). Add fruits - cook until thick and clear. Seal in jars. Cover with paraffin.

Vi Epperson

Wine Jelly

"Serve with egg custard or whipped cream."

Yields 8 to 10 jelly jars

1 box (4 packages) granulated gelatin
1 pint cold water
2 lemons (juice)
1 pint dry sherry
2½ cups sugar
1 pint boiling water

Mix gelatin in 1 pint cold water, let stand 5 to 10 minutes. Add sugar and lemon juice and mix well. Pour in 1 pint boiling water and heat on stove over very slow heat, stirring till dissolved. Add 1 pint dry sherry.

Lacey Barkley

Pepper Jelly

"Colorful addition to a party table. Serve over cream cheese with crackers."

Yields 10 small jars

1½ cups white vinegar
1½ cups finely chopped bell peppers
¼ cup finely chopped red hot peppers
   or ¼ teaspoon cayenne pepper
6½ cups sugar
1 bottle liquid fruit pectin
Green or red food coloring

Bring vinegar, peppers and sugar to a rolling boil in a heavy saucepan. Boil for 3 minutes. Add the pectin very slowly, stirring constantly; then boil for 1 more minute. Add the food coloring. Strain and pour into sterile jars and cover with paraffin.

Anne Butler

The Pink House *is Harmony Grove's finest private residence.*

Barbecue Sauce for Grilled Chicken

"Can be refrigerated for about a week."

Serves 32

1 pound margarine
Juice of 3 lemons
1 cup white vinegar
1 3-ounce jar prepared mustard
4 tablespoons Worcestershire sauce

Melt margarine. Add other ingredients, then bring to a boil. Mop warm sauce on chickens as they grill. Add red and black pepper to sauce if desired. Makes enough sauce for 8 chickens.

Polly Bishop

▲ To lower fat content, use lowfat margarine.

Barbecue Sauce for Baked Chicken or Pork

"Will keep in the refrigerator for at least several weeks."

Yields 1 quart

⅓ cup chopped onion
3 tablespoons margarine
1 cup catsup
⅓ cup vinegar
2 tablespoons brown sugar
½ cup water
2 tablespoons prepared mustard
1 tablespoon Worcestershire sauce

Slowly cook onion in margarine in a saucepan until tender. Add remaining ingredients. Cover and simmer for 15 minutes.

Joyce Moorman

▲ To lower fat content, use lowfat margarine.

Barbecue Sauce for Pork

"The barbecue sauce can be kept in refrigerator several days and freezes well."

Yields 1 quar

1 cup pork stock, all fat removed
1 cup vinegar
1 cup catsup
1 small onion, chopped very fine
2 teaspoons mustard
2 tablespoons Worcestershire sauce
Salt, red and black pepper
1 tablespoon horseradish
2 tablespoons chili sauce
1 teaspoon steak sauce
1 teaspoon brown sugar
1 bay leaf
Dash of nutmeg and allspice

Cook about 10 minutes in porcelain pan. Season liberally with red and black pepper and salt. Thicken with flour paste. Pour this over the well-cooked, sliced pork from which all fat has been removed. Place in a warm oven until sauce thoroughly penetrates meat.

Helen Lashley

Seafood Cocktail Sauce

"Enough for about 3 pounds of shrimp."

Yields ¾ cup

½ cup tomato catsup
½ lemon, cut into pieces
½ tablespoon horseradish
¼ cup chili sauce
½ teaspoon Worcestershire sauce

Put all ingredients into blender container and process until smooth. Serve with shrimp, oysters, lobster and crab. Keeps several months in refrigerator.

Justine Jones

Herbs

When trying a recipe, try an herb of your own.

Basil - complimentary to green salads, potatoes, noodles, tomatoes, peas, all kinds of squash, lamb, fish, cheese.

Bay leaves - vegetables, tomato sauces and juices, fish, stews.

Chervil - eggs, cheese, spinach, tossed salads, cream soups.

Chives - sauces, beef, veal, poultry, tomatoes, vegetables, salads.

Dill - potatoes, fish, green salads, cottage cheese, bread, tomatoes, cream cheese, Cheddar cheese.

Fennel - soups, fish dishes, sweet pickles, bread.

Garlic - lamb, beef, veal, sauces, stews, mayonnaise.

Marjoram - roast, beef, lamb, pork, eggs, vegetables, vegetable soups.

Mint - fruits, lamb, ice cream, potatoes, peas, candies, cake frostings, vinegar-oil dressing (for fruit).

Oregano - tomatoes, sauces, fish, pork chops, veal chops, pizza.

Onion - sauces, beef, veal, poultry, tomatoes, salads, vegetables.

Parsley - lamb, beef, veal, vegetables, cheese, seafood, eggs. This is a very healthy herb.

Rosemary - veal, lamb, pork, fish, spinach, cauliflower, cabbage.

Saffron - rice, shell noodles.

Sage - stuffings.

Savory - poultry, quail.

Scallions - sauces, beef, veal, poultry, tomatoes, vegetables, salads.

Tarragon - vinegar, salads, tomatoes, sauces for meats and vegetables, soups, stuffings, chowders.

Thyme - all meats, stews, vegetable soup, eggs, egg dishes, cheese dishes.

Oven Chart

Meat	Temperature	Time in Minutes
Fish		
Fillet	400	20
Steaks	400	30
Whole fish	400	10 per pound
Roasts		
Beef, rib		
Rare	325	20-25 per pound
Medium	325	25-30 per pound
Well done	325	30-35 per pound
Ham	325	25-30 per pound
Leg of Lamb	300	30-35 per pound
Pork Loin	350	30-40 per pound
Veal	325	30-35 per pound
Chicken	325	30-45 per pound
Turkey,		
8-12 pounds	325	20-25 per pound
12-20 pounds	325	15-20 per pound

Table of Equivalents

Measurements and Equivalents

Dash — less than ⅛ teaspoon

Trace — less than ⅛ fl. teaspoon

3 teaspoons — 1 tablespoon

2 tablespoons — 1 liquid ounce — ⅛ cup

4 tablespoons — 2 liquid ounces — ¼ cup

5 tablespoons plus 1 teaspoon — ⅓ cup

8 tablespoons — 4 liquid ounces — ½ cup

16 tablespoons — 8 liquid ounces — 1 cup

2 cups — 16 liquid ounces — 1 pint

2 pints — 32 liquid ounces — 1 quart

2 quarts — 64 liquid ounces — ½ gallon

4 quarts — 128 liquid ounces — 1 gallon

Beans — 16 ounces dry — cooked 6 to 7 cups

Butter or margarine — ¼ pound stick — ¼ cup

Cheese — hard — 4 ounces, — shredded — 1 cup
cottage — 8 ounces — 1 cup
cream — 8 ounces — 1 cup

Chocolate — 1 ounce — 1 square
morsels — 6 ounces — 1 cup

Coconut — 3 ounces — shredded — 1 cup

Coffee — 1 pound — brewed — 4 cups

Cranberries — 12 ounces — fresh — 3 cups

Cream — 1 cup — unwhipped
2 cups — whipped
sour — 8 ounces — 1 cup

Crumbs (fine, dry) —
3 slices bread — 1 cup
28 saltines — 1 cup
22 vanilla wafers — 1 cup
14-15 graham crackers — 1 cup

Dates or candied fruit — 8 ounces chopped — 1 cup

Egg — whites — 8 to 10 — 1 cup
yolks — 12 to 14 — 1 cup

Flour — sifted — 1 pound — 4 cups
unsifted — 1 pound — 3½ cups

Garlic — 1 clove — powdered — ⅛ teaspoon

Gelatin, unflavored — 1 envelope — 1 tablespoon

Herbs — 1 tablespoon fresh — dried — 1 teaspoon

Lemon juice — 1 medium lemon — 3 tablespoons

Lime juice — 1 medium lime — 2 tablespoons

Macaroni — 1 cup — cooked 2 cups

Meat — 1 pound chopped — cooked 3 cups
1 pound ground — cooked 2 cups

Mushrooms — 4 ounces canned — fresh 8 ounces

Noodles — 1 cup —cooked — 1¾ cups

Nuts — 4 ounces — chopped — 1 cup

Onion — ¼ cup fresh — dried 1 tablespoon

Orange juice — 1 medium orange — ½ cup

Raisins — 16 ounces — 2½ to 3 cups

Rice — 1 pound — 2 cups
1 cup — cooked 3 cups

Spaghetti — 1 pound — cooked 8 cups

Sugar — granulated — 1 pound — 2½ cups
packed brown — 1 pound — 2¼ cups
confectioner's — 1 pound — 4 to 4½ cups

Table of Party Equivalents

How much liquor to buy for a party

If You're Entertaining	Pre-Dinner Cocktails	For a Party
4 People	8 to 12 Drinks (one fifth required)	12 to 14 Drinks (one fifth required)
6 People	12 to 18 Drinks (two fifths required)	18 to 24 Drinks (two fifths required)
8 People	16 to 24 Drinks (two fifths required)	24 to 32 Drinks (two fifths required)
12 People	24 to 36 Drinks (three fifths required)	36 to 48 Drinks (three fifths required)
20 People	40 to 60 Drinks (four fifths required)	60 to 80 Drinks (four fifths required)
25 People	50 to 70 Drinks (five fifths required)	75 to 100 Drinks (five fifths required)
40 People	80 to 120 Drinks (eight fifths required)	120 to 160 Drinks (eight fifths required)
	To be safe - use quarts for fifths.	

To help you plan your party....

Champagne
1 case (12 fifths) serves 50 people (82 drinks)
Our Champagne Fountain will operate with as little as 3 bottles of champagne and as much as 5 gallons.

Liquor
Plan on approximately 2 drinks per hour per person.
There are 28 drinks per quart of liquor.
In order of preference: Vodka - Scotch - Gin - Bourbon

Punch
24 people per gallon of punch.
Cocktail Napkins
2 to 3 per person for a 3 hour party.
Coffee
1 pound of coffee makes 60 cups.

Table of Substitutions

Baking powder — ¼ teaspoon baking soda plus ½ teaspoon cream of tartar — 1 teaspoon
Cornstarch — 2 tablespoons flour — 1 tablespoon

Flour — ½ to ⅔ tablespoon cornstarch (for thickening) — 1 tablespoon
1 cup plus 2 tablespoons sifted cake flour — 1 cup
cake flour — 1 cup minus 2 tablespoons sifted all-purpose flour — 1 cup

Milk — ½ cup evaporated plus ½ cup water — 1 cup
Sour Milk — 1 cup sweet milk plus 1 tablespoon lemon juice or vinegar — 1 cup
Sugar — 1⅓ cups brown sugar or 1½ cups confectioner's sugar — 1 cup

Blender Sour Cream

⅓ cup cottage cheese
¼ cup buttermilk, skim milk or water
½ teaspoon lemon juice
Salt (optional)

In blender container, process ingredients until smooth. Serve immediately or refrigerate.

Candied Strawberries

"Good for eating or decorating a serving tray."

2 6-ounce boxes of strawberry gelatin
1 14-ounce package flaked coconut
1 can sweetened condensed milk
Juice of 1 lemon

Mix 1 box of gelatin, coconut, milk and lemon juice. Shape this into strawberries and roll in second package of gelatin. Top each strawberry with a mint leaf. These can be made ahead and frozen for a long time.

Sweetened Condensed Milk Substitute

¼ cup hot tap water
¾ cup granulated sugar
1¼ cups nonfat dry milk

Process water and sugar in blender for one minute with on/off speed or until sugar has partially dissolved. Add dry milk powder slowly while continuing to blend. Refrigerate at least 24 hours before using. Refrigeration is the secret of this imitation. Makes 1½ cups and can be used in all recipes that call for condensed milk.

Fried Noodles

2 cups spaghetti
Oil

Instead of buying more expensive Chinese noodles, cook spaghetti until almost done. Rinse, drain, then fry in deep oil.

Entertaining Ideas

We would like to leave you with a few more thoughts and helpful hints. Happy cooking.

Appetizer Ideas

Cover a block of cream cheese with any of the following:
    Crab meat topped with cocktail sauce and served with crackers
    Chutney and toasted almonds to spread on crackers
    Hot pepper jelly and serve with crackers
    Saturate a block of cream cheese with soy sauce and roll in sesame seeds.

Form seasoned cream cheese in a ball around drained, smoked oysters.

Mix three cups of mayonnaise and one cup of horseradish to always have on hand to dress rare roast beef.

Marinate canned or fresh mushrooms in Italian dressing overnight and serve with toothpicks.

Wrap melon balls in thin strips of Smithfield ham and secure with picks.

Top party rye bread with tomato sauce, oregano, pizza fixings and grated Mozzarella to broil golden brown.

Vertically slice large French rolls, spread each slice lightly with butter. Dot with: tuna, cubes of sharp Cheddar cheese, ham and a dash of catsup. Sprinkle with oregano and sprinkle generously with Parmesan cheese. Broil slowly until golden brown.

In a double boiler melt a roll of jalapeño cheese with a can of chili with beans; serve in a chafing dish with tortilla chips.

Sandwich suggestions:

Freeze bread slices for easier cutting of fancy shapes. Edges will be smooth.

Cut white bread with Christmas tree cookie cutter, spread with Roquefort cheese mixture, cream cheese with onion, or anchovy and cheese mixed. Garnish with slices of stuffed olives, shreds of carrot, and very small pearl onions. Use chopped black walnuts for the bottom of tree base.

Flower - cut bread with a scalloped edge cookie cutter. Color cream cheese with green food coloring, spread on each scallop to form petal shape, garnish with blanched almonds (split) and use grated orange rind to form center of flower. Or you can use cream confectioners' sugar, butter and lemon juice, spread on bread and garnish with the halves almond halves and grated lemon rind.

Star - cut bread with a star shaped cookie cutter. Mix cream cheese with onion, cayenne, and a little salt. Cover entire surface of bread, garnish with chopped parsley and slices of hard-boiled egg. Top with a sprinkle of paprika.

Ribbon - use a whole loaf of unsliced bread. Remove crusts and cut into 4 pieces horizontally. Mix cream cheese and mayonnaise with a different food coloring for each layer. The cream cheese can be spiced with onion juice, red pepper, or lemon juice. Alternate the colored layers. Chill thoroughly, then cut sandwiches ½-inch thick vertically, cutting each sandwich into thirds.

Always serve one sweet with cocktails; such as a tray of petite chocolates or candied nuts.

For chocolate fondue, combine 12-ounce package of semisweet chocolate bits with 1 cup of light cream in a fondue pot. Suggested dunkers are: marshmallows, cubed angel food cake, pineapple chunks, maraschino cherries.

For melon balls with white crème de menthe - using at least 4 melons, make into balls. Combine 1 (6-ounce) can frozen lemonade with ¼ cup crème de menthe and pour over the balls when ready to serve.

Strawberry macaroons - Take 2 macaroons and stick bottoms together with strawberry jam in between. Heat in a 350 degree oven for 10 minutes and dust with confectioner's sugar while still warm. Serve warm.

Serving fruit juices is a nice alternative and/or addition to punch or mixed drinks. To prepare frosted glasses for serving your juice in an exceptional manner, dip a glass upside down in water, then twist the rim in granulated sugar. Place in the freezer overnight. Fill with juice of your guests' choice.

Salad Ideas:

Fresh spinach, mandarin oranges, sliced red onions and a tangy red salad dressing combine for a real tasty salad.

Chilled asparagus served on a bed of lettuce topped with mayonnaise and lemon juice. Garnish with sliced hard-boiled eggs or pimento strips.

Chicken salad can be given a special flavor with the addition of lemon juice and nutmeg.

To add a little zest to chicken salad, blend a small amount of soy sauce and curry powder with mayonnaise for the dressing.

Garnish your salads with frosted grapes. Frost grapes with slightly beaten egg white, sprinkle with sugar and let dry.

Crab meat combined with celery, mayonnaise, salt, pepper and grapefruit sections is a marvelous seafood salad.

Any canned fruit served with a mixture of cream cheese, juice of the fruit and pecans, served on a bed of lettuce.

Serve fruit salads from melon bowls or pineapple boats.

Greens match up well with apple or pear wedges, grapes, berries, citrus slices and dried fruits.

For fascinating flavors in salad, add fresh or dried herbs such as dill, chervil, rosemary, chives, mint, basil or parsley.

For variety in tossed lettuce salad, add watercress, tender spinach leaves, celery tops or Swiss chard. Add unusual vegetables such as thin strips of raw jícama or sweet potatoes, enoki mushrooms, chopped raw fennel, hearts of palm or roasted sweet red pepper strips.

When lacking vinegar as an ingredient for dressing use lemon juice. Try ¼ cup lemon juice, ¾ cup salad oil, 2 teaspoons salt, ½ teaspoon pepper, 1 teaspoon lemon peel, and any herbs of your choice.

Vary the flavor of French dressing by putting a clove or garlic in the bottle.

Salad dressing - try matching equal parts of flavored vinegar such as raspberry, champagne or red-wine vinegar to one part oil such as hazel hunt, walnut or olive oil. Shake or mix to combine. Add a little sugar, lemon, salt or pepper to taste.

Another salad dressing - stir together a creamy low-fat dressing with milk and Dijon-style mustard (about a tablespoon each) to an 8-ounce carton of plain yogurt. Season with a teaspoon each of honey and dried herb.

Vegetables
A pinch of sugar gives vegetables a fresher taste, but does not make them sweet.

Mix hot, buttered rice with raisins and curry to accompany lamb, chicken or veal.

Petite green peas, canned mushrooms, fresh pepper, bacon pieces and butter mixed together and heated in a 325 degree oven is an easy and fancy dish.

Serve buttered peas that have been sprinkled with fresh ground nutmeg or chopped fresh mint.

Canned asparagus may be topped with Parmesan cheese and butter then broiled until golder brown to serve at once.

Peel fresh tomatoes by plunging them into boiling water for a minute, remove immediately and peel. Chill until ready to use.

Reheat baked potatoes by dipping in very hot water and baking again in a moderate oven.

Baking Cakes and Cookies
Add the following to any cake mix and notice the difference: ½ teaspoon dry yeast dissolved in ½ cup warm water, add 2 teaspoons lemon juice to the yeast mixture. To this mixture add enough milk to make amount of liquid called for in the cake mix directions.

To prevent nuts and fruits from sinking, shake in flour before adding to batter.

Cheesecake tips:
Let the cream cheese and eggs stand at room temperature for 30 minutes before using.

Mix the filling ingredients only until they are combined. Do not overbeat as that can cause the cheesecake to puff, then fall and crack.

Keep the oven humid during baking to help prevent the cheesecake from cracking. Place a shallow pan of water on an oven rack below the cheesecake.

Test for doneness near the end of the baking time by gently shaking the pan. When fully baked, a one-inch area in the center will jiggle slightly (two-inch area for sour cream cheese-cakes). This soft center will firm after cooling. The traditional knife test for doneness does not work for cheesecakes.

Cheesecake tastes best at room temperature. Remove it from the refrigerator about one hour before serving.

Decorate with fresh cranberries dipped in white corn syrup, then into granulated sugar. Arrange them on the cheesecake with fresh mint leaves.

Colored sugar for decorating cookies: Combine ¼ teaspoon food coloring, ¼ teaspoon water, ¼ teaspoon vanilla and ¼ cup granulated sugar. Mix well. Spread thinly on waxed paper to dry. Rub between hands occasionally to prevent lumping.

To soften brown sugar which has hardened: Place ½ cup water in a 1 cup measure and microwave on high until boiling, 1 to 2 minutes. Place brown sugar in a microwave-safe container next to water. Microwave on high until soft, 2 to 3 minutes per pound.

When chopping nuts in food processor: Add a bit of sugar specified in recipe to keep them from sticking.

For soft cookies that get hard: Place an apple quarter in cookie tin for a day. When crisp cookies get soft, place in 300 degree oven 3 to 5 minutes. Cool completely on rack before serving.

Hummingbird Water

1 cup sugar
4 cups water

Combine sugar and water and bring to a full boil and turn off burner and let cool. If using a gas burner boil for 1 minute, no longer. You may add a small amount of red food coloring, but it is not necessary to attract birds except, perhaps at first. Store cooled liquid in refrigerator. Some authorities recommend a 3 cups of water to 1 cup of sugar mixture to initially attract hummingbirds, but switch to the 4 to 1 mixture over the long run. Feeders should be put out at the end of April and taken down by late September.

Bluebird Picnic

1 cup sugar
1 cup raisins
½ cup shortening
½ cup water
2 cups flour
½ teaspoon baking powder
1 teaspoon baking soda
½ cup chopped nuts

Set aside (in a bowl) flour, baking powder and soda. Boil sugar, shortening, raisins and water for 5 minutes. Add to dry ingredients and mix well. Add nuts. Spoon into a well-greased 8 x 8-inch pan. Bake at 350 degrees for 20 to 25 minutes. Serve in pieces on a feeder tray.

Grease Paint For Clown Faces

White:
2 teaspoons shortening
5 teaspoons cornstarch
1 teaspoon flour
2 to 3 drops glycerin for smoothness
Food coloring

Mix first three ingredients together. Add glycerin. Add food coloring for color.

Brown:
1 teaspoon shortening
2½ teaspoons cocoa
2 to 3 drops glycerin

Mix first two ingredients. Add glycerin. Both wash off with baby oil, cold cream or shortening.

Tooth Powder

Use a blender which has a glass container. Pour 1½ cups salt (if you have sensitive teeth use half this amount) into blender and turn it on high. Turn it off and shake the container (leave lid on). Repeat the process of blending and shaking until salt in pulverized into a fine, fine powder. Next add a 1-pound box of baking soda to blender. Cover and blend some more. Shake the blender until soda and salt are mixed. If you want to flavor, divide mixture in half and add ⅛-ounce bottle oil of cloves to ½- and ⅛-ounce bottle of wintergreen to the other half. Vanilla flavoring can also be used, some people prefer plain.

Play Clay

½ cup salt
1 cup flour
2 tablespoons cream of tartar
1 cup water
1 tablespoon cooking oil
Food coloring for desired shade

Mix dry ingredients. Add water, oil and food coloring. Cook on medium heat, stirring constantly until it forms a ball, leaving sides of pan. Cool. Store in closed container.

Christmas Tree Preservative

2 gallon bucket ¾ full hot water
1 pint clear Karo syrup
2 ounces bleach
2 pinches epsom salt
½ teaspoon 20 Mule Team Borax

Mix all ingredients in bucket. Make a fresh cut on the end of the tree so it will absorb solution. Put tree in bucket until ready to bring in the house. Use solution to water tree during the season.

Homemade Furniture Polish

⅓ cup boiled linseed oil
⅓ cup turpentine
⅓ cup white vinegar

Mix well. Apply with a soft cloth. Wipe dry with a clean cloth. This can also be used with fine steel wool to remove stains and spots. It is excellent to brighten up furniture.

"In rural communities everywhere, the church has been a central gathering place for generations. People come seeking spiritual growth and direction as well as a place to unite in worship and fellowship. I have found churches to be one of my favorite subjects to paint. This painting was inspired by a church in southside Virginia. The umbrellas, some bright and bold while others are more somber, may be symbolic of the unique souls beneath them."

Eldridge Bagley

"SOUL COLORS"
Appears through the courtesy of the painting's owner, Julia J. Norrell.

Peebles Inc.
Harmony Grove Cookbook
One Peebles Street
South Hill, VA 23970-5001

Please send _____ copy(ies) of **The Harmony Grove Cookbook** @ $ 19.99 each $ _____
Postage and handling @ $ 3.00 each $ _____
Residents of DE, KY, MD, NC, NJ, SC, TN and VA
add applicable sales tax @ $ _____ each $ _____
TOTAL $ _____

Name _____

Address _____

City _____ State _____ Zip Code _____

Make checks payable to **PEEBLES INC.** or use your

☐ Peebles Card   ☐ Discover Card   ☐ MasterCard   ☐ Visa

Account No. _____ Exp. Date _____

- -

Peebles Inc.
Harmony Grove Cookbook
One Peebles Street
South Hill, VA 23970-5001

Please send _____ copy(ies) of **The Harmony Grove Cookbook** @ $ 19.99 each $ _____
Postage and handling @ $ 3.00 each $ _____
Residents of DE, KY, MD, NC, NJ, SC, TN and VA
add applicable sales tax @ $ _____ each $ _____
TOTAL $ _____

Name _____

Address _____

City _____ State _____ Zip Code _____

Make checks payable to **PEEBLES INC.** or use your

☐ Peebles Card   ☐ Discover Card   ☐ MasterCard   ☐ Visa

Account No. _____ Exp. Date _____

Peebles Inc.
Harmony Grove Cookbook
One Peebles Street
South Hill, VA 23970-5001

Please send _____ copy(ies) of *The Harmony Grove Cookbook* @ $ 19.99 each $ _____
Postage and handling   @ $ 3.00 each $ _____
      Residents of DE, KY, MD, NC, NJ, SC, TN and VA
                add applicable sales tax @ $ _____ each $ _____
                                    TOTAL $ _____

Name _____

Address _____

City _____ State _____ Zip Code _____

Make checks payable to **PEEBLES INC.** or use your

☐ Peebles Card   ☐ Discover Card   ☐ MasterCard   ☐ Visa

Account No. _____ Exp. Date _____

- -

Peebles Inc.
Harmony Grove Cookbook
One Peebles Street
South Hill, VA 23970-5001

Please send _____ copy(ies) of *The Harmony Grove Cookbook* @ $ 19.99 each $ _____
Postage and handling   @ $ 3.00 each $ _____
      Residents of DE, KY, MD, NC, NJ, SC, TN and VA
                add applicable sales tax @ $ _____ each $ _____
                                    TOTAL $ _____

Name _____

Address _____

City _____ State _____ Zip Code _____

Make checks payable to **PEEBLES INC.** or use your

☐ Peebles Card   ☐ Discover Card   ☐ MasterCard   ☐ Visa

Account No. _____ Exp. Date _____